THE HIGH CITADEL

Books by Joel Seligman

Taming the Giant Corporation (with Ralph Nader
    and Mark Green)
The High Citadel: The Influence of Harvard
    Law School

THE HIGH CITADEL

The Influence of Harvard Law School

By Joel Seligman

With the Assistance of Lynne Bernabei

Introduction by Ralph Nader

Houghton Mifflin Company Boston   1978

This book is also dedicated to Mary
"Du meine Seele, du mein Herz . . ."

Library of Congress Cataloging in Publication Data

Seligman, Joel.
    The high citadel.

      Bibliography: p.
      Includes Index.
      1. Harvard University. Law School. 2. Law—Study
and teaching—United States. I. Bernabei, Lynne,
joint author. II. Title.
KF292.H34S44   340'.07'1173   78–2360
ISBN 0–395–26301–8

Printed in the United States of America

P 10 9 8 7 6 5 4 3 2 1

A portion of this book has appeared in *Juris Doctor.*

PREFACE

Fifty-six years ago, A. Z. Reed culminated eight years of study of legal education for the Carnegie Foundation with the publication of his seminal work, *Training for the Public Profession of the Law.* Eloquently, Reed urged lawyers and the law-teaching profession to recognize the unique public responsibilities of the bar:

> Whatever incidental purposes are cherished by particular law schools, the main end of legal education is to qualify students to engage in the professional practice of the law. This is a public function, in a sense that the practice of other professions, such as medicine, is not. Practicing lawyers do not merely render to the community a social service, which the community is interested in having them render well. They are part of the governing mechanism of the state. Their functions are in a broad sense political. This is not due primarily to the circumstance that a large proportion of our legislative and administrative officials, and virtually all our judges, are chosen from among this practically ruling class. Nor is it due entirely to the further circumstance that the growth of our law in the form of judicial decisions that interpret and declare its actual content is necessarily greatly influenced by arguments of counsel. It springs even more fundamentally from the fact, early discovered, that private individuals cannot secure justice without the aid of a special professional order to represent

and to advise them. To this end lawyers were instituted, as a body of public servants, essential for the maintenance of private rights. From their earliest origins the law has accorded to these "officers of the court" certain special and exclusive privileges, which set them apart from the mass of the people as truly as if they were, in a strict sense, public officials.

This book embodies a similar sentiment. Its ambition is to further the transformation of the American legal profession from an expensive provider of a vital service to one that would be available to all regardless of means and whose behavior would be more consistent with American law's ideal of "equal representation." This transformation has in part already begun, due to the federal government's growing subsidy of legal services and recent United States Supreme Court decisions which have proscribed minimum-fee schedules and state bans on attorney advertising. *The High Citadel* was written in the hope that law schools can awaken to a broader sense of *their* public responsibilities. Institutions with the reputation of Harvard Law School should act as the conscience of the legal profession, using their independence and prestige as a means to cleanse the practice of law of excessive self-interest and stressing to their students the ethical responsibilities of the individual attorney.

It is the basic theory of this book that law schools will not be equal to this responsibility until they are fundamentally changed. By focusing on Harvard's model of legal education in the first nine chapters of this book I hope to demonstrate why this is so, and to make the case for the fresh start in legal education that I urge in the final chapter.

This book has been written not without a sense of affection for Harvard Law School. No one can graduate from the School — as I did — without being touched by it. Harvard Law School is a great school in the same sense that the Sorbonne or Oxford are great schools. Its example has advanced university-level education. This is both Harvard Law School's finest virtue and its deepest tragedy. A great school can enjoy a respect for novel ideas, a joie de vivre, and a commitment to pluralism that less secure institutions cannot. But all great schools are also prisoners of their history. Inevitably there is a fear of fundamental change, based upon the simple reasoning, "If the school has been successful in the past, why tamper with it?" I well remember the first advice I received as a student at Harvard Law School, "Old ways are best."

Unfortunately, old ways are best only if the circumstances that produced them remain static. When these circumstances change, old ways can be stultifying. Harvard Law School today confronts this dilemma. Relevant circumstances have changed faster than the School has. For Harvard to remain the leader among American law schools it must make fundamental reforms. Great schools, when solvent, are not noted for their enthusiasm for taking chances.

The second lesson I learned in Cambridge was that "reasonable people can differ." It is a lesson I have taken more to heart. In all probability, some faculty members and alumni will vehemently disagree with portions of this book, but I trust they will not doubt my good intentions just as I have not doubted theirs. Debate will be reserved for principles and proving facts. What is significant in the law is rules — not individuals. That was the most important lesson I learned at Harvard, and the Law School will survive — and, one can hope, profit by — my application of this principle to the School itself.

Let me elaborate by offering a special word about one man. So far, the most influential post-World War II figure in the history of American legal education has been Harvard Law School's former Dean, Erwin Griswold. Like some of his predecessors as dean, Griswold is a giant of legal history, rightfully ranked with Christopher Columbus Langdell, Roscoe Pound, and James Landis in the small circle of men who most powerfully left a mark on Harvard Law School and, indirectly, on all American law schools.

This book is very critical of Dean Griswold. I trust it will be recognized that my criticisms are of Griswold's ideas concerning legal education, not of Griswold personally. I can say without equivocation that I never enjoyed interviewing any individual quite so much as Erwin Griswold. He is extraordinarily candid, direct, and impressive. Invariably, professors and students recall Griswold as "formidable" or a "powerful personality." To talk with him — after his twenty-one years as Harvard Law School's dean and six years as solicitor general of the United States — is a little like journeying to Mount Olympus to go one-on-one with Zeus. Nonetheless, neither my interview with Griswold nor my subsequent review of his relevant writings significantly changed my opinions of his manner of running a law school. Although I was moved by Griswold's honesty and gruff charm, I disagree with many of his theories about legal education. This book, in a sense, is a description of our differences. In a broader sense, it elaborates on a series of debates that currently divides the law-teaching profession. In adversity are books born.

Much has been made of the celebrity of Harvard Law School's graduates. Although only one United States President — Rutherford B. Hayes — graduated from the Law School, fourteen of the last eighty-eight justices of the Supreme Court have been associated with the Law School. They include such giants of the bar as Joseph Story, Oliver Wendell Holmes, Jr., Louis Brandeis, and Felix Frankfurter. Secretaries of State Elihu Root, Henry L. Stimson, and Dean Acheson matriculated at Harvard Law. So did Elliot Richardson, who during the Nixon and Ford administrations held four different cabinet posts; Franklin Roosevelt's Attorney General, Francis Biddle, Ford's Secretary of Transportation, William Coleman, and Carter's Secretary of Health, Education, and Welfare, Joseph Califano.[1]

To some degree, such glories are fortuitous. The greater signif-

1. During Watergate, the involvement of the Law School in national politics was especially prominent. Richard Kleindienst, class of 1950, was the first attorney general to be convicted of a crime. But the Law School also graduated James St. Clair, President Nixon's chief defense counsel; Senators Sam Ervin and Edward Gurney of the Senate Select Committee; the committee's chief counsel, Sam Dash; Congresswoman Elizabeth Holtzman of the House Impeachment Committee; Watergate Special Prosecutor Archibald Cox; his first three assistant prosecutors, James Vorenberg, Philip Heymann, and Stephen Breyer; and all three Saturday Night massacrees: Cox, Richardson, and Deputy Attorney General William Ruckelshaus. Later, John J. McCloy, a graduate and former CIA director, supervised the most intensive investigation of illegal corporate campaign contributions associated with the scandal. Harvard Law School Research Fellow Raoul Berger wrote widely read books on impeachment and executive privilege.

icance of Harvard Law School to this study is institutioned. To what extent has the model of legal education developed at Harvard influenced other American law schools and, concomitantly, American law, and what are the consequences of this influence? In this light, it is not important that some Law School alumni became famous. What is important is the degree to which Harvard Law School has affected the legal profession and the substance of American law.

I do not pretend to have "scientifically" or fully answered these questions. I doubt anyone can. But it is my hope that by my assembling the evidence available, reasonable conclusions can be drawn as to how law schools might better contribute to a more democratic and egalitarian system of law and legal practice.

Throughout the two years I worked on this book, I often reminded myself that it is easier to criticize than to build, and that educational theories with a distressing frequency have been more successful in journal articles than in practice. A sense of my own limits and those of Lynne Bernabei; and the other Harvard law students who worked with me during this project persuaded me it was better to focus this project exclusively on the Harvard model of legal education per se, bypassing such intriguing related topics as the Law School's International Legal Studies program, the Law School's governance and faculty consulting. I think the project benefited by our studying only those aspects of Harvard Law School that have been widely emulated.

Yet humility alone, John Kenneth Galbraith, that modern patron saint of gadflies, has warned, is a much overrated virtue. A dozen times during my research senior law professors at Harvard and other law schools told me that when they were younger they had considered proposals similar to those in the final chapter of this book but had not effectively lobbied for them. So I would prefer to close this Preface with a favorite campaign story of Adlai Stevenson, Jr. It seems that Pericles, the troubled leader of Athens during the city's golden age, once came upon the youthful Alcibiades, his most vociferous critic. "You know, Alcibiades," the exasperated Pericles exclaimed, "when I was your age I talked exactly as you do." Without a moment's hesitation, Alcibiades replied, "Ah, to have known you when you were great!" Now classicists may scoff that Alcibiades reached a sad end, but they cannot doubt that he received the best education in the law that his generation could provide. This book is dedicated to my true teacher in the law, Ralph Nader.

J.S.
Cambridge, Massachusetts
January 1978

CONTENTS

INTRODUCTION

"What is the purpose of the Harvard Law School?" asked Robert Hutchins before a crowded gathering in Austin Hall over two decades ago. "What kind of question is that?" whispered a classmate sitting next to me. Wanting to listen to the next words of the great iconoclast of the educational world, I chose not to reply. In retrospect, perhaps, I should have whispered back: "It is *the* question."

It is *the* question for reasons beyond the rarely disputed belief that Harvard Law School is *the* Law School and has been for nearly a century. It is *the* question because this Cambridge institution has greatly influenced both the curriculum content of most of the country's law schools and the training of students who become powerful members of the most central profession in our society. And, because the question was so basic, it was asked only once during my years at the Law School — by Hutchins, former dean of the Yale Law School at the age of twenty-nine.

You do not attend Harvard Law School to look at horizons or distant mountain peaks. You do not go there to engage in a pervasive study of justice. Nor do you go there to learn how to comfort the afflicted and afflict the comfortable. The consensus of most law professors is that you go there to encounter and master the techniques of legal reasoning. That process did not include the pondering of basic questions that might draw students to examine the raw power that distorts, nullifies, or delays legal justice.

It did not, and it does not, for Harvard Law School has proven remarkably predictable year after year. In 1969 I had the occasion to make the following observations, which I would like to cite at some length because, unfortunately, they are almost as descriptive today as they were then.

•

It was a similar ritual every year. About 550 new law students would file into venerable Austin Hall at Harvard Law School on a September day and hear the no-nonsense dean, Erwin N. Griswold, orient them. The good dean had the speech down to a practiced spontaneity. He advised them that at that instant they had become members of the legal profession, that law firms were the backbone of the profession, that there were no glee clubs at the Harvard Law School and that the law was a jealous mistress. Thus was launched a process of engineering the law student into corridor thinking and largely non-normative evaluation. It was a three-year excursus through legal minutiae, embraced by wooden logic and impervious to what Oliver Wendell Holmes once called the "felt necessities of our times." It is not easy to take the very bright young minds of a nation, envelop them in conceptual cocoons and condition their expectations of practice to the demands of the corporate law firm. But this is what Harvard Law School did for over a half century to all but a resistant few of the 40,000 graduates.

The Harvard Law pattern — honed to a perfection of brilliant myopia and superfluous rigor — became early in the century the Olympian object of mimicry for law schools throughout the country. Harvard also did everything it could to replicate its educational system through its production of law school teachers, casebooks, and an almost proselytizing zeal. This system faithfully nourished and fundamentally upheld a developing legal order that has become more aristocratic and less responsive to the needs and strains of a complex society. In turn, the established legal order controlled the terms of entry into the profession in ways that fettered imagination, inhibited reform, and made alienation the price of questioning its assumptions and proposing radical surgery.

Unreal as it may appear, the connection between the legal establishment and the spectacular increase in the breakdown of the legal system has rarely been made outside the fraternity. This is due to the functional modesty of the profession, its reluctance to parade itself as the shaper, staffer, and broker for the operating legal framework in this country. What is not claimed is not attributed. This escape from responsibility for the quality and quantity of justice in the relationships of men and institutions has been a touch stone of the legal profession.

Anyone who wishes to understand the legal crises that envelop the contemporary scene — in the cities, in the environment, in the courts, in the marketplace, in public services, in the corporate-government arenas, and in Washington — should come to grips with this legal flow chart that begins with the law schools and ends with the law firms, particularly the large corporate law firms of New York and Washington.

Harvard Law's most enduring contribution to legal education was the mixing of the case method of study with the Socratic method of teaching. Developed late in the nineteenth century under Dean Christopher Columbus Langdell, these techniques were tailor-made to transform intellectual arrogance into pedagogical systems that humbled the student into accepting its premises, levels of abstractions, and choice of subjects. Law professors take delight in crushing egos in order to acculturate the students to what they called "legal reasoning" or "thinking like a lawyer." The process is a highly sophisticated form of mind control that trades off breadth of vision and factual inquiry for freedom to roam in an intellectual cage.

The study of actual law cases — almost always at the appellate court level — combines with the Socratic questioning sequence in class to keep students continually on the defensive, while giving them the feeling that they are learning hard law. Inasmuch as the Socratic method is a game at which only one (the professor) can play, the students are conditioned to react to questions and issues that they have no role in forming or stimulating. Such teaching *forms* have been crucial in perpetuating the status quo in teaching *content*. For decades, the law school curriculum reflected with remarkable fidelity the commercial demands of law firm practice. Law firm determinants of the content of courses nurtured a colossal distortion in priorities both as to the type of subject matter and the dimension of its treatment. What determined the curriculum was the legal interest that came with retainers. Thus, the curriculum pecking order was predictable — tax, corporate, securities, and property law at the top, and torts (personal injury) and criminal law, among others, at the bottom. Although in terms of the seriousness of the legal interest and the numbers of people affected, torts and criminal law would command the heights, the reverse was true, for the retainers were not as certain nor as handsome. Courses on estate planning proliferated; there were none for environmental planning until a few years ago. Other courses dealt with collapsible corporations, but the cupboard was bare for any student interested in collapsing tenements. Creditors' rights were studied deeply; debtors' remedies were passed by shallowly. Courses tracking the lucre and the prevailing ethos did not embrace any concept of professional sacrifice and service to the unrepresented poor or to public interests being crushed by private power. Such service was considered a proper concern of legal charity, to be dispensed by starved legal aid societies.

The generations of lawyers shaped by these law schools in turn shaped the direction and quality of the legal system. They came to this task severely unequipped except for the furtherance of their acquisitive drives. Rare was the law graduate who had the faintest knowledge of the institutionalized illegality of the cities in such areas as building and health code violations, the endemic bribing of officialdom, the illegalities in the marketplace, from moneylending to food. Fewer still were the graduates who knew anything of the institutions that should have been bathed in legal insight and compassion — hospitals, schools, probate and other courts, juvenile and mental institutions, and prisons. Racialism, the gap between rich and poor, the seething slums — these conditions were brought to the attention of law firms by the illumination of city riots rather than the illumination of concerned intellects.

Even the techniques of analysis — the ultimate pride of the law schools — were seriously deficient. Techniques that concede to vested interests a parochial role for the law and that permit empirical starvation of portions of their subject matter become techniques of paralysis. This was the case in the relation of tort courses and motor vehicle injuries. Law as prevention, law as incorporator of highway and vehicle engineering facts and feasibilities was almost totally ignored. The emphasis was on legal impact after crashes occurred, so as to assign liabilities and determine damages between drivers. Another failure in analysis was thematic of the entire curriculum. Normative thinking — the "shoulds" and the "oughts" — was not recognized as part and parcel of rigorous analytic skills. Although the greatest forays in past legal scholarship, from the words of Roscoe Pound to those of Judge Jerome Frank, proceeded from a cultivated sense of injustice, the nation's law schools downplayed the normative inquiry as something of an intellectual pariah. Thus the great legal challenges of access to large governmental and corporate institutions, the control of environmental pollution, the requisites of international justice suffered from the inattention of mechanized minds. There was little appreciation of how highly demanding an intellectual task it was to develop constructs of justice and injustice within Holmes' wise dictum that "the life of the law is not logic, it is experience." Great questions went unasked, and therefore unanswered.

Possibly the greatest failure of the law schools — a failure of the faculty — was not to articulate a theory and practice of a just deployment of legal manpower. With massive public interests deprived of effective legal representation, the law schools continued to encourage recruits for law firms whose practice militated against any such representation even on a sideline, *pro bono* basis. Lawyers labored for polluters, not antipolluters, for sellers, not consumers, for corporations, not citizens, for labor leaders, not rank and file, for, not against, rate increases or weak standards before government agencies, for highway builders, not displaced residents, for, not against, judicial and administrative delay, for preferential business access to government and against equal citizen access to the same government, for agricultural subsidies to the rich but not food stamps for the poor, for tax and quota privileges, not for equity and free trade. None of this and much more seemed to trouble the law schools. Indeed, law firms were not even considered appropriate subjects of discussion and study in the curriculum. The legal profession — its organization, priorities, and responsibilities — were taken as given. As the one institution most suited for a critical evaluation of the profession, the law school never assumed this unique role. Rather, it serviced and supplied the firms with fresh manpower selected through an archaic hierarchy of narrow worthiness topped by the editors of the school's law review. In essence it was a trade school.

The strains on this established legal order began to be felt with *Brown vs. Board of Education* in 1954. *Brown* rubbed the raw nerves of the established order in public. The mounting conflict began to shake a legal order built on deception and occult oppression. The ugly scars of the land burned red. Law students began to sense, to feel, to participate, and to earn scars of their own. Then came the Kennedy era with its verbal eloquence, its Peace Corps — overseas and later here. Then came Vietnam and Watts, Newark and the perturbation became a big-league jolt. Law students began to turn away from private practice, especially at the Ivy League law schools. Those who went directly to the firms were less than enthusiastic. The big corporate firms in New York and Washington began to detect early signs that their boot camps were not responding to the customary Loreleis of the metropolitan canyons. Starting salaries began to reflect the emergence of a seller's market. Almost two years ago, the big New York Cravath firm set a starting salary of $15,000 a year and many firms followed. Still the law graduate detour continued. The big firms began to promise more free time to engage in *pro bono* work — the phrase used to describe work in the public interest such as representing indigents. The young graduates were still dissatisfied —first over the contraction of the promises and second over the narrow interpretation given to *pro bono* work.

At the same time, more new or alternative career roles in public service began to emerge. Neighborhood Legal Services, funded by OEO, was manned by 1800 young lawyers around the country at last count. The draft is driving many graduates into VISTA programs. There are more federal court clerkships available. And the growth of private, public-service law institutions such as Edgar Cahn's Citizen's Advocate Center and the Urban Law Institute headed by his wife, Jean Cahn, are not only providing such career roles but articulating their need throughout the country.

Meanwhile back at the law schools, student activism has arrived. Advocacy of admission, curriculum, and grading reform is occurring at Harvard and Yale. Similar currents are appearing at other law schools. New courses in environmental, consumer, and poverty law are being added to the lists. The first few weeks of the present school year indicate that the activists' attention is turning to the law firms that are now coming on campus to recruit. In an unprecedented move, a number of detailed questionnaires, signed by large numbers of students, are going out to these firms. The questions range far beyond the expected areas of the firms' policies on minority and women lawyers, and *pro bono* work. They include inquiries about the firms' policies on containing their clients' ambitions, on participation in law-reform work, on conflict of interest issues, on involvement in corporate client and political activity, and on subsidizing public-interest legal activity. Such questionnaires are preliminary to the development of courses on law-firm activities, and to more studies of specific law firms, which began this past summer with a study of the largest Washington, D.C., firm, Covington and Burling.

The responses that the firms give to these questionnaires, and whatever planned response the students envisage for those firms who choose not to reply, will further sharpen the issues and the confrontations. The students have considerable leverage. They know it is a seller's market. They know how vulnerable these very private firms are to effective public criticism. Status is crucial to these firms. Status is also a prime attraction for competent law school graduates.

In recent months, there has been much soul-searching among the larger firms. Memos suggesting various opportunities for *pro bono* work by younger associates have been circulating between partners. A few decisions have been made. Some New York and San Francisco firms are considering or have instituted time off allowances ranging from a few weeks a year to a sabbatical. Piper & Marbury, a large Baltimore firm, has announced its intention to establish a branch office in the slums to service the needs of poor people, without charging fees if there is an inability to pay any- thing. Arnold and Porter, the second largest Washington, D.C., firm, has appointed a full-time *pro bono* lawyer and is permitting all firm members to spend, if they wish, an average of 15 percent of their working hours on public service activities. Hogan and Hartson, the third largest D.C. firm, is setting up a "Community Services Department" to "take on public interest representation on a non-chargeable or, where appropriate, a discounted fee basis," according to the firm's memorandum on the subject.

The Hogan and Hartson memorandum is a fairly candid docu- ment. Like other firm memorandums on *pro bono* ventures, there is the acknowledgment that such a move "may have a favorable impact upon recruitment." The executive committee of Hogan and Hartson concedes that "there is a tendency among younger lawyers, particularly those with the highest academic qualifica- tions, to seek out public-service-oriented legal careers as an alter- native to practice in the larger metropolitan law firms." In its internal firm statement, the committee notes that it "regards the relative disfavor into which the major law firms have fallen to be attributable, at least in part, to the feeling among recent law school graduates *that these firms have failed to respond to the larger problems of contemporary society."* (Their emphasis.) Some statistics impressed the senior partners: the University of Michigan Law School reports that 26 of its 1969 graduates entered Wall Street law firms as compared with an average of 75 in preceding years. Harvard Law School reported that the percentage of its graduates entering private law practice declined from 54 percent in 1964 to 41 percent in 1968, and an even more significant decline is ex- pected in the next few years.

It is too early to appraise these programs because they have not yet gotten underway. The likelihood that serious or abrasive conflict of interest situations will arise depends on the kind of *pro bono* work seclected. If this work deals with "Band-Aid law" in the slums on a case basis, few conflict of interest problems should arise. On the other hand, should the *pro bono* lawyers grapple with the financial institutions who fund the slum moneylenders for example, or strive toward structural reform of a legal institution, then the probability of conflict is increased.

Because of the enormously greater cost-benefit that attached to the more basic *pro bono* efforts, the external and internal pressures on the firm's leaders will be in that direction. This could lead to more profound clashes between the firm's allegiance to its paying clients and its recognition of public service responsibilities. With additional law-student and younger-lawyer demands for cash contributions for scholarships to minority law students, for admission of more minority lawyers to firm membership, and for senior partners to pay "reparations" out of their own salaries to assist the legally deprived — all demands made or in the process of being made — the pressure may soon exceed the firms' thresholds of tolerance. At that point the experiment in *pro bono* may terminate.

In the succeeding eight years, it has become clear that the pressure did not exceed the firms' tolerance; instead the *pro bono* interest waned. The demands of aroused law students, stimulated by the draft, the civil rights marches, and the Vietnam war, declined. As record numbers of students were graduated from the law schools, a buyer's market developed. And as starting salaries by the largest firms climbed toward $25,000 and beyond for the "top" law graduates, the rewards for conventional thinking became persuasive. Gone were the outside provocations of the Sixties which shook the law school communities and spurred the thinking of new thoughts and the opening of new vistas. Nothing internal to these communities emerged as a replacement. True, some changes resulted from the tumult of a decade ago — courses that took into account disenfranchised peoples, more clinical education, and wider curricula options. By and large, however, the law schools, again insulated from the outside society, returned to the task of producing legal technicians unperturbed by the larger sores and failings of the legal system.

I think it fair to say that the motive force for what changes occurred in legal education several years ago came from the law students themselves. Only a few members of the faculty were supportive. Recently, however, there has been a quiet reassertion of the traditional pedagogy, content, and method — a coming of a period of "normalcy." Once again, with few exceptions, the law schools are unwavering mirror images of the distribution of power and rewards in the outside politico-legal world. What is additionally revealing about the present state of legal education and law school life generally is the anomie. A listlessness prevails at a time in American history when widely reported corporate crime waves and government illegalities provide a most fundamental affront to the rule of law. The necessity of reform is clear. But instead of these tragic events, contributing to an intellectual and normative ferment, with suitable scholarship and involvement, the law school environment appears becalmed and incapable of being stirred to high ideals and resolves.

Is it unfair to expect law schools to be in the vanguard of examining and trying to resolve legal injustices? Would such inquiries detract from the honing of legal skills and demean the intellectual rigor of legal education's subject matter? To ask the questions is to answer them. If law schools are to give their students opportunities to understand legal reality, the traditional emphasis must change. Subject matter that is either so technical or so appellate as to be quarantined from the reality of the field must surrender to the sidewalk facts that shape or distort the law. This is not to suggest the wholesale replacement of existing legal courses with legal ethnography. It is to argue for a broader and more balanced empirical content to such courses as taxation, securities regulation, trusts, corporations and property. It is to plead for a finer sensitivity to the demonstrable client biases of currently taught courses — in part because the studied cases were initiated that way, in part because of the uniform experience of most law professors, and in part because that is what accords with the commercial demands of law practice. And it is to advocate full-time lawyer roles as representatives for the unrepresented. The profession is already amply permeated with a retainer astigmatism without making it the unspoken premise of legal education.

The facile belief that technical competence and normative inquiry are a zero-sum game has helped make Harvard Law School one of the nation's great wasting assets. After all, how has its narrow definition of academic excellence over the years helped resolve the major challenges to the justice system in America? Very little, especially as compared to the expectation that Harvard's size and status excites. There is a broad consensus about these major challenges — about how citizen access to justice mechanisms are often frustrated and how the maldistribution of corporate, bureaucratic, and technological power injure the innocent. But consensus of judgment has not been translated into a consensus for a changed legal education experience. Upon his leaving the deanship of the Harvard Law School, Erwin Griswold lamented the attrition of idealism between the time the students entered the school and the time they graduated. "What do we do to them that makes them turn another way?" he asked, to his credit.

A useful way to respond to the Dean's query is to recall what episodes or professors did quicken the idealism of Harvard Law students through its history. Certainly Dean Griswold's solid defense of the Fifth Amendment during the latter years of the McCarthyite period was an inspiration by conviction. While a student, I was told that it took courage for the Dean to write the tract. The magnificent and humane Zack Chafee, whether teaching Equity, an all too neglected course, or elaborating the "blessings of liberty" to nonlawyer audiences, presented the force of noble example. Roscoe Pound's breadth of vision together with this cross-cultural and disciplinary embrace counseled students not always to look at the law writ small.

Furthermore, instances of past student involvement while at the Law School could serve similar exemplary purposes today. Particularly in the Sixties, the causes of civil rights, antiwar, and environment enlisted important frontline student engagement.

What is there to transform a law school into a pulsating forum for thought and involvement in those "felt necessities" of the times? What does it take to combine logic and experience and values during those formative law school years? It takes leadership, a cultivated sense of justice, tolerance, and a modest amount of nerve. It takes deep diversity among the faculty and a climate of recognizing socially important work, not only with consultantships and publications. It requires a breaking down of the tunnel vision symbolized by the tunnel architecture of the Harvard Law School building complex. It invites empathy with the aggrieved and deprived. It calls for a program of visiting workers, farmers, victims of the law, and other people to mix with law students in classes and other school activities. It beckons Harvard Law School to have a sense of vision and a sense of its civic importance.

In the past few years, the Law School has reached the attention of the public overwhelmingly through two books that described the pressured life of first-year law students. One might have expected a broader view of an institution with 1600 or more students, a large faculty, and a very large sway over American legal education. The time for preening is past. The crisis of legal education and the law that helps nourish and staff is too apparent and too endemic. It is time for self-examination.

Joel Seligman, a Harvard Law graduate '74, came to his subject with considerable sympathy. Assisted by several law students, he spent months going through historical documents, Law School records, and sometimes difficult interviews. His study is of the Harvard model of legal education as instrument, motivation, and subculture. While focused on Harvard, his analysis is relevant to the whole spectra of American legal education. His interest is at the nucleus, however, from Harvard Law School's founding in the late nineteenth century to its present plight as a stagnating phenomenon still clothed with ermine.

The High Citadel is a pioneering historical criticism with a major proposal for a different kind of legal education. The broader infrastructure of the Law School — alumni, law firms, corporations, and other constituencies — was not the chosen emphasis of this study. Instead Seligman examined that part of the Harvard Law School that would most likely invite searching dialogue among students, faculty, administrators, and lawyers across the country.

Should the book succeed in engaging their serious attention, the audience for its concerns will expand well beyond our profession. It will reach the people who can be served so much better by the law writ large in the consciences of its practitioners.

RALPH NADER
Washington, D.C.
December 1977

Part I

BUILDING THE CATHEDRAL

1

DISSOLUTION THEN DRIFT:

The Last Ten Years at Harvard Law School

What do we do to them that makes them turn another way?

ERWIN GRISWOLD

A decade of dissolution began that crisp autumn day. A decade first of stridency, then of drift. A decade in which the basic premises of American legal education, and implicitly those of American law, would be challenged, would ossify, then slowly begin to change.

It was September 22, 1967, the 150th anniversary of the founding of Harvard Law School. For close to 100 years, Harvard Law School had stood as the high citadel of American legal education. Its admissions procedures, faculty selection, curriculum, teaching methods, and placement practices had served as a model for the education of lawyers in the greater than 160 law schools in the United States. This was especially true in the twenty or twenty-five "national" law schools that together with Harvard composed the principal training schools for the nation's most influential private and government attorneys.

Yet the greater significance of the School had been political. In the popular imagination, few institutions had been more closely associated with liberal intellectual beliefs. Since the turn of the century, the writings and actions of the Law School's faculty and graduates had frequently defended such democratic concepts as judicial restraint, freedom of speech, equal protection, federalism, and the rule of law. If it would have been fair to characterize the disparate intellects of Harvard Law School's most celebrated professors and alumni as adhering to a common faith, it would have been that of constitutional liberalism.

Inherent in the structure of the Law School's curriculum and practices, however, was a paradox. Whatever the intellectual beliefs of some of its alumni, Harvard Law School's historic function had been to prepare students to practice in the nation's leading private law firms: To this date, in Wall Street's Dewey, Ballantine, Bushby, Palmer, and Wood; Boston's Ropes and Gray; and Washington, D.C.'s Covington and Burling, half or more of the partners are graduates of Harvard Law School.

On that crisp September day, few men better personified this paradox than the Law School's Dean, Erwin Griswold. A self-styled Charles Evans Hughes type of Republican, Griswold had established his public reputation during the McCarthy era by defending the Supreme Court's 1954 school desegregation decision and witnesses' rights to plead the Fifth Amendment privilege against self-incrimination. Yet no Harvard Law School dean had ever made so plain his enthusiasm for big-city law practice. Law firms, Griswold stressed, were the backbone of the profession. Since his election as dean twenty-one years earlier, Griswold had attempted to reconcile the conflicting demands of democratic liberalism and corporate-law practice by emphasizing that law is a value-neutral craft.

"There are no glee clubs at Harvard Law School," the no-nonsense dean had admonished each year's freshman class, and they had always understood what he meant. "This is a law school for lawyers who will practice law in the grand manner [where] the essence of the preparation must be in the fundamentals: straight thinking and cliché avoidance." Characteristically, he expected the *Harvard Law Review* to be on his desk by the tenth of the month.

That fall morning, Griswold led the sesquicentennial celebration. To the music of trumpets, orchestra, and choir, the academic procession formed in front of weather-beaten Austin Hall, the Law School's oldest remaining class building. In the background stood the sturdy white wood-frame Gannett House, home of the *Law Review* and the Legal Aid Bureau. Near it, the dark bricks of Hemenway Gymnasium, and Hastings Hall, built in 1910, which, with its spacious common rooms, fireplaces, and hand-lathed wooden appurtenances, offered a stunning contrast to the "Skinner boxes" of the newer dormitories.

Between rows of students, Griswold, Harvard University President Nathan Pusey, and the faculty celebrants proceeded the short distance to a canopied, crimson-trimmed platform erected on Holmes Field before the entrance to Langdell Hall. Langdell then was the heart of the Law School, including the largest classrooms, the library, and most faculty offices. Within its cavernous halls, three generations of students had studied the law while before portraits of the giants of Harvard Law School: Joseph Story, Christopher Columbus Langdell, Learned Hand, Oliver Wendell Holmes, Jr., and Felix Frankfurter. Soon, Erwin Griswold would be known best by his portrait, too.

For this was Erwin Griswold's last hurrah at Harvard Law School. The previous year, for the first time in his deanship, the Placement Office, the honoraries selection, the grading system, and the curriculum "all," asserted the student newspaper, the *Harvard Law Record*, "came under [the students'] Blitzkrieg attack." Even the faculty had advised reform. Styling himself "a gadfly," Professor Clark Byse had recommended "intensive" questioning of student recruitment — "The admission of students is too important to be left to deans" — the first-year curriculum, the second year's required courses, the third-year paper, and the entire concept of grades and examinations. Later Byse would make criticisms more personal, suggesting that no dean should serve more than ten or twelve years, for "thereafter he may tend to regard proposals for change or innovation as implied criticisms of his stewardship and, therefore, may be unduly resistant to proposals which are necessary for the ongoing renewal of any institution." The Harvard Law School Griswold knew seemed to be slipping away. Griswold had appointed Byse to chair a Joint Student-Faculty Committee to preside over the "intensive" questioning. Just one week after the sesquicentennial, Griswold flew to

Johnson City, Texas. There, President Johnson announced Griswold's nomination as solicitor general. The Senate swiftly confirmed the nomination, and in October Griswold left Harvard Law to serve in the Johnson and Nixon administrations. He later joined the Washington office of a corporate-law firm from his home town of Cleveland.

But that September day, as Griswold took his place to speak alongside Supreme Court Justice William Brennan, sociologists Talcott Parsons and David Riesman, Law School faculty members, and others, the dean's thoughts were very much on Harvard Law School. "For some years now I have been concerned about the effect of our legal education on the idealism of our students. I have great faith in our students. They are surely as good, as earnest, as sincere, as their predecessors who have come here through the years. They bring to this school a large measure of idealism. Do they leave with less? And if they do, is that something we can view with indifference? If they do, what is the cause? What do we do to them," Griswold asked, "that makes them turn another way?"

Nineteen months later, Harvard Law School all but ground to a halt. Shortly after the police were called in to arrest and expel students who occupied Harvard's University Hall in the early morning hours of April 10, 1969, Law School students met and decided to hold their own all-night meeting in the Law School library.

Tempers flared. Students threatened not to take exams, demanded the abolition of first-year grades, called for greater participation in making Law School decisions, and railed at the "hostility" and "impersonality" of the faculty. Under pressure, the Law School faculty voted not to condemn the occupation of University Hall, but privately professors complained, "the guns were being put to our heads," the students acted like "spoiled brats." Professor Ernest Brown resigned. "For the first time," another professor commented, "I've heard colleagues I love and respect say, 'Why am I here?' "

To many in the class of '69, the most vivid memory of Harvard Law School would be the all-night meeting in the library when Professor Detlev Vagts stood on a desk and fielded student questions like a cornered Mr. Chips. Derek Bok, the young reform-minded dean shortly to become University president, would write the alumni, "Paradoxically, though some law students honored the strike, most teachers reported that class attendance, if anything, seemed to have increased. Moreover, though many meetings and colloquia took place outside of class, law students did not seem to be preoccupied by ROTC, expansion or the other issues debated in the university. They were concerned instead, and often passionately so, with law school problems."

Undoubtedly the Vietnam War was an important cause of the students' fervor. As many as 325 of the Law School's 1600 students left in 1967–1968 because of the draft. Hundreds marched in moratoriums against the war. In the aftermath of the shooting of four students at Kent State, 700 students passed a resolution to join a nationwide strike, and the faculty reluctantly agreed to allow students to take examinations off the campus so they could participate in the strike. Vietnam even motivated the *Harvard Law Review* to publish its first editorial on a foreign-policy issue, which concluded that the war was "immoral," while judiciously noting that a minority of the editors had opposed this statement because "readers might be offended by it."

But there were more enduring causes of the faculty-student schism than the Indo-China War. In the decade following Griswold's departure, these stresses became increasingly evident.

In the late 1960s and early 1970s, women and minority students first came to the Law School in significant numbers. Before 1950, not one woman law student had been admitted. As late as 1967, less than 4 percent of the class was female. In 1975–1976, that figure grew to 21 percent. Similarly, before 1963, often only a single black had been accepted in each year's class of 550. A recruitment program gradually increased that number: Three blacks were admitted in 1963; the next year, twelve. By 1975–1976, fifty-three blacks, fifteen Chicanos, seven Asian Americans, and two native Americans were admitted in a class of 552.

Simultaneously, the admissions process became more competitive. In 1960, nearly one of every two applicants was accepted. By 1974, the odds for the 7011 applicants were about one in nine. The median LSAT (entrance examination) score for the entering class rose from 630 in 1960 (approximately the 92nd percentile) to 725 in 1974 (approximately the 98th percentile). This furthered a profound change in the character of the student body. The new students had been raised on competition. Dr. Alan Stone, a psychiatrist on the Law School faculty, described interstudent relations in terms of "enmity, friction, hostility, distaste, contempt and the lack of group cohesiveness and morale." Many students feared, especially in the first year, "that one is about to be found out as a fraud," and desired, above all else, a release from competition.

During this same period, skyrocketing tuition and living costs transformed Harvard Law School into a debtors' colony. In the mid-1960s, tuition was $1582; ten years later, tuition and the Health Service Fee had doubled to $3161. The basic budget for an unmarried student was estimated to be $7000 a year. Including estimates of the cost of attending college developed by the College Board, it would cost an unmarried student between $35,000 and $49,000, as well as seven years of lost or forgone income, to attend four years of college and three years at Harvard Law School.

In this decade, even more substantial changes occurred among the faculty. Since Dean Langdell had chosen James Barr Ames as his first acolyte in 1873, faculty appointments had been made on the basis of "academic brilliance" rather than more worldly success as a legal practitioner. Such judgments usually rested on one's scoring well enough on first-year examinations to be classified in the top 5 percent or so of each class invited to write and edit the *Harvard Law Review*. Among the uninvited were brilliant lawyers, like Clarence Darrow, whose academic record was embarrassing but who could plead a case as skillfully as any lawyer of his generation, and legislative specialists, arbitrators, and government attorneys who had honed talents unrelated to making the *Review*.

Under Dean Griswold, the School's approach to faculty selection had come to resemble admission into an exclusive club. A potential faculty member needed not only the imprimatur of a *Law Review* editorship, but also recommendations from a select circle of the School's senior law professors and outside judges and attorneys, constituting a *Law Review* "old boy" network.

Derek Bok and Albert Sacks, Griswold's successors as dean, opened up the faculty to new voices. Each was sympathetic to the need for the Law School to adopt an affirmative-action program. Harvard Law School named its first two non-visiting female professors in 1972. Weeks later both were named to the Admissions Committee, and in January 1973, Jeanne Kettleson became the first woman to hold the position of assistant dean. By 1975, there were three women professors and three women assistant deans among the Law School's seventy or so professors and senior administrators. In 1969, Walter Leonard, a graduate of Howard Law School, had been chosen as Harvard Law School's first black assistant dean. Two years later Derrick Bell became the school's first black professor. The Law School named its second and third black professors in 1975–1976.

Bok and Sacks also presided over the appointment of several assistant professors with public-policy or humanities backgrounds who disputed Griswold's narrower, craft-oriented approach to the law. By the mid-1970s, such professors as Morton Horwitz, Roberto Unger, Gary Bellow, and Duncan Kennedy formed a politically critical minority faction of the faculty. Sacks furthered the Law School's pluralism by naming former student radical Douglas Phelps to be the School's first Alternative Careers administrator.

Seemingly, Harvard Law School was greatly transformed in the decade after Griswold resigned. From virtually the moment he left, parietal hours were all but abandoned in the dorms. In 1973, the Law School's Dorm Council demanded that the University health services distribute contraceptives to its students "at cost" in light of an "epidemic" of venereal disease. Between 1968 and 1970, most male students stopped wearing coats and ties to classes. In April of 1969, the faculty voted to end Saturday classes.

New rituals, new organizations rose to replace traditional ones. In the spring of 1966, the *Harvard Civil Rights-Civil Liberties Law*

Review was established to rival the more conservative *Harvard Law Review*. By 1970, 350 Law School students were helping the poor through one of three legal-aid societies; others defended the criminally accused and prison inmates through four voluntary-defender organizations. Students had formed a Black Law Students Association, a Women's Law Association, an Environmental Law Society, a student-run law firm to advise state and local governments, a Committee for Research on the Draft, and an underground newspaper called *The Outlaw*. There were still, alas, no glee clubs at the Harvard Law School.

But women, after a determined battle, won the right to shower in Hemenway Gymnasium, and in 1974, the *Harvard Law School Bulletin* ran a three-part article called "Law Schools and Indian Tribes," a notable departure for the alumni magazine from its usual fare of faculty appointment and charter-flight announcements.

A more fundamental attack on the curriculum, teaching methods, and purpose of Harvard Law School, however, failed.

For decades legal education had been criticized for being too tense and too tedious. As the old saying went, "In the first year they scare you to death; in the second year they work you to death; and in the third year they bore you to death." As the practice of law became more specialized and admission to the top law schools more restricted, the tedium seemed less defensible.

Succeeding Erwin Griswold, Derek Bok, in his first annual report as dean, urged considering the reduction of the curriculum from three years to two, more specialization, and the imparting of more new skills. "Taken together these three models create a long agenda for legal educators to consider," Bok argued. "A single school could simultaneously offer a two year degree for the student impatient with academic life and eager to practice, a program of specialization for students — young and old — who have set their minds upon a definite field of practice, and a wide-ranging program of analytical skills for those envisioning extensive work in business and government."

A movement for a two-year curriculum soon began. At Harvard Law School, Professor Charles Fried suggested "a real possibility that our society is requiring young men and women to serve time too long in institutions of higher learning." Professors Cavers, Keeton, Bator, and Breyer all voiced interest in variants of a two-year plan. Elsewhere, the Carrington committee presented to the influential Association of American Law Schools a model two-year law school curriculum. Thomas Ehrlich, then dean of Stanford Law School, and fellow Stanford Law Professor Herbert Packer recommended it in their 1972 study, *New Directions in Legal Education,* as did future Attorney General Edward Levi while he was president of the University of Chicago.

By early 1972, the stage was set for the rule-making Council on Legal Education and Admissions to the Bar of the American Bar Association to vote on permitting experimental two-year plans. On Friday, February 4, 1972, several of the nation's law school deans crowded into a New Orleans hotel room. And that is where the music died. By then Derek Bok had been elevated to the presidency of Harvard University, and Albert Sacks installed as the Law School's dean. From the first day of his deanship, Sacks opposed reducing the three-year course. In New Orleans, he led the charge against the two-year proposal. Conceding that law schools in general had problems developing "meaningful" third-year programs, he argued that Harvard was now turning its attention to this problem by designing specialized research and clinical programs. "But we need time to try." Nearly every law school dean sided with Sacks in his opposition to the curricular reform. Ideas which Harvard Law School giveth, Harvard Law School also can taketh away.

So Harvard Law School went eclectic. Retaining its three-year curriculum — and all of its tuition base — it broadened the course elective system until it became more varied than the special-interest amendments in a Senate tax reform bill. Students could now choose courses in Technology and the Environment; Suburbs and Cities; Work, Wages, and Welfare; and Television and the Law.

A significant change did occur in the way a few courses were taught. The great pedagogical contribution Harvard Law School had made to graduate education was to join the case study to the Socratic method. Instead of asking students to memorize rules of

law, in the 1870s Dean Christopher Columbus Langdell institutionalized a system of requiring them to study actual court decisions under the pointed quizzing of professorial discussion
leaders.

But Socratic questioning when conducted by some professors
seemed to ridicule and depoliticize student reasoning. By the late
1960s there was a sense, as one student article put it, that 100
years with the case method was "long enough." One professor
tried to deactivate resentment of Socratic questioning by instituting the "hassle-free pass" — allowing students who didn't know
or didn't care not to answer a question without being "hassled."

But the more significant reform was substantive. Aided by an
initial $175,000 grant from the Council on Legal Education for
Professional Responsibility, Harvard Law School spirited Professor Gary Bellow from the University of Southern California Law
School to teach and administer a second- and third-year Clinical
Legal Education program. Originally the intent of the council
was to provide greater legal services for the poor. Bellow, a vet-
eran of the War on Poverty, shared this aim. But he also believed that clinical education was a method that should "be applied to the whole curriculum." Linking classroom instruction to
the actual representation of clients seemed to many students a
more effective — and more humane — means of learning law.
Their determination in the face of short-lived fund cutbacks and
former Dean Griswold's icy admonition that he hoped "Harvard
Law School won't go overboard on clinical legal training" kept
the program alive, and by the mid-1970s it had been expanded.
Nonetheless, Bellow's frustration with the peripheral importance
that Harvard Law assigned to clinical and legal education persuaded him in 1977 to announce his intention to form a separate
law institute.

An even more intense decade-long battle was waged over
grades. As in Plato's *Republic* or Hermann Hesse's *Glass Bead
Game*, a primary function of the Law School is selecting a few ex-
ceptionally talented students for special training and opportunities. Most are chosen on the basis of first-year grades — about
twenty-five students with the highest marks in each class of 550

are offered membership on the *Harvard Law Review*. Under Griswold, the next-ranked students were invited to join the Board of Student Advisers and the Legal Aid Bureau. For many first-year students this procedure resulted in a year of stomach-clutching anxiety, for second- and third-year students, humiliation or anger. Yet the harsh judgments of the grading system had been generally accepted over the years with scant debate. Credentialism, historically, also has been a true faith of Harvard Law School.

The opening salvo of the student "Blitzkrieg" near the end of the Griswold administration was a protest letter concerning grades. When Griswold responded by establishing Professor Byse's Joint Student-Faculty Committee, the *Record* commented: "Many find the [grading] system contains 'inherent absurdities' such as siphoning off students from the top one and two percent of the college graduates of the nation and then giving the majority of them C averages that numerically appear to be D or F averages on most commonly recognized grading scales." Other students made a more telling point; law school written examinations "leave unmeasured more legal skills than they measure" since they examine only legal writing ability.

During the months after Griswold left, the faculty adopted a policy of grade "inflation," leading to four out of five students averaging a B or better where formerly half of a typical class had a C average or worse. Dean Bok was pleased. In his first address to an entering class, he praised the new grading system: "We've fuzzed it up quite well."

Students disagreed. In February 1969, a committee of first-year students in consultation with 150 members of their class wrote a report entitled "The Trouble with Grades." Arguing that "under the current system . . . grades create a status hierarchy with few winners but many losers," the students claimed that year-end examinations at Harvard Law School failed to achieve any of their declared aims:

> We believe that the system draws critical distinctions among students prematurely, at the expense of developing

> talents over a three-year period. We believe that the system is a detrimental force in the lives of many first-year students; that it creates unnecessary tension, anxiety, and fear of failure in the minds of many of our classmates; that it encourages us to compete, to score points on each other, rather than to communicate and work in cooperation with one another. We believe that individual talents and interests go unrecognized and are often inhibited by the monolithic structure of the first year and its over-emphasis on final grades. Finally, we believe that the present grading system offers students too little evaluation too late.

The students recommended greater faculty evaluation of their work through written comments and the elimination of all grades except notations of "pass" or "fail."

Dean Bok quickly agreed "with the main thrust of these criticisms." A Special Faculty Committee recommended, and the faculty, shortly after the all-night study-in "put the guns to their heads," accepted, a series of measures including one giving first-year students the opportunity to elect "pass-fail" grades as an alternative to nine-tier (A+, A, A−, B+, etc.) or four-tier (high, satisfactory, low, fail) grade reporting. Although *Law Review* members would continue to be chosen on the basis of grades, members of the Board of Student Advisers and the Legal Aid Bureau would not.

Many of the faculty were outraged by this "caving in" under pressure. Archibald Cox vigorously dissented from the Special Faculty Committee's recommendations, which he felt "devalue[d] all grades and all grading." The professor stated his belief "in the importance of grades to the vital spirit of the law school": "They are essential to set and sustain an unreachable goal of excellence in *disciplined* intellectual performance in law; they make it plain that this is an institution where only performance counts, and this opens opportunities to hundreds of young men and women who would not otherwise enjoy them."

But students were just as upset that a mandatory pass-fail system — at least for the first year — had not been initiated. Two hundred students met early in the 1969–1970 term to protest the optional pass-fail system. A poll in January 1970 found 51 percent of the first-year class favored mandatory pass-fail; only 5 percent preferred the options adopted by the faculty.

The suicide of a student in April 1972, allegedly because he could not handle the pressure of the first year, touched off even more strident protests. A classmate recalls, "Everyone was in a state of shock, especially in our section. We walked around in a daze. We were hysterical."

A heated meeting was held in which several students pleaded with their professors to grade on a pass-fail basis. The professors refused. Seventy-one percent of the class signed a petition demanding this grading system. (The next year, 69 percent of the freshman class indicated the same preference.)

A month after the meeting, a *Harvard Law Record* editorial entitled "Grades Should Stay" was attacked by an assistant editor "as gratuitous mollycoddling of the faculty at a time when the overwhelming majority of students remains disgruntled by the present state of affairs . . ." The Law School Council also weighed in: "The cynicism and hostile disinterest that the experience of the first year generates under the present system is legendary. To those involved in the process the cost in anxiety and humiliation is substantial. The present grading system is the core of the problem."

In April 1973, Professor Jerome Cohen's Committee on First Year Evaluation and Related Matters, after eight months of study, recommended semesterization of the first year with grades in the first semester recorded on a modified mandatory pass-fail basis. After four lengthy meetings, the faculty voted to accept semesterization but eliminate pass-fail grading altogether. That single decision gnawed at students like a festering sore for the rest of the post-Griswold decade.

The other half of the rewards system at Harvard Law School is placement. Accompanying the protests against the Vietnam War was increased student hostility toward the large corporate law firms that employ many Harvard Law School students after graduation. In 1969, for example, twenty students picketed Milbank, Tweed, Hadley, and McCloy, an old-line Wall Street firm, because it represented the Chase Manhattan Bank, which was alleged to have "played a leading role in furnishing American economic and political support to South Africa." The following interview season students picketed a leading Boston firm, Ropes and Gray, for representing a coal company allegedly exploiting miners. Law students distributed a questionnaire to firms interviewing at Harvard Law School that was designed to probe "their internal operations and philosophical bases."

More significant, fewer students accepted corporate-law-firm job offers. Where 61 percent of the graduating class of 1960 had gone directly to law firm practice, only 44 percent did so in 1967 and 1968. And those students who did, extracted concessions. Washington firms such as Arnold and Porter, and Hogan and Hartson, established opportunities for young associates to do *pro bono* work through community-services offices. So did the Baltimore firm of Piper and Marbury, Boston's Foley, Hoag, and Eliot, and numerous firms in San Francisco and New York. Hogan and Hartson, for one, was not unaware that *pro bono* opportunities "may have a favorable impact upon recruitment."

But the primary response from Wall Street was meretricious. Rather than helping law students in their effort to solve "the larger problems of contemporary society," the firms bought them off. Wall Street's leading firm, Cravath, Swaine, and Moore, raised the "going rate" for first-year associates from $12,000 to $15,000 early in 1968 because of its difficulties in attracting a sufficient number of qualified law graduates. Other firms quickly fell in line. In October 1968, the "going rate" was hiked to $18,000, and by 1977, had reached $25,000.

Harvard Law School students could be bought — but they didn't like it. Sixty-seven percent of the class of 1973 went into private firms; fewer than 5 percent joined legal-aid or public-interest groups. Some even agreed with Donald Solomon, class of 1973, that "these statistics are nauseating."

It is somewhat saddening to think that ⅔ of the seats in every law school are warmed by people whose ultimate goal is not to serve any public interest but to resist collective bargaining, regulate the regulatory agencies, pollute with impunity and fight liability for defective products and industrial accidents . . .

Certainly it is too late "at this point in time" to claim ignorance of the crimes committed by our large corporations and so often justified by their counsel, or of the viable alternatives available in a legal practice. Perhaps the public should be warned that, on balance, Harvard Law School may be hazardous to their health.

From outside the citadel came voices even more critical of Harvard's model of legal education. For years, University of Miami Law School Dean Soia Mentschikoff warned first-year law students' wives: "Your husbands are going to change, their personalities are going to change in law school. They'll get more aggressive, more hostile, more precise, more impatient."

Then, in 1970, Yale law student — now Harvard Law Professor — Duncan Kennedy set out to explain the process à la Holden Caulfield. "How the Law School Fails: A Polemic" portrayed law school in terms of a "degredation ceremony . . . First year students when acting as a group in class are as cruel if not crueler than the teachers. They howl with glee when one of their number is dismembered. Many times during the first year I felt ashamed that my own laughter was uncontrollable, that the slight hysteria in the room infected me too. But the teacher who provokes, orchestrates and then openly revels in these displays should be far more ashamed."

The following year, Harvard Law School graduate John Jay Osborn, Jr., novelized Kennedy's polemic in *The Paper Chase*. To many law students, the snide Professor Kingsfield was a caricature, just like Osborn's description of some students as "robot pimps." But John Houseman's Academy Award–winning performance in the film version popularized the Kingsfield characterization, and many students did agree with the novel's leitmotiv, "something is happening to your mind."

By 1976–1977, student-faculty relations at the Law School had settled into an uneasy routine. Yale Law School had developed a mandatory pass-fail grading system for first-year students and a four-tier grading system for second and third years in 1968. Stanford Law School's *Law Review* had become voluntary in 1969. Harvard's grading system had ossified, although *Law Review* membership was broadened to include ten students chosen by a writing competition. Antioch and Northeastern had structured entire law schools along the lines of the legal-clinic approach. Harvard still offered only a few clinical-law courses.

Certainly, there had been reforms. In March 1971, Professor Byse delivered a memorable address outlining seventeen separate steps the School had taken in the previous five years to insure that "the evolutionary process has worked." Yet the nature of Harvard Law School's reforms to that date seemed more accurately depicted by former student David Kirp:

> . . . Most law schools have confronted vociferous demands for change in a manner which should be dear to every lawyer's heart: They have accommodated themselves to those demands, giving away points about which they really don't much care — adding extra courses, enrolling a limited number of formally less qualified students, abandoning class ranking, experimenting with alternative pedagogical approaches — while continuing to control those matters which still count for a great deal — faculty appointments, the selection of non-exceptional students, and the structure of the core curriculum.

By April 1975, when sixty students confronted Harvard University's Visiting Committee with a four-hour presentation of grievances, there was an obvious staleness to their effort. Demonstrably, Washington attorney Joseph Califano, Jr. (now Secretary of Health, Education, and Welfare), federal court of appeals Judge Shirley Hufstedler, and others "were impressed with the level of preparation of the students, the sincerity with which they held certain convictions, and the contrast with prior years when presentations tended to be more emotional than rational." In the best Harvard Law School tradition, the students presented their familiar concerns: The faculty had too little contact with the students, faculty selection was "prejudice[d] against practicing lawyers," there were too few clinical courses, more women should be admitted, the Placement Office allegedly was uncooperative with blacks, all members of the *Law Review* should be chosen on the basis of a writing competition. The committee listened patiently and, after expressions of sympathy, unanimously agreed that the present *Harvard Law Review* selection system should be maintained. Months later, Dean Sacks issued the text of the committee's report, including a list of the actions taken in response. The actions ran along the lines of encouraging the faculty to consult more often with students and describing recent increases in the number of clinical law courses.

After a decade, the periphery of Dean Griswold's Harvard Law School had altered, but the center had not. Harvard Law School, as the dean once put it, continued to teach law "in the grand manner."

2

LAYING THE FOUNDATIONS:

The Law School Model of
Christopher Columbus Langdell

And whoever labors on this edifice, with usefulness and distinction, whoever clears its foundations, strengthens its pillars, adorns its entablatures, or contributes to raise its august dome still higher in the skies, connects himself, in name, in fame, and character, with that which is and must be as durable as the frame of human society.

DANIEL WEBSTER, eulogy for Joseph Story

Christopher Columbus Langdell is widely regarded as having transformed Harvard into the first modern American law school during the twenty-five years he was dean, from 1870 to 1895. He extended classwork from eighteen months to three years and implemented a standardized curriculum. The first career law professors were hired. Rigorous examinations and the college-degree admission requirement were initiated. Now-familiar institutions — the *Law Review,* elective courses, moot courts, the Law School Alumni Association — were created or shaped to their present form by Langdell. Most celebrated was his transformation of the method of law school teaching from the study of general principles in textbooks to the study of actual law cases guided by the "Socratic" questioning of law professors. In the seventy years after Langdell stepped down as dean, the Harvard Law School "model" of legal education was emulated by virtually every American law school.

But the intellectual origins of American legal education were British. From England, the United States inherited two conflicting approaches to legal education. Prior to the American Revolution, most English attorneys served a five-year apprenticeship as an "articled" clerk to a practitioner before being admitted to the bar. Their education was primarily self-acquired. The law student would learn what he could by copying and rewriting legal documents, attending trials, and reading a small number of highly technical outlines of the common law of England.

Beginning with a series of lectures delivered at Oxford in 1753, William Blackstone attempted to reform English legal education and, more important, "to mark out a plan of the laws of England, so comprehensive, as that every title might be reduced under some one or other of its general heads, which the student might afterwards pursue to any degree of minuteness; and at the same time so contracted, that the gentleman might with tolerable application contemplate and understand the whole."

Blackstone was unsuccessful in persuading the English legal community that law was best taught in universities. But between 1765 and 1768, he published his four-volume *Commentaries on the Laws of England*, which provided a systematic outline of English law and described what Blackstone termed the "natural foundations of justice."

The root of Blackstone's "science" was his faith that the common-law judges of England possessed the "reason" to apply natural law "in every circumstance of life." Over time, the random decisions of these judges, formed with due regard for earlier, related decisions, amounted to a body of social rules: an unwritten constitution of property and civil liberties laws described in Blackstone's *Commentaries*.

The United States imported both the apprenticeship and university modes of legal education. Usually practicing attorneys made poor law teachers, but a few had a flair and enthusiasm for instructing students. Among these was Tapping Reeve of Litchfield, Connecticut. Around 1784, Reeve ceased to be an attorney who taught students on the side and instead became a full-time teacher of law. The Litchfield School, however, continued to be administered like a law office. Students continued to draft pleadings and conveyances. But Reeve supplemented this "practical" education with weekly examinations and a series of lectures roughly paralleling Blackstone's *Commentaries*. By 1798, when Reeve was appointed a judge, Litchfield had a national reputation. Before it closed its doors in 1833, the school had matriculated over a thousand graduates, including two men who became vice-president of the United States, three who sat on the United States Supreme Court, 101 who were elected to the United States House of Representatives, and 28 who were elected to the United States Senate. Not surprisingly, Litchfield also encouraged the formation of at least twenty other "practical" law office type schools.

Simultaneous with the American development of apprenticeship, legal education, and the Litchfield type of school were the beginnings of university legal education. In 1779, Thomas Jefferson reorganized William and Mary College to include a chair in law. Sharing Blackstone's view that law was a liberal art, he encouraged George Wythe, the first American professor of law, to lecture not only on municipal law (meaning Blackstone) but also government.

Relatively few students attended such lectures prior to the Civil War, but the influence of the university law schools soon became significant. The United States began without any written court records. The commentaries on United States law written by the first law professors provided the early framework of the American legal system. In 1803, St. George Tucker, Wythe's successor at William and Mary College, published an edition of Blackstone's *Commentaries* with notes adapting it to American usage, which "fixed the Blackstone tradition in this country," in the words of legal historian A. Z. Reed. Twenty-three years later, one-time law lecturer, later New York State's Chancellor, James Kent, began publishing the four volumes of his *Commentaries* on American law, which were also conceived in the general spirit of Blackstone's *Commentaries*. But within a few years after Kent's

Commentaries were published, the intellectual leadership of the American legal profession gravitated north to Cambridge.

As early as 1775, Edmund Burke observed in the British House of Commons that almost as many copies of Blackstone's *Commentaries* had been sold in the Colonies as in England. It was probably knowledge of Blackstone's books or of his professorial chair at Oxford that persuaded Isaac Royall, a wealthy owner of West Indian sugar plantations living in Medford, Massachusetts, to bequeath to Harvard College in 1778 over 1000 acres of Massachusetts Bay land to endow "a Professor of Laws in said College or a Professor of Physick and Anatomy which ever the said Overseers and Corporation shall judge to be the best for the benefit of said College . . ." Since Royall had been loyal to the British during the Revolutionary War, it was not until 1815 that courts permitted Harvard University to complete the sale of his lands and appoint the first professor of law under Royall's bequest.

Harvard Law School officially opened in 1817 under the tutelage of Isaac Parker, chief justice of Massachusetts, and Asahel Stearns, a local Federalist politician who had recently lost his seat in Congress. For a dozen years the school foundered, graduating only twenty-five students between 1817 and 1829, apparently because of its inability to compete with the better-known and more practice-oriented Litchfield type of law school.

But in 1829, with the aid of a $10,000 contribution from lawyer–law author Nathan Dane, Harvard University hired United States Supreme Court Justice Joseph Story to lecture at the Law School whenever his judicial duties allowed. Story was a judge with a national reputation, recognized as one of the most erudite legal thinkers of his day. In 1845, when Story died, over 140 students were attending the School.

But Story's primary reason for accepting the School's offer was to write. Throughout the sixteen years he lectured in Cambridge, the justice was assisted by a full-time professor, giving Story time to complete his books, "sound and useful law being the object." Between 1832 and 1845, he published nine *Commentaries: The Law of Bailments* (1832), *The Constitution* (1833), *Conflicts of Law* (1834),

Equity Jurisprudence (1836), *Equity Pleading* (1838), *Agency* (1839), *Partnership* (1841), *Bills of Exchange* (1843), and *Promissory Notes* (1845). These *Commentaries* provided the United States with its first general outline of commercial law.

Like Blackstone, Joseph Story believed the real source of American law — unless a legislature explicitly stated otherwise — stemmed from a transcendent natural law knowable through a judge's reason. In *Swift* v. *Tyson,* one of his most celebrated Supreme Court decisions, Story elaborated this view. Section 34 of the United States Judiciary Act of 1789 provided "that the laws of the several States, except where the Constitution, treaties, or statutes of the United States shall otherwise require or provide, shall be regarded as rules of decision in trials at common law in the courts of the United States, in cases where they apply." But Story did not construe the term "laws" to include state judicial decisions — only state statutes. "In the ordinary use of language it will hardly be contended that the decisions of courts constitute laws. They are, at most, only evidence of what the laws are, and are not of themselves laws." Then what was the law? In the instant case, "The law respecting negotiable instruments may be truly declared [to be] not the law of a single country only, but . . . principles established in the general commercial law" and applicable throughout the entire "commercial world."

Consistent with his imposing view of federal common law, Story organized a two-year curriculum at Harvard Law School that totally omitted the study of state government and state statutory law. Instead, Harvard concentrated on the study of commercial law, contracts, property, and courtroom procedure. By this curriculum, and to a larger extent in his *Commentaries* and judicial decisions, Story associated Harvard Law School with a polar position in one of the great political debates of the Jacksonian period. The common (or judge-made) law of England had not been well received in the United States. On a visceral level, this antagonism reflected the patriotic hatred of the British engendered by the last colonial years and the Revolutionary War. But the enduring hostility to the common law was based on other considerations. To the Jeffersonian Democrats, judge-made law grounded in judicial interpretation of the law of nature posed a threat to their conception that all political power under the federal and state constitutions emanated from "the consent of the governed" and that laws might be amended whenever the voters or their legislators saw fit. This philosophical position was transformed into the political question: Who would design the property laws of the new Republic — democratically elected legislatures or appointed judges?

Historian Perry Miller has explained that at an early point the conservative or Federalist lawyers

> rallied once more to the figure who had so often provided their strength and consolation: Blackstone. Here he was of tremendous help, for he freed them from allegiance to the notion that property rights derived from the Lockean social compact or that they were in any sense dependent on the society's recognition that the owner had made something his own by mixing his labor in it. Not at all, said Blackstone: the concept of property exists even before there is any society at all; to protect the individual in the enjoyment of this absolute right, vested in him by the immutable law of nature, governments are created. The law "will not authorize the least violation of it; no, not even for the general good of the whole community."

When the Jefferson Democrats succeeded the Federalists in the White House and many state legislatures, this view of judicial supremacy became the cornerstone of the Federalist platform. Fortified by Blackstone, Federalist judges ignored or overruled debtor, banking, and other property-related statutes that they found contrary to the "eternal principles of justice, which no government has a right to disregard."

Over time, the "doctrinal" writings of Kent and Story Americanized Blackstone and strengthened the autonomy of the judicial lawmaking process. Blackstone had argued that law was a science, and had rationally assembled the English common law. The understanding of this science was the special competence of judges and lawyers, not legislatures. By calling upon the legislatures to recognize that the "scientific arrangement and harmony of principles" could be developed comprehensively only in the *Commentaries,* the conservative legal profession, in effect, freed much of American law from legislative supervision. Perceiving this process in 1831–1832, Alexis de Tocqueville would assume, "Lawyers consequently form the highest political class . . . the most powerful, if not the only counterpoise to the democratic element. In that country we easily perceive how the legal profession is qualified by its attributes, and even by its faults, to neutralize the vices inherent in popular government. When the American people are intoxicated by passion or carried away by the impetuosity of their ideas, they are checked and stopped by the almost invisible influence of their legal counselors."

Even as Tocqueville penned these oft-cited words, a sustained movement against the autonomy of the American legal profession lawmaking was beginning. During the age of Jackson (roughly, 1830–1860), state legislatures asserted themselves, broadly challenging Tocqueville's "highest political class" and the economic interests they represented. For the first time, legislatures performed a significant role in making property laws through the adoption of restrictive general incorporation acts. Property qualifications were no longer required to secure the right to vote. In some states, judges for the first time were popularly elected.

The single reform, however, that most directly affected legal education was the easing of bar admission standards. In 1800, fourteen of the nineteen states and organized territories required of lawyers a definite period of preparation (typically two, three, or five years) in law office or law school study. By 1840, such training was necessary in no more than eleven of the thirty jurisdictions; by 1860, a definite period of study was necessary in only nine of thirty-nine jurisdictions.

In the western states, where the bar admission requirements were the weakest, Abraham Lincoln wrote, in an 1858 letter, that "the cheapest, quickest and best way" to become a lawyer was to "read Blackstone's *Commentaries,* Chitty's *Pleadings,* Greenleaf's

Evidence, Story's *Equity* and Story's *Equity Pleading,* get a license and go to the practice and still keep reading." Lincoln's own bar examination was so casual a formality that Lincoln had difficulty believing that he "was really being examined at all." University legal education remained at most "a holding operation in the decades before the Civil War." Almost immediately after Story's death in 1845, the number of enrolled students at Harvard Law School dropped sharply. Where 163 students had attended the School in 1844, only 100 enrolled in 1849, and for twenty-five years thereafter the Law School experienced a decline.

Lacking Story's national reputation, his successors shortened the curriculum to eighteen months, abolished examinations, and allowed students to enter or leave at midterm and to stay for as long or short a period as they wished. Perhaps this was as well as Harvard Law School could have done during the Jacksonian period. Dependent upon tuition for their entire support, the faculty strained all conventions to entice as many students as possible to study as long as they could pay their way. "It was," noted A. Z. Reed, "a question merely of dollars and cents."

In 1869, less than half the graduating students had college degrees. "Everything about the school was stereotyped," declared the Law School's official *Centennial History.* "For twenty years the language of the catalogue as to entrance, course of study, and degree was not changed by a letter. There was no recorded faculty meeting during the entire period . . . Library rules were made in theory by the corporation, in practice by the janitor."*

The School was apparently also an unpleasant place in which to study. Where Story had lectured, succeeding professors employed the "textbook method" — students had to memorize as-

---

* The janitor, an immigrant named John Sweetnam, possessed an impressive command of Latin as well as an autocratic personality. Ostensibly hired to open the doors in the morning and lock them at night, he attended all lectures and criticized each speaker's delivery and doctrine, seemingly making him the true but unheralded father of the Law School's Socratic method. According to historian Charles Warren, Sweetnam "exercised a general supervision over all matters connected with the School, and in his later years became a terror to everyone in or near it. But he was at last displaced by the wave of reform that swept over the School about 1870."

signed portions of textbooks. During the recitation periods, professors explained the text and quizzed students to determine how accurately they had memorized their assignments. Oliver Wendell Holmes, Jr., who entered the Law School in 1864, recalled bitterly, "One found oneself plunged in a thick fog of details — in a black and frozen night, in which were no flowers, no spring, no easy joys. Voices of authority warned that in the crush of that ice any craft might sink. One heard Burke saying that law sharpens the mind by narrowing it. One heard in Thackeray of a lawyer bending all the powers of a great mind to a mean profession. One saw that artists and poets shrank from it as from an alien world . . ."

However, the faculty did continue Story's scholarship. In the 1840s, Professor Simon Greenleaf began publishing a multivolume treatise on evidence. Attorney Theophilus Parsons, who served between 1848 and 1869, published prominent texts on contracts, mercantile, and maritime law. And Emory Washburn, a former governor of Massachusetts, published a seminal volume, *Real Property.* Parsons and Washburn no doubt sincerely believed, as they reported to the Visiting Committee of Harvard University's overseers on October 21, 1869, that "the condition of the school at the present time is eminently satisfactory."

This opinion was not widely shared. In October 1870, Oliver Wendell Holmes, Jr., and Arthur Sedgwick, both Harvard LL.B.'s of 1866, published an unsigned article in the *American Law Review* that began:

> For a long time the condition of the Harvard Law School has been almost a disgrace to the Commonwealth of Massachusetts. We say "almost a disgrace," because, undoubtedly, some of its courses of lectures have been good, and no law school of which this can be said is hopelessly bad. Still, a school which undertook to confer degrees without any preliminary examination whatever was doing something every year to injure the profession throughout the country, and to discourage real students. So long as the possession of a degree signified nothing except a residence

for a certain period in Cambridge or Boston, it was without value . . .

When a faculty member responded defensively, Holmes and Sedgwick published a second article noting that students were virtually unable to check out books from the library. Reports of this nature so concerned the Visiting Committee that it recommended in 1869 to the college's new President, Charles W. Eliot, the creation of a committee to review "the condition and prospects of the law school . . ." This derogatory recommendation prompted Professor Parsons, the leader of the faculty, to resign. It was in such circumstances that Christopher Columbus Langdell arrived at Harvard Law School.

Christopher Columbus Langdell was an unlikely revolutionary. Existing portraits invariably show him as an old man: gray-haired, with a long white beard, his dark recessed eyes squinting. In Harvard's law library, an "official" portrait painted in 1892 portrays Langdell seated bolt upright in a nondescript black suit before a green baize desk on which are arranged three law books, some papers, a gold watch, and a walking cane. A photograph accompanying an 1889 magazine article adds only the further information that Langdell then wore small-lensed wire-framed glasses.

Throughout his life, Langdell followed a policy of "never complain, never explain," so the comparatively little known about his personal life is the gossamer-hued accounts of his admirers, principally those of his protégé, James Barr Ames. Born in 1826 in New Boston, New Hampshire, to an impoverished but literate farming family, Langdell lost his mother when he was seven. A few years later, his father ceased to provide a home for Langdell and his two sisters, and thereafter they lived with various families, "working in the summer and going to the district school in the winter."

His elder sister commented that around the age of sixteen Langdell "opened his heart to me for the first time, and it was also the first time he had made known his aspirations to any human being. He told me that he had a very strong desire for a college education, but did not see how it could be accomplished." To save money, Langdell taught school, and for several months worked in one of Manchester, New Hampshire's textile mills.

Encouraged by a prominent local attorney, Langdell entered Exeter in the spring of 1845. When he failed to win a scholarship in July of that year, he suffered "the keenest disappointment of his life," explains Ames. "Almost heart-broken, he sat down upon the steps of the Academy building and burst into tears." Both sisters, however, contributed money from their earnings as millworkers so that Langdell could remain at Exeter. With these sums, plus what Langdell himself earned doing part-time work at the Academy, he was able to hold out until the following July, when he did win a scholarship.

In 1848, Langdell, who was considerably older than his classmates, entered Harvard College as a sophomore. He was a relentless scholar, refusing, among other things, to march in the University's annual parade, because, as Langdell remarked to a classmate, "I preferred to study." At the end of his first year he ranked second in his class. But in December of his second year, he dropped out, partly for monetary reasons, partly because he had decided to become a lawyer. After working as a private tutor, he returned to Exeter. There he paid a fee and began reading law in a local law office. An Exeter acquaintance recalled watching Langdell saw wood while reading a law book at the same time.

In November 1851, Langdell enrolled in Harvard Law School. Although the course was only a year and a half long, Langdell stayed three years, supporting himself by serving as the Law School's librarian and helping Professor Parsons prepare his treatise on contracts. By then, Langdell had become a fanatic student. He so constantly worked in the library and so late at night that classmates gossiped that he slept on a library table. Once a classmate found him in a library alcove totally absorbed in an ancient collection of English cases. Langdell suddenly glanced up and said, in a tone of mingled exhilaration and regret, "Oh, if only I could have lived in the time of the Plantagenets!" For all his studiousness, Langdell seems to have been liked. Fifty years later, a fellow student would remember:

The Librarian was no less a personage than C. C. Langdell, a book worm if there ever was one . . .

He always wore a green lined dark shade. Under his
auspices there were a dozen of us who clubbed together.
There I saw his "case system" in the making, although at
the time I did not realize it. Over our sausage and buck-
wheat, or whatever it was, we talked shop, nothing but
shop, discussed concrete cases, real or hypothetical, criti-
cised or justified decisions, affirmed or reversed judgments.
From these table-talks I got more stimulus, more inspiration, in fact, more law, than from the lectures of Judge
Parker and Professor Parsons.

As a student, Langdell was regularly referred to as a genius.

But when Langdell began his career in 1854 as a New York
City lawyer, he was initially a failure. A friend later wrote he
retreated from courtroom practice after being bested by "the
tricks of the legal sharper." This was a polite way of saying that
Langdell was not a very effective trial lawyer. During the four
years of his solo practice, he seems to have spent much of his time
reading in the New York Law Institute library. The librarian soon
fell into the habit of referring attorneys with questions to Langdell: "That young man knows more about the law on such a matter than anyone else." One such attorney, William Stanley, received so much valuable advice from Langdell that he invited
Langdell to become his partner in 1858.

With Stanley and other partners in the firm, Langdell apparently formed a relationship similar to that between the attorneys in Dickens's novel *A Tale of Two Cities*. While the others
appeared in court or met with clients, Langdell did the research
and wrote the briefs.

He always harbored a healthy respect for the dollar. Indeed,
a striking aspect of Langdell's few reports about the Law School
is his focus on tuition fees received, surplus, and endowments.
Nevertheless, his practical concern for making ends meet was
far overshadowed by his love of books. In one writing, Langdell
discounted all other problems at Harvard Law School in the pe-

riod after Story died to emphasize that the worst failing of his predecessors was that they allowed the library to deteriorate: "If the professors had taken a strong and active interest in the care and preservation of the books, the evil day might have been deferred; but, as it was, the condition of the library had become so ruinous . . . that some radical change in its administration was imperatively called for." By his own account, his first acts as dean were to reorganize the library and hire a full-time librarian.

Langdell's arrival as a professor in 1870 was fortunate if not miraculous. On May 19, 1869, Harvard College's Board of Overseers elected as president Charles William Eliot, a thirty-five-year-old professor of chemistry, with well-known progressive views on education. Eliot soon grew dissatisfied with the condition of the Law School and sought out Langdell. "I remembered," explained Eliot,

> that when I was a junior in college, in the year 1851–1852, and used to go often in the early evening to the room of a friend who was in the Divinity School, I there heard a young man who was making the notes to "Parsons on Contracts" talk about law. He was generally eating his supper at the time, standing in front of the fire and eating with a good appetite a bowl of brown bread and milk. I was a mere boy, only eighteen years old; but it was given me to understand that I was listening to a man of genius. In the year 1870 I recalled the remarkable quality of the young man's exposition, sought him in New York, and induced him to become Dane Professor.

Assured of Eliot's support for his strongly held beliefs about legal education, Langdell swept into the Law School like a whirlwind. On February 21, 1870, Langdell began as a professor. On September 27, the Law School's faculty held its first formal meeting. With Eliot presiding, the faculty elected Langdell to be the Law School's first dean.

Langdell's first curricular reform was to restore examinations. Even before he officially began as dean, Langdell placed in the

Law School's 1870 circular the notice that "the faculty reserve the right of basing their recommendations for a degree upon a final examination." Both students and alumni were outraged, contending that examinations were unnecessary; that success in passing them would not guarantee success in the actual practice of law, which, after all, was the reason students attended Harvard Law School; that it was undignified to test whether students had seriously examined the law, each student's word that he had being sufficient (a powerful argument in the gentlemanly Boston and Cambridge of the 1870s); and that examinations would injure the Law School by decreasing attendance and consequently reducing its income (also a powerful argument since the Law School then was losing money). Undeterred, Langdell instituted written examinations in June 1871.

Simultaneous with his investment as dean, Langdell announced that the LL.B. degree would be granted only to those students completing certain mandatory courses within the framework of a two-year course of study. As modified in 1871–1872, all students were required to study seven courses familiar to law students to this day: Real Property, Contracts, Torts, Criminal Law, Civil Procedure, Evidence, and Equity. Students could also elect Constitutional Law (previously emphasized), Personal Property, Bailments, Marine Insurance, Corporations, Shipping and Admiralty, and Conflict of Laws. Theoretical courses such as Jurisprudence and International Law were dropped. As early as 1876, the Law School encouraged students to pursue a three-year course of study, an approach not formally required until 1899.

But Langdell's most controversial innovation was to change the way law was taught. The 1870–1871 catalog described the method of instruction in much the same terms as in catalogs for the previous forty years: "Instruction will be given in recitations; by lectures and exposition; by moot courts; by cases assigned to students for written and oral opinions and by exercises in drawing pleadings at common law and equity." This was a ceremonious way of stating that Professor Washburn would continue to lecture and quiz students to see how well they had memorized the legal rules described in the assigned reading. But there followed an ambiguous additional sentence: "Each instructor will adopt such mode of teaching the subjects of which he has charge as in his judgment will best advance the pupils in his course." With that enigmatic introduction, Langdell's most celebrated reform, the case method, was born.

In Langdell had come the first day of his Contracts course to face his already confused students. He opened a pamphlet containing a number of old English decisions that the students earlier had received. There was no explanation of why these cases were to be studied or what, if any, relation existed among the cases.

"Mr. Fox," Langdell had begun, "will you state the facts in the case of *Payne* v. *Cave?*" Fox did his best to state the case. Langdell asked a second student to present the argument of the plaintiff. He then inquired whether a third student agreed with the second student. Langdell posed a dozen more questions. By this time, the students were thoroughly bewildered. Langdell had not once stated the law pertaining to the case or the significance of the decision. He never did.

Rather, after the long, inconclusive discussion of *Payne* v. *Cave,* he proceeded to a second case. After class, the indignant students held a meeting. Students demanded: "What do we care whether Myers agrees with the case, or what Fessenden thinks of the dissenting opinion? What we want to know is: What is the law?" Attendance in Langdell's class plummeted. Students criticized the "useless" preparation for the "grammar-school recitation." The evaluation of a few short cases often occupied several lectures.

Indeed, one of the ironies of Langdell's experiment was that although his methods would ultimately be adopted by most law professors, Langdell himself was not a very inspiring teacher. Even his admirers conceded that he always progressed deliberately, ponderously, extracting every possible legal principle from each case.

The slow pace of his course was compounded by the opacity of his method — why was he asking all these questions? — and his disturbing tendency to lapse into silence in the middle of a class, absorbed in thought, to reconsider his own views. It was believed he did not respond to students' questions because he did not know the answers. On one occasion when a student elicited an immediate response from Langdell, he turned Langdell's method against him, posing additional questions to show that Langdell's answer contradicted the decisions of several previous cases. There was "a hurricane of derisive clapping and stamping," a classmate recalled. Another wrote, "Langdell was routed." Yet, the next day, the "old crank" returned to the same cases.

By the end of the year, the class had shrunk to seven or eight students. This lack of attendance was considered proof of the failure of his method. It soon affected the reputation of Harvard Law School as well. Between the 1870–1871 school year and that of 1872–1873, the number of students enrolled shrank from 165 to 117 — fewer than either Langdell or President Eliot had anticipated. In 1872, Boston University opened a new law school to compete with Harvard because "many students who would have liked to attend some law school were deterred" by the impracticality of the nearby law school in Cambridge. By the fall of the 1873–1874 school year, it was rumored that Langdell would be fired if enrollment continued to decrease.

Enrollment increased. Gradually, the advantages of Langdell's technique became appreciated. By teaching students law from court decisions, an original source, Langdell taught students legal reasoning more effectively than did the textbook professors. Louis Brandeis, who studied under Langdell in 1875, would later glorify the dean's method: "[From cases] the authors of text-books had gained their knowledge of the law, and there only can others acquire it. No instructor can provide the royal road to knowledge by giving to the students the conclusions deduced from these sources; his chief aim should be to teach the student to think in a legal manner in accordance with the principles of the particular branch of the law. He should seek to inculcate and develop in legal reasoning the habit of intellectual self-reliance." Brandeis recognized the maddening slowness of Langdell's method as its greatest strength. "When the end of the chapter of cases is reached, the student stands possessed of the principles in their full development. Having attended as it were at their birth, having traced their history from stage to stage, the student has grown with them and in them; the principles have become a part of his flesh and blood; they have *pro hac vice* created a habit of mind. Like swimming or skating, once acquired, they cannot be forgotten, for they are a part of himself."

But students were absorbing far more than a reasoning process. Bound up with Langdell's curriculum and methods were political beliefs every bit as conservative as those of Joseph Story. However, where Story, like Blackstone before him, emphasized the natural-law basis of the "scientific" organization of the common law, Langdell treated philosophical first principles as implied, and focused on the process of discovering these principles. As Langdell explained in his most often quoted statement:

> Law, considered as a science, consists of certain principles or doctrines. To have such a mastery of these as to be able to apply them with constant facility and certainty to the ever-tangled skein of human affairs, is what constitutes a true lawyer; and hence to acquire that mastery should be the business of every earnest student of law. Each of these doctrines has arrived at its present state by slow degrees; in other words, it is a growth, extending in many cases through centuries. This growth is to be traced in the main through a series of cases; and much the shortest and best, if not the only way of mastering the doctrine effectually is by studying the cases in which it is embodied.

To assert that judges by their reasoning had developed doctrines that should be applied "with constant facility and certainty to the ever-tangled skein of human affairs" was to revive the natural-law argument for judicial supremacy, albeit with a glossy "law is a science" label. Langdell's political position was particularly evident in his curriculum. Emphasized was a national common law, which theoretically controlled the courts of every state. Within particular courses, the study of statutes was sometimes entirely eliminated. For example, in Langdell's *Summary of Equity*

Pleading (1877) he suggested the reader "bear in mind that it is the object of these sheets to aid the student in acquiring a knowledge of the equity system as such; and with this view the writer confines himself to the system as it existed in England from the earliest times to the end of Lord Eldon's chancellorship." This prompted one law review to wonder (no doubt mindful of the legislative activity of the Jacksonian period) why "the study of equity pleading at Harvard University in 1877 should be limited to the system as it existed prior to 1827."

Even before the 1873–1874 enrollment increase, Langdell took the next step in building his new model of legal education. In 1872, Professor Nathaniel Holmes, an exponent of the old textbook style of teaching, resigned, partially due to his discomfort with Langdell's reforms. A year later, with President Eliot's backing, Langdell persuaded a reluctant Harvard Board of Overseers to appoint his recent student, James Barr Ames, an assistant professor and offer him a five-year contract. For Langdell, the appointment of the twenty-six-year-old Ames was crucial to fully converting Harvard Law School to the case method. As long as the faculty largely consisted of famous retired judges, the lecture system would predominate. Langdell campaigned, ". . . A teacher of law should be a person who accompanies his pupils on a road which is new to them, but with which he is well acquainted from having often traveled it before. What qualifies a person, therefore, to teach law, is not experience in the work of a lawyer's office, not experience in dealing with men, not experience in the trial or argument of cases, not experience, in short, in using law, but experience in learning law."

Harvard's Board of Overseers was dubious, and in December 1873 appointed, in addition to the youthful Ames, James Bradley Thayer, a forty-three-year-old Boston attorney, to a full professorship. Initially Thayer relied on the lecture method.

Ames, employing Langdell's case method more effectively than Langdell, soon proved to be a popular instructor. With enrollment increasing slightly between 1873–1874 and 1874–1875 (from 141 students to 144) and significantly in 1875–1876 (to 173), Langdell was able to extend his control over the faculty. In 1875, the practice of employing Boston attorneys as part-time lecturers at the Law School was abandoned. At the same time, the School hired John Chipman Gray, one of the first editors of the then prestigious *American Law Review* and a founder of the Boston firm of Ropes and Gray, as a full professor. Gray used the lecture method. But the following spring seventy-six-year-old Professor Washburn resigned. At his retirement, wrote Harvard legal historian Charles Warren, "the old order of things in the Law School may be said to have passed away. The new regime, now had full swing, and Dean Langdell assumed unfettered sway among his associates."

Langdell began pressing for an even more controversial aspect of his model: fully transforming Harvard Law School into a graduate school. Before Langdell arrived in 1870, entrance to the school was "free." That is, there was no prerequisite of a college degree, students could come and go as they chose throughout the school year. In his annual report as dean in 1873, Langdell specified three measures necessary to "enable us to turn out a much higher grade of young lawyers than has hitherto been known in the United States . . . First, requiring a good academic education as a condition of admission; secondly, abolishing the practice of admitting students to advanced standing; thirdly, establishing a three years' course." For the next twenty years, Langdell struggled to "raise standards" along these lines.

In February 1875, the Law School adopted the regulation that all future students must be college graduates or pass an entrance examination. Since the entrance examination required applicants to translate (without the aid of a dictionary) Latin passages from Caesar's *Commentaries,* Cicero's *Orations,* or the *Aeneid* of Virgil, and answer legal questions based on Blackstone's *Commentaries,* it is probable that virtually every applicant would have had to be a college graduate.

President Eliot was delighted. His academic governing board soon approved the new requirement, with Eliot reporting: "The University in taking this action is only doing its duty to the learned professions of Law and Medicine, which have been for fifty years in process of degradation through the barbarous practice of admitting to them persons wholly destitute of academic culture . . . to their own lasting injury and that of the community . . ." Eliot then advanced the unexpected — though, as it turned out, wholly accurate — argument that raising standards was also good business for the University: "An institution which has any legal prestige and power, will make a money profit by raising its standard, and that either at once or in a very short time. Its demand for greater attainments on the part of its students will be quickly responded to, and this improved class of students will in a marvelously short time so increase the reputation and influence of the institution as to make its privileges and its rewards more valued and more valuable . . ."

The Harvard Board of Overseers, nonetheless, was outraged. To suggest just ten years after the assassination of Abraham Lincoln that Lincoln should not have been permitted to become a lawyer because he neither graduated from a college nor spoke Latin was political sacrilege even in Brahmin Boston. Following an angry meeting, the board insisted that the Law School rescind its new admission standard.

Langdell bided his time. In 1876, the Board of Overseers approved a Law School rule encouraging each student to study three years to earn an LL.B. degree. This rule coupled with the weakened economy of the late 1870s and early 1880s reduced attendance for the next decade. Not until 1887–1888 did the enrollment again exceed the 1876–1877 registration. But during these years, Langdell continued to build. In 1881–1882, Boston attorney Louis Brandeis convinced classmate William Weld to contribute $90,000 of his recent inheritance to Harvard Law School, enabling the School to endow a fifth professorial chair.

In that same year, other contributions facilitated the expansion of the library and construction of a new building, Austin Hall. Alumni financial support for the School was formalized through the establishment of the Harvard Law School Association.

During the 1880s, the faculty reluctantly agreed to an elective system. Langdell essentially believed that the subject fields of the common law were just as eternal as their underlying principles. But the students, by petition, requested that advanced courses be offered in such developing areas of commercial law as insurance, banking, patents, railroad, and mining law. These second- and third-year optional courses were added to the curriculum, but it is a mark of Langdell's faith in the common law that Harvard long limited its elective courses to a small number of optional courses in Commercial and Property Law.

In 1886, the *Harvard Law Review* was organized. Eight third-year students, with the financial support of Boston alumni, began publishing a student-edited magazine of legal commentary. From the outset, articles and book reviews solicited from professors and attorneys on legal topics were subjected to criticism by student editors. Students also contributed notes analyzing prominent court decisions. In 1902, membership on the *Review* was limited to the highest-ranked students in the first-year class.

Competition "to make the *Review*" coupled with a fear of failing examinations soon set the tone of the School. In 1942, Professor Edward H. (Bull) Warren characterized Harvard Law School in his *A Spartan Education:* "It was fashionable to work. Gone was the college distinction between sports and grinds. Over three quarters of the students worked hard. Sixty hours a week was common; seventy hours a week not infrequent." In large measure, the motivation was *Law Review.* Felix Frankfurter recalled his roommate pointing out the editor of the *Harvard Law Review.* "If he'd said, 'That's the Archangel Gabriel,' he couldn't have been more awed. 'My God,' I said to myself, 'the head of the *Harvard Law Review.* He must be a giant." Years later, Frankfurter recalled his "quasi-religious feelings about Harvard Law School . . . the most complete practice in democracy" that Frankfurter claimed he ever knew:

> You very quickly got into the atmosphere. There was a dominating atmosphere, first, of professionalism, and what I think is an indispensable quality of true professionalism, the democratic spirit. What mattered was excellence in your profession to which your father or your face was equally irrelevant. And so rich man, poor man were just irrelevant titles to the equation of human relations. The

thing that mattered was what you did professionally. If a man was respected, it was because he was very good either because he showed up very well in the classroom or in private discussion, or, after the first year, which was the novitiate year, the very good men were defined by the fact that they got on the *Harvard Law Review*. This was determined entirely on the basis of your work as a student by examinations at the end of the year. Election to the *Harvard Law Review* followed academic rank, an automatic affair.

By the late 1880s, enrollment at Harvard Law soared, and Langdell was again able to lobby for "raised standards." In 1895–1896, the School passed a rule restricting admission to "graduates of approved colleges" and "persons qualified to enter the senior class of Harvard" unless an applicant passed an admission test comparable to the one Langdell had proposed in 1875. There was an immediate national outcry. In 1896, only seven of the seventy-four existing law schools required a high-school diploma for admission. The *American Law Review* reflected the mood of many practitioners: "The crimes that have been committed against the youth of our race under the plea of *mental discipline* pass all computation. They have been drilled in Greek for mental discipline; they have been drilled in the higher mathematics for mental discipline; and they have been drilled in this and in that useless study for mental discipline, when they could best get the mental discipline which a lawyer needs by studying law . . ." The *Michigan Law Review* took issue with the Frankfurter-Langdell conception of democracy: The "Harvard idea seems to be to exclude all but a privileged class from admission to the practice of law." The *Chicago Legal News* agreed: "Harvard may never have knocking at its classic doors the future Marshall, Webster, or Lincoln, because this mental giant has not in his pocket the A.B. degree."

To the Harvard Law School faculty, this reaction seemed exaggerated. Seventy other law schools still did *not* insist on college degrees. The year before the rule went into effect, 80 percent of Harvard's law students had college degrees.

But critics of the new procedure feared that a Rubicon was

being crossed. And they were right. In the fifteen years from 1896 to 1910, only forty-nine of the 3488 students admitted to the School entered without a college degree. In 1909, the alternative of passing "a satisfactory examination in simple French and Latin and in Blackstone's *Commentaries*" was dropped.

In 1895, Langdell, his eyesight deteriorating, retired as dean and was succeeded by his protégé, James Barr Ames. By then, Langdell's model of legal education had been established. And the School, Langdell took pride in noting, had succeeded "in a pecuniary sense." Enrollment had tripled. The library had been expanded from 10,000 to 34,000 volumes; the faculty from three to eight professors; a new building had been constructed and maintained; and Langdell still had been capable of increasing the School's endowment from $37,000 to $360,000 and converting its 1870 deficit into a $25,000 surplus.

In a broader sense, Langdell had answered what Louis Brandeis called "the much debated question whether the law school or the lawyer's office afforded the best opportunity for legal training." For by 1895, "the prevailing opinion among lawyers" was that "a thorough knowledge of legal principles is essential to higher professional success, and this knowledge . . . can rarely be attained except as the result of uninterrupted, systematic study, under competent guidance." In the next seven decades, Langdell's model of legal education would spread from Harvard Law School and become the model for virtually every American law school.

Initially, the "Harvardization" of American law schools was related to the perceived superiority of the case method of teaching. In 1889, Eugene Wambaugh, a graduate of Harvard Law School, was appointed a professor of law at the State University of Iowa, where he introduced the technique. The following year, Harvard Law Professor William Keener was named dean of Columbia Law School. Keener was a strong advocate of Langdell's theories, and when, in 1891, the former Dean, Theodore Dwight, and other long-time Columbia law professors resigned to form a rival law school, Keener restaffed Columbia with professors who shared his views. In 1892, Professor Wambaugh left Iowa to found the law school of the Western Reserve University along Harvard lines. John Henry Wigmore, a Harvard Law School graduate of 1887, brought the case method to Chicago's Northwestern University in 1893. After Langdell's retirement, the spread of the case method quickened. By 1902, twelve of the ninty-eight law schools had unequivocally accepted the case system; by 1908, over thirty. Beginning in 1912, the method was employed even at Yale.

As the reputation of Harvard's case method grew, law schools began adopting other aspects of Langdell's model. Future United States President William Howard Taft, while dean of the Law School of the University of Cincinnati, for example, wrote in 1896:

> In the conduct of the Law School, the Faculty decided that its wisest course would be to follow as closely as circumstances would permit, the course and methods of study prevailing at the Harvard Law School . . .
>
> In the study of Contracts, Torts and Property, the instructors have adopted the Case System as it is pursued at Harvard and the same books of select cases are used by the students . . . For the first year's work we follow the Harvard curriculum exactly . . .

Six years later the University of Chicago invited Harvard Law Professor Joseph Beale, Jr., to introduce the case method at its law school. Beale, however, was adamant that the curriculum be limited to "strictly legal subjects." If Chicago supported Professor Ernst Freund's proposal "that 2/9 of the work leading to the degree should consist of subjects belonging properly in the departments of political science or sociology" then Beale would not come. Chicago relented, abandoning such "heretical" courses as American Political Theory and Jurisprudence and the notion that a political scientist might teach at a law school.

Most law schools, impressed by the national prestige and financial success of Harvard Law, followed its curriculum without a struggle. In 1891, the United States commissioner of education published a report showing that coincident with the rise of Harvard Law School under Langdell was a diminution of "nontechnical" subjects taught at the university law schools. By 1920, nearly every American law school had assimilated Harvard's core curriculum, although many law schools offered a greater number of electives.

The three-year law school course was standard by the 1920s. Even the practice of hiring full-time career law professors made headway, although slowly. By 1907, in thirty-eight law schools responding to a national survey, 31 percent of their instructors taught full time.

Only Harvard Law School's college-degree requirement was not swiftly adopted. Not until 1916 did another law school enforce the same rule. As late as 1921, only 5 of the 150 then existing law schools had followed suit.

Langdell's model had a conservatizing influence on the profession and American law. In the decades after the Civil War, not only the size but the character of the American legal profession changed. By the close of the nineteenth century, the profession was bifurcating into two types of practice. A minority of lawyers working in New York, Chicago, and other large cities increasingly specialized in representing corporate clients. Some of these attorneys were employed directly as general counsel by railroads and other large firms. More joined together in partnerships and served as outside advocates and counselors to several firms simultaneously. The overwhelming majority of attorneys in 1900, however, remained solo "general" practitioners, whose principal function was courtroom advocacy rather than boardroom counseling.

At about the turn of the century, a number of the new corporate partnerships became convinced that Harvard Law School provided the most effective preparation for their type of practice. As a result, Harvard Law graduates initially received higher salaries than graduates of other law schools. In an unashamedly acquisitive age, such a reputation was no small matter. Harvard Law School could brag that it attracted students from every state of the Union. Law schools desirous of preparing their graduates to serve in the best-paying firms were inclined to follow Harvard's lead.

Since the substance of a Harvard Law education was uncritical, a consequence of the Harvardization of American legal education was to export a model that defined its success in terms of securing the most remunerative employment for law graduates, rather than reforming the acquisitive enthusiasms of the profession or criticizing the generally conservative property rules of American law.

This conservatizing influence also was evident as Langdellian ideas came to dominate the literature of the law. As the United States industrialized, the *Commentaries* of Blackstone, Kent, and Story grew progressively out of date. At the same time, the number of volumes of printed court decisions, warned one scholar, were "becoming alarmingly numerous." Lawyers, argued another, were in danger of being "overwhelmed by their number and variety." This "fearful calamity" threatened the bar's "being buried alive, not in the catacombs, but in the labyrinths of the law." In 1820, when these lamentations were first voiced, there were fewer than 200 volumes of American law reports. By 1910, there were over 8000.

Langdell solved the problem of the multitude of printed court decisions with his theory that "law, considered as a science," consisted only of a discrete number of "principles and doctrines." With the invention of the casebook in 1871, Langdell offered a new basis for organizing the doctrines of the law, at approximately the time when the old commentaries were becoming seriously dated. By reaffirming the concept of eternal legal first principles, Langdell freed his votaries from the responsibility of hunting down every relevant case. They merely need cull from "scientifically" selected leading cases principles that then could be applied to related fact situations. At the conclusion of his massive casebooks, Langdell sometimes attached a summary that reduced an entire field of law to twenty or thirty pages of doctrine. Langdell's theory of a general body of legal principles applicable in all jurisdictions, in effect, brought order out of chaos.

By the early twentieth century, Langdell's casebook approach to teaching law was well established. In 1908, for example, the *Harvard Law Review* advertised eighty-three separate casebooks. In addition, a series of thirty volumes "covering the fundamentals of the law for the purpose of classroom instruction" was then being prepared under the general editorial supervision of James Brown Scott, a Langdellian theorist at the George Washington University Law School.

But the very certainty of the casebook approach insured its conservatism. By insisting that the appropriate knowledge of a field of law could be abstracted from a set of leading cases, the early casebook authors denied students the opportunity to engage in the more speculative study of what *should* be the ends of law, and under what circumstances should the premises of judges be questioned.

Nonetheless, in the first decades of the century, the writings of such Harvard Law School casebook authors as Joseph Beale, Jr., and Samuel Williston articulated an orthodox view of law throughout the legal profession. Their Langdellian philosophy that the law, in the phrases of Beale, must be uniform, general, continuous, equal, certain, pure, and free from "warping by bad precedent" achieved a political significance. In 1902, the Commission on Uniform State Laws turned to Harvard Law School's Samuel Williston to draft a Uniform Sales Act. The commissioners endorsed Williston's act in 1906, and by 1941 the proposed legislation had been enacted by 38 states. Williston's effort was succeeded by a series of related commercial law proposals. But the high-water mark of Langdell's "formal" approach came with the founding of the American Law Institute in 1923. Significantly influenced by such Harvard Law School draftsmen as Beale, Williston, and Austin Scott, its purpose was to "restate" the law, not for enactment by legislatures but for direct application by the courts. Contracts, property, torts, agency, and corporations law were reduced to simple rules (called black-letter law), then explained by a logical commentary. The social or economic consequences of the rules were all but ignored; the basic aim of the *Restatements* was to achieve a uniform judge-made law in all state jurisdictions. To this date, both law students and law courts are still weaned on the *Restatements*. Their significance cannot be overstated. A taught tradition, Roscoe Pound once wrote, is the most enduring form of law.

3

THE EARLY ASSAULTS ON THE CITADEL, AND ROSCOE POUND

I suppose that all struggle for law has been conscious; that very little of it has been blind or merely instinctive . . . but in very few ages of the world has the struggle for change been so widespread, so deliberate, or upon so great a scale as that which we are taking part in. The transition we are witnessing is no equable transition of growth and normal alteration; no silent, unconscious unfolding of one age into another, its natural heir and successor. Society is looking itself over in our day from top to bottom; is making fresh and critical analysis of its very elements; is questioning its oldest practices as freely as its newest; scrutinizing every arrangement and motive of its life; and stands ready to attempt nothing less than a radical reconstruction, which only frank and honest counsels can hold back from becoming a revolution.

WOODROW WILSON, address to the
American Bar Association, 1910

From its introduction, Langdell's model of legal education was vigorously opposed. The initial critics came from within the Harvard community, but over time, their voices were joined by the faculties of other leading law schools until a broad counter-movement gained force during the 1920s and 1930s.

Oliver Wendell Holmes, Jr., was the intellectual godfather of four decades of Langdell critics. Before his appointment to the Massachusetts Supreme Judicial Court in 1882, Holmes had briefly taught at Harvard Law School and had been genuinely impressed by Langdell's case method: "After a week or two, when the first confusing novelty was over, I found that my class examined the questions proposed with an accuracy of view which they never could have learned from text-books, and which often exceeded that to be found in the text-books." But Holmes never considered teaching methods terribly important, since "ability and industry will master the raw material with any mode." In 1880, he deprecated the premises of Langdell's contracts casebook as those of a false prophet:

> It may be said without exaggeration that there cannot be found in the legal literature of this country such a *tour de force* of patient and profound intellect working out original theory through a mass of detail and evolving consistency out of what seemed a chaos of conflicting atoms. But in this word "consistency" we touch what some of us at least must deem the weak point in Mr. Langdell's habit of mind. Mr. Langdell's ideal in the law, the end of all of his striving, is the *elegantia juris,* or *logical* integrity of the system as a system. He is, perhaps, the greatest living legal theologian. But as a theologian he is less concerned with his postulates than to show that the conclusions from them hang together.
>
> If Mr. Langdell could be suspected of ever having troubled himself about Hegel, we might call him a Hegelian in disguise, so entirely is he interested in the formal connection of things, or logic . . .

But that is not what a legal system is. "The life of the law," Holmes wrote in this book review and again in his landmark work, *The Common Law,* "has not been logic: it has been experience." The source of the law is not some "brooding omnipresence in the sky"; there is no "transcendental body of law outside of any particular State but obligatory within it unless and until changed by statute"; the actual basis of law has always been "felt necessity . . . No one will ever have a truly philosophic mastery over the law who does not habitually consider the forces outside of it which have made it what it is. More than that, he must remember that as it embodies the story of a nation's development through many centuries, the law finds its philosophy not in self-consistency, which it must always fail in so long as it continues to grow, but in history and the nature of human needs."

Sixteen years later Holmes sharpened his criticism of Langdell's philosophy and attempted to redirect "the path of the law." The appropriate rules for society, Holmes contended, will not be written as long as law is studied as a series of historical generalizations:

> It is revolting to have no better reason for a rule of law than that so it was laid down in the time of Henry IV. It is still more revolting if the grounds upon which it was laid down have vanished long since, and the rule simply persists from blind imitation of the past . . .
>
> I look forward to a time when the part played by history in the explanation of dogma shall be very small, and instead of ingenious research we shall spend our energy on a study of the ends sought to be attained and the reasons for desiring them. As a step toward that ideal it seems to me that every lawyer ought to seek an understanding of economics. The present divorce between the schools of political economy and law seems to me an evidence of how much progress in philosophical study still remains to be made. In the present state of political economy, indeed, we come again upon history on a larger scale, but there we are called on to consider and weigh the ends of legislation, the means of attaining them, and the cost.

In the early twentieth century, the political campaign for progressive legislation paralleled an intellectual movement for what future Harvard Law School Dean Roscoe Pound labeled "sociological jurisprudence." In Pound's view, a tradition of "mechanical jurisprudence" led to "the backwardness of law in meeting social ends." It was necessary for law to "look to economics and sociology and philosophy" and appreciate the actual social effects of legal doctrines — for "law is a means, not an end."

Pound's goal was to realign judge-made legal doctrine with contemporaneous philosophical, political, and ethical ideas. When he wrote of the need for "social engineering," he explicitly meant lawmaking by enlightened judges. But his intellectual successors rarely held so modest a view.

In the 1920s, a group of law professors, popularly known as "Legal Realists," initiated a brusk, often free-swinging attack on the conventional wisdoms of the American legal system, assaulting judge-made law with special ferocity. Not only did some scholars who considered themselves "Realists" argue that the place of first principles was very slight, but the Realists tended to combine their relativistic approach to morals and ethics with a sweeping skepticism about whether judges really understood the process by which they made decisions, or whether "traditional legal rules" accurately describe "what either courts or people are actually doing."

Borrowing economic, statistical, anthropological, and psychological techniques, some Realist scholars attempted to reformulate law as a social science. But the aspect of the Realist movement most significant to legal education was the attempts at Columbia and Yale to redefine the curriculum and purposes of a law school.

In 1928, after three years of preparation, Columbia Law School's faculty published a *Summary of Studies in Legal Education*, advocating the reformulation of law school curricula along "functional" lines. The traditional common-law categories of law school curricula (for example, Contracts, Property, and Agency), the study urged, should be supplanted by new "functional" categories that more precisely described American law — such as Form of Business Unit, Labor, The Family and Familial Property, and Finance and Credit. These topics, in turn, would be explored within the context of a curriculum that also included a history of thought in the social sciences ("The subject-matter should disclose what effects on current practices in legal thinking flow from the coming of the scientific habit of thought into the field of the social sciences"); sociology ("A knowledge of modern society organized in terms of social agencies, social processes and social ends . . ."); and methods of legal study ("These include the ability to use a case and a statute as tools for getting new knowledge; to use objective sampling methods besides the case method; to use the objective methods, accounting and statistics; to use the historical method; and to understand the limitations and uses of the various logical forms of thought").

A related effort was made to transform the literature of law school study. In 1930, Columbia Law School's Karl Llewellyn published his *Cases and Materials on Sales,* the first of a new generation of casebooks.

Where the typical Langdellian casebook consisted of a series of law cases organized by doctrinal rubric, Llewellyn placed the study of *Sales* cases within a framework of economic and business considerations. In many instances, the judge's reasoning was omitted; Llewellyn focused on the judge's actual rule and the underlying fact situation. British legal historian William Twining explains: "Behind this were two ideas . . . first the idea that at least as much significance should be attached to what judges do . . . as to what they say by way of justification. Secondly, the idea that the facts of cases have a significance that transcends their significance as precedents and illustrations of doctrine; they are concrete illustrations of business situations, which give a flavour of practice beyond the particular legal issues involved . . ."

As fundamental a shift as the proposed Columbia Law School curriculum and literature represented, the faculty's desire to redefine the purpose of a law school was even more radical. Rather than settle for Langdell's "pecuniary" satisfaction in graduating students destined to become well-paid private attorneys, Columbia Law School's faculty aspired to define itself as "a great center of legal research in law as an aspect of social organization," and to have "this school render unique service in the preparation of persons for public service in law."

In such academic committee prose are political impulses clothed. Columbia law student — now Columbia Law School professor — Herbert Wechsler recalls, "For a law student vintage 1928 to 1931 . . . those were creative and exciting years in the development of legal thought, years in which a new faith was being nurtured in the schools." Wechsler described the articles of the new faith: First, "a frontal challenge to the concept of the common law as a closed legal system, yielding answers to all questions by conformity to earlier decisions or deduction from the principles that they declared." Second, a recommendation of judicial receptivity to statutory changes of the common law. "The epitomization of this aspect of the creed was, perhaps, the paper read by Mr. Justice Stone [former dean of Columbia Law School] in 1936 at the Harvard Tercentenary. 'A statute,' he said, 'is not an alien intruder in the house of common law, but a guest to be welcomed and made at home there as a new and powerful aid in the accomplishment of its appointed task of accommodating the law to social needs.' " Third, "unqualified disdain for the then dominant interpretation of the Constitution by the Supreme Court of the United States precluding any major governmental action in the ordering of the economy, despite the magnitude of the abuse and dislocation incident to the development of an industrial society."

Following a celebrated faculty split in 1928, several Realists on the Columbia faculty angrily stalked off to the Johns Hopkins Institute for the Study of Law to embark on empirical research, or to Yale Law School. Nonetheless, by 1932 Columbia Law School had added "functional courses" to its curriculum, including: Landlord and Tenant, Trial Practice, Business Organization, Corporate Finance, Industrial Relations, Trade Regulation, and Evidence. Novel courses in Legal History, Legislation, Comparative Law, Administrative Law, and Accounting were also offered.

But the momentum for curricular reform slowed. Yale Law School, briefly directed by twenty-eight-year-old Dean Robert Hutchins, established the Institute of Human Relations to bring together scholars of various disciplines "to correlate knowledge of the mind and body and of individual and group conduct and to study further the interrelations of the many factors influencing human actions" and applied several of the earlier Columbia

Law School curricular ideas. But this activity was, Yale Law Professor Robert Stevens would report forty years later, "intellectual excitement for the few." A Harvard Law School faculty committee report coolly noted in 1932 that Yale Law School — replete with student research projects, small group seminars, a student-faculty ratio of only fifteen students to each professor — cost well over twice a Harvard Law School education. Yale Law student tuition fees covered only 48 percent of the school's budget (compared with 99 percent at Harvard). The obvious implication was that the interdisciplinary aspects of legal realism could exist only if subsidized.

Because Columbia's "functional" curriculum was never wholly adopted by any other law school, and certain of the more free-wheeling Realists spent the 1930s decade embroiled in bitter, sometimes internecine, polemics, some scholars have concluded that the Legal Realist movement itself was unsuccessful. But Realist theories have continued to influence legal thought, in part, because the social reform legislation of the Franklin Roosevelt presidency, coupled with a series of Supreme Court decisions in the late 1930s, put to rest the uncritical acceptance of Langdellian ideas within the law-teaching profession.

If the first assault on the Langdellian method of legal education attacked Langdell's philosophy, the second challenged the practicality of Langdell's methods. This attack appeared most memorably in a series of slashing law review articles written by Legal Realist Jerome Frank. Frank argued, "American legal education went badly wrong some seventy years ago when it was seduced by a brilliant neurotic. I refer to the well known founder of the so-called case system, Christopher Columbus Langdell."

> His pedagogic theory reflected the man. The experience of the lawyer in his office, with clients, and in the courtroom with judges and juries, were, to Langdell, improper materials for the teacher and his student. They must, he insisted, shut their eyes to such data. They must devote themselves exclusively to what was discoverable in the li-

brary. The essence of his teaching philosophy he expressed thus: "First that law is a science; second, that all the available materials of that science are contained in printed books." This second proposition, it is said, was "intended to exclude the traditional methods of learning law by work in a lawyer's office, or attendance upon the proceedings of courts of justice."

This, Frank suggested, was like confining future horticulturists to the study of cut flowers or architects to the study of pictures of buildings.

Believing "that something of immense worth was lost when our leading law schools wholly abandoned the legal apprentice system," Frank urged, first, that a considerable portion of teachers in any law school should have not less than five to ten years' actual legal experience: "So long as teachers who know little or nothing except what they learned from books under that case system control a law school, the actualities of the lawyer's life are there likely to be considered peripheral and as of secondary importance." Second, the case system should be revised to include *complete* records of cases — starting with the filing of the first papers, through the trial and appeals to the upper courts. "A few months properly spent on one or two elaborate court records, including the briefs (and supplemented by reading of textbooks as well as upper court opinions), will teach a student more than two years spent on going through twenty of the casebooks now in use." Third, students should supplement their study of cases by making "frequent visits, accompanied by law teachers, to both trial and appellate courts." But better, fourth, each law school should sponsor a legal clinic (similar to the clinics in medical schools) where teacher-clinicians supervise students in providing services typical of law offices, as well as aiding governmental agencies, legislative committees, or other quasi-official bodies. In this way, students could actually learn such essential legal skills as brief-writing, contract negotiation, and client counseling.

A third criticism of the Harvard Law School model of legal

education was that it resulted in the denial of legal representation to all but the richest citizens, to the serious prejudice of the poor and middle-income classes. In1919, Reginald Smith, himself a Harvard Law graduate, published *Justice and the Poor*, in which he argued that due to the unequal availability of legal counsel, "the law itself becomes the means of extortion . . . Because law is all-embracing, the denial of its protection means the destruction of homes through illegal foreclosures, the loss through trick or chicanery of a lifetime's savings, the taking away of children from their parents by fraudulent guardianship proceedings. Hundreds of thousands of men, many of them immigrants, have been unable to collect their wages honestly earned."

Smith's book was a revelation to many and had a significant influence in speeding the growth of legal-aid societies, small claims courts, and voluntary criminal defender organizations. But the perennial underfinancing of such lawyers and courts resulted in the continuation of unequal legal representation. A 1938 survey by the National Resources Committee found that virtually all legal representation was provided for the 13 percent of the families from the highest income groups. Of the 73 percent of families with annual incomes between $500 and $2500, one third of this group could afford a home and over half of them an automobile, but only 1.5 percent felt they could afford an attorney.

The effect of four decades of criticism of Langdell's Harvard Law School model separated the Law School's Langdellian methods from the underlying Langdellian principles, but these methods were retained and little changed. As a result, the study of law at Harvard became more practical and less principled; the intellectual coherence of Langdell's Law School was succeeded by a model without a unifying theory. Much of this change occurred during the deanship of Roscoe Pound, from 1915 to 1936, a period of extraordinary financial success for the Law School, but also a period of bitter faculty differences.

Dean Langdell had been succeeded by his protégé, James Barr Ames, who, in turn, had been followed by Ezra Ripley Thayer in 1910. The deanships of these two men occurred during a time of intellectual ferment, a time when the social sciences in general were in revolt against formalism; a time in politics aptly named the progressive era.

The fervor of the political climate was early assimilated by the leading law schools. William Draper Lewis of the University of Pennsylvania Law School criticized the "total absence of any idea that there exists any obligation on the part of the Bar towards the community . . . If, as a profession, we are to awake to our failure to perform our public duties, it is the small class of men who are devoting their lives to legal teaching who must point the way." One private attorney who did awake to his "public duties" was Louis Brandeis, a millionaire Boston practitioner who led a series of pioneering legal challenges as a self-styled "people's attorney." Brandeis similarly described the value of a law school professorship "as a fulcrum in efforts to improve the law and through it — society."

Receptivity to such progressive sentiments, in part, prompted Harvard Law School in 1910 to hire Roscoe Pound. Four years later, the School reached out to Felix Frankfurter, a rising progressive political official in Washington. Although friends urged Frankfurter to remain in government, he accepted the Law School's job offer because Cambridge was "the center of the liberal movement . . ." and because "our universities increasingly should *be* in politics."

A further impact of the progressive movement was the opening of a Legal Aid Bureau at Harvard Law School in 1913. But the School was not initially very enthusiastic about legal aid. In 1918, an "official" history of Harvard Law School reassured alumni readers that for the 27 members of the bureau (out of a school with close to 800 students) there was a "sacrifice of comparatively little time . . . Members of the Bureau are on duty at the consultation office for two hours on alternate weeks. If the burden upon one man becomes too heavy, a portion of his cases are assigned to another." With considerably more enthusiasm the history noted that in 1913 several students who were members of the Massachusetts militia had been excused from taking final examinations so that they could help suppress the textile workers during the celebrated strike at Lawrence, Massachusetts. For regardless of the intellectual ferment of the period, Harvard Law School remained essentially a training institution for large-firm private practitioners. That was the path to success: In 1895–1896, when Langdell resigned as dean, there had been a record-breaking 475 students enrolled. By conserving his law school model, Ames and Thayer steadily increased enrollment to 730 by 1914–1915. Crowning their efforts had been the construction of a new and much larger law school building, Langdell Hall, in 1906. The spirit of the common law as interpreted by Christopher Columbus Langdell was still very much alive at Harvard Law School in 1915 when Ezra Ripley Thayer suddenly died and Roscoe Pound became dean.

At the time, Roscoe Pound was the best known law professor in the country. His articles and public speeches attacking "mechanical jurisprudence" and endorsing "sociological jurisprudence" had made him an idol of the law-teaching profession. Nonetheless, he was an unfortunate choice to become dean of Harvard Law School. A Law School faculty including such dominant personalities as Joseph Beale, Jr., Samuel Williston, Edward H. (Bull) Warren, and Felix Frankfurter would have been difficult for any dean to lead, but Pound, by background and temperament, was particularly unsuited for the job. Having attended Harvard Law School for a single year in 1890, Pound was an intellectual outsider on the faculty. His formative years had been spent in Nebraska, where he earned a doctorate in botany while supporting himself as an attorney. He then served as a law school professor, a state law commissioner, and dean of the University of Nebraska College of Law. An extraordinarily well-read academic, he was perhaps the greatest scholar in European legal history this country had produced to that date. But the very breadth of his reading contributed to the idiosyncratic nature of his thought. Pound defied political and jurisprudential categories. Able at one moment to advance progressive political ideas with allusions to Roman and continental law, he was equally able in the next to attack the Legal Realists and the New Deal on equally opaque grounds.

To complicate matters, Pound tried to run Harvard Law School the way he had run the law school at the University of Nebraska. As W. Barton Leach, who joined the faculty in 1929, observed, "Pound ran the Law School as if he had just bought 51 percent of the stock. He neither sought nor tolerated opposition."

Yet Dean Pound became increasingly timid in confronting outside critics of the School. Early in his deanship Pound sided with seven of the other eight law professors supporting Senate confirmation of Louis Brandeis's nomination to the Supreme Court against the opposition of Harvard University President Lowell and several prominent alumni of the Law School. Shortly thereafter, the World War I Red scare began. Government reports, sympathetic to business employees, that Felix Frankfurter had prepared were criticized, by Frankfurter's account, as "manifestations that the Bolshevik Revolution was coming to America." Frankfurter recalled that Pound, rather than "brushing them off . . . or quietly disposing of" alumni complaints, traveled to Washington to discuss his troubles with Justice Brandeis. Brandeis was incredulous. "Well, what are you worried about?" he had asked. "Hasn't Frankfurter got tenure?" "Oh yes," Pound replied, "but they'll want to take away his courses in public law by which he might corrupt the young and their outlook on American law." Such scenes turned Frankfurter against Pound, causing him to assert years later, undoubtedly with some overstatement: "Pound was a scare cat. He was timid. Not only was he timid, but he wanted to be all things to all men. He was afraid to stand up to people. He wanted to be thought well of by everybody. He was a near genius. He once told us at a faculty meeting when he did something that ordinary people don't do, "Well, you have to pay a price for genius."

Over time, others on the faculty were alienated. In 1920, Pound, Frankfurter, Zechariah Chafee, Jr., and nine distinguished lawyers and political scientists signed a report entitled "To the American People," criticizing the excesses of the Red deportation drive of Attorney General A. Mitchell Palmer. Pound had worked enthusiastically on the document, being genuinely indignant at Palmer's wholesale violation of American constitutional rights. But Austen G. Fox, a prominent Harvard Law alumnus and opponent of the Brandeis nomination, submitted a petition to the Harvard University Board of Overseers condemning five members of the Law School faculty, including Pound, Frankfurter, and Chafee.

On Sunday, May 22, 1921, a "heresy trial" was held before the Harvard Law School Visiting Committee in which Fox, supported by several alumni, assumed the role of prosecutor and Harvard University President Lowell made the defense. Against all the professors but Chafee, Fox's case quickly crumbled. By advancing the argument that Chafee had intentionally misstated the truth about the Federal Espionage Act in a law review article and a 1920 book, *Freedom of Speech,* Fox persuaded five of the eleven members of the Visiting Committee to vote against Chafee. Chafee was positively buoyant about his six-to-five victory: "With Lowell's energetic support we threw the Wall Street invaders back with heavy losses."

Pound, however, seems to have been deeply scarred by the wartime hysteria. Even before he helped write the anti-Palmer report, he had attempted to resign both as dean and professor of Harvard Law School. "I doubt if an intellectually honest man can justify himself in teaching in this country in the next decade." Supreme Court Justices Holmes and Brandeis, among others, convinced Pound to stay, but after the "heresy trial" Pound was reluctant to involve himself in public controversies. He refused to be drawn into the national debate over the Sacco-Vanzetti case — even, in 1926, when a celebrated article Frankfurter wrote defending the pair (which Pound considered accurate and fair) was attacked by Northwestern University Law School Dean Wigmore, an attack that Pound privately called "a disgrace to legal scholarship." Similarly, in the late 1920s, Pound did not publicly respond to President Lowell's periodic outbursts of anti-Semitism. According to one Pound biographer, "Others shared Frankfurter's disgust that Pound, the most powerful dean at Harvard, failed to wage a vigorous campaign when Lowell objected, on two occasions, to appointing Jewish scholars to the law faculty. Both incidents created enormous ill will and added to the mounting dissatisfaction with Pound's leadership."

This dissatisfaction intensified in June 1934, when Pound visited Germany and Austria coincident with the assassination of

Austrian Chancellor Engelbert Dollfuss by Austrian Nazis. Pound blandly remarked that his principal impressions were of domestic peace. He saw no soldiers, noticed no tension, and described Hitler as "a man who can bring them [the Central Europeans] freedom from agitating 'movements.'" The following September, Pound accepted an honorary degree from the University of Berlin. Even Dean Pound's most fervent admirers wondered why he seemed to condone National Socialism.

But Pound had begun to lose control long before Felix Frankfurter complained that Langdell Hall was being "turned into a Nazi holiday." Pound disapproved of Franklin Roosevelt's New Deal and was especially irritated by Felix Frankfurter's role as a close adviser to the president. Despite the fact that Pound had taken several long absences from the Law School to aid the Hoover administration, the dean tried to reduce Frankfurter's trips to Washington on the grounds that they interfered with Frankfurter's classes. The death of Pound's wife in 1928 may have deepened his sense of isolation and his belief that his colleagues were suspicious of him because he was neither an easterner nor a Harvard man. An official history of Harvard Law School described matters ever so delicately: "As the 1930s wore on, the Law School machine creaked a bit . . . In 1930 [Dean Pound] passed his sixtieth year, and his ability under stress to tolerate differences with close associates . . . began bit by bit to slip away from him."

Against this background, the equivocal nature of Pound's deanship is somewhat more comprehensible. By conventional criteria, Pound was a successful dean. Between 1916 and 1936, Harvard Law School's enrollment doubled, the number of faculty members quadrupled, and the endowment, stimulated by a massive fund-raising campaign in the mid-1920s, increased over sixfold. So enriched, the Law School built new wings on Langdell Hall and increased the volumes in the library from 290,000 to 433,000.

But the character of the Law School's expansion belied the figures. Above all else, Pound sought to develop research institutes and graduate training in legal research. This ambition was inextricably tied to his personality and his idiosyncratic view of the law. Pound agreed with the Legal Realists: "We must study the law in action as well as the law in books. We must study the work of our agencies of making law and of applying law as well as the work of the courts in finding and interpreting the law." But Pound stopped short of the Realists' campaign to limit judicial prerogatives or encourage legislation. Possessing an abiding faith that only scholars (or judges with the aid of scholars) could properly apply the law, Pound sought to modernize the common law. Sharing Beale's distaste for local law, the dean avidly supported the codification projects of the American Law Institute. In his dean's report of 1925–1926, Pound declared his personal faith in and ambition for Harvard Law School.

> We shall achieve nothing by denouncing the exuberance of legislative activity, the revival of personal justice through administrative activity, or the rejection of reason and tendency to individualize with reference to results in each case, that now marks so much of judicial justice, unless we provide for the causes of these things. They can be provided for effectively only by making provision for studying them under conditions insuring permanence of tenure, continuity of treatment, possibility of dealing with them as a whole rather than in detached fragments, and a body of workers whose results will command public confidence. In other than English-speaking lands this task of legal preparedness, as it might be called, is committed to a public ministry of justice. Very likely the genius of English-speaking peoples calls for spontaneous individual enterprise rather than for an official bureau . . . Perhaps the nearest to a ministry of justice that we can come, while avoiding the setting up of any official bureau, is to provide adequately for the work of legal research in our national law schools.

The implications of attempting to transform Harvard Law School into an unofficial "ministry of justice" were complex. To achieve this goal, Pound needed to raise a great deal of money. So he supported increased enrollment and time-consuming fund-raising drives. These efforts made Pound more dependent on the good will of his alumni. During the 1925–1927 drive, when Harvard Law School set a target of $5,400,000, Pound described the goal of creating an institute to study the administration of criminal law in a pamphlet entitled "For the Safety of the Citizen and the Protection of Business." The subtitle proposed, "A Plan to Eliminate from the Administration of Justice in This Country Many Elements of Delay, Waste, Friction and Uncertainty which are threatening the General Security and Hampering Commerce and Industry." This was the manner in which a conservative Wall Street attorney would have defined "the crime problem." Since Pound felt it necessary to gain the financial support of such Wall Street attorneys, this may have been another reason why he was reluctant to defend Sacco and Vanzetti.

The greater concern of Harvard Law School, however, remained training law students, and Pound's view was consistently that "radical changes in the curriculum are not called for . . . As the American law teachers of one hundred years ago assured the definite reception of the common law so the law teachers of today and tomorrow may assure its preservation." This approach, in part, was grounded in Pound's appraisal of the employment market and his desire to generate funding for sophisticated research:

> . . . We ought not to expect every graduate of a national law school to become a great law reformer, any more than we should expect every graduate to become a great legal scholar or law teacher. We should seek to turn out well trained, competent practitioners, filled with what is best in the spirit of the profession, conscious of the need of improvement in our administration of justice, and alive to the possibilities of law reform, but withal sound lawyers with a mastery of the materials and the technique with which reforms must go forward. Also we must seek to turn out from time to time a chosen few, whom nature meant for

such things, specially trained in the problems and methods of creative lawmaking. Likewise we must seek from time to time to turn out another chosen few, of pronounced scholarly bent, specially trained to become legal scholars and teachers.

If law students desired to learn more about history, economics, politics, psychology, and sociology, then, Pound wrote, let them study these topics in college. For most law students courses in Jurisprudence, Philosophy of Law, Comparative Law, Theory of Legislation, Administrative Law, or Criminology would be "pretentious," as would "premature so-called research" by law students, except for graduate students "of high rank who showed special aptitude therefor." "Legal clinics" or a system of "legal internes" were equally objectionable, since they would result in students "doing a little of everything and very little of anything."

Throughout Pound's deanship there were no important revisions of the curriculum. As with the common law itself, a few elective courses were introduced incrementally. Arguably, this was prudent. Harvard Law School had become the leader among American law schools because it had demonstrated to the big-city law firms that it best prepared students for their type of practice. To propose broad changes in the curriculum would have invited alumni opposition.

But the pace of change under Pound was too slow even for members of the faculty who shared his sense of the importance of "the fundamentals." A 1932 Harvard Law School Faculty Committee Report clearly shows that at least the authors of the report (Professors Dodd and Simpson) were intrigued by many of the innovations developed by the Legal Realists at Columbia and Yale. The report was written shortly after Pound had published a controversial law review article that had sweepingly attacked the Legal Realist movement. In response, Karl Llewellyn published an indictment of Pound entitled "Some Realism About Realism," which convincingly illustrated that whatever the Realist movement was, Dean Pound had misrepresented it. For good measure, Llewellyn published a second piece, "On What Is Wrong with So-called Legal Education," which with a bluntness uncharacteristic of law review articles asserted that legal education at the Harvard type of law school if "viewed in critical aloofness" was "blind, inept, factory-ridden, wasteful, defective, and empty. If you prefer verbs: it blinds, it stumbles, it conveyor-belts, it wastes, it mutilates, and it empties."

When Roosevelt was elected president in 1932, Pound's position became untenable. The New Deal oriented Harvard Law School toward Washington for the first time. In Roosevelt's first term, Professors Landis, Sayre, and Magruder left the Law School to serve in the federal government. Frankfurter declined Roosevelt's offer to be solicitor general in 1933 but began his legendary role as a job-broker. Twenty-eight of forty-three *Harvard Law Review* editors graduated between 1930 and 1932 were employed by the federal government in the following decade. This statistic underscored the half-jocular claim of the period that "the most direct route to Washington was to go to Harvard Law School and turn left."

The reorientation of some Harvard law professors and students toward Washington accelerated the pressure for curricular change. In 1934–1935, a faculty committee on the curriculum "pursuant to a resolution adopted by the Faculty" invited criticism on every premise of Pound's Harvard Law School. Merely posing such questions involved a repudiation of Pound and a bow to the Legal Realists, but the committee candidly stated its concern that Harvard Law School maintain "its past and present position of leadership in American legal education."

The ensuing student criticisms of the Law School were searing, despite the fact that the vast majority of students were destined for private practice and were, as Professor Arthur Sutherland noted in an official history, "quite conservative." The Student Advisory Group told the Committee on the Curriculum that Langdell's vaunted case method had "broken down . . . In the first place, the classes are so large that anything like a general discussion is out of the question . . . In the second place, students, especially in the last two years, do not read their cases." The extended study of old English cases was boring. "Above all, something must be done to make law school more interesting in the second and third years." A student could master the case method "thinking-like-a-lawyer" technique in one year. Thereafter, "to have nothing to look forward to but more cases and still more cases in monotonous sequence ad nauseam is the last word in dismal outlooks."

Other voices were more caustic. Felix Frankfurter sat down for six hours with five third-year students and the preceding year's editor-in-chief of the *Harvard Law Review*. Afterward, he sent the Committee on the Curriculum his conclusions. "At the end of the second year men 'are sick' of reading cases . . ." Frankfurter suggested to the students that "the real question" in the third year was the difference in interest between public-law courses (such as the seminar on Public Utilities that Frankfurter taught) and private-law courses (the Langdellian Commercial Law courses that Pound had retained). "Public law courses," Frankfurter believed, "gave one a sense of reality, dealt with things that were alive here and now, that really will matter tomorrow, and involved complicated facts that were themselves intrinsically interesting." To Frankfurter's astonishment, "this opinion was severely challenged." Frankfurter realized then that the third year was "largely a bore" for "the great muck of the class" who failed to make the *Law Review* hierarchy, since no attempt was made to give them any "stimulus or exhilaration or a feeling of excitement about the law and their future share in it." This did not mean that the *Law Review* grading competition was invidious, but rather that "we have been all oblivious of the subtle but powerful changes due to the size of the student body":

> Twenty-five years ago Austin Hall housed a community. A good many of the students knew each other, but in any event, they felt they were part of a common household. They at least saw each other, recognized each other, saw members of the faculty from day to day and lived under the same rather small roof, engaged in a common enterprise. Very little such feeling exists today. The dominant note of the place is impersonal. The professors are comfortably separated from the life of the students and are

rarely seen going to and fro as we used to see Ames and
Gray and Williston and Beale go to and fro in old Austin.
That physical separation is symbolic of much. The vast-
ness of the reading room, the great mass of students who
are necessarily total strangers to each other, the lack of any
common life not only of the School as a whole but of individual classes — all make against having that feeling of at-
homeness without which there can be no inner peace and
satisfaction. In a word, men are overwhelmed by the size
and impersonality of the place . . .

Students on the *Harvard Law Review* concurred: "Under the
present system large classes militate against an effective function-
ing of the school." Recent law graduate David Riesman, then
clerking for Supreme Court Justice Brandeis, did not agree. The
law school failed, he believed, because it no longer had a theoretical framework: "Most first-year students (including myself) fail to
see the woods for the trees when thrown into five case courses
without an understanding of what the system means or what its
objectives are. Indeed, they graduate with very little understanding of the development of the law, of its main figures, of its more
general concepts."

The following year, 1936, Dean Pound resigned and went away
for half a year of rest. He remained to the day he resigned, and
indeed to the day he died in 1964, one of the most admired
American legal theorists of the twentieth century. Even while he
was losing the support of the professors, he was popular among
the students, being the most approachable member of the faculty.
But, by 1936, it was plain his days of academic leadership were
behind him. He remained independent to the end. His last major
task as dean had been to organize a law school conference to cele-
brate the three-hundredth anniversary of the founding of Harvard
University. At the height of the constitutional crisis concerning
the New Deal legislation, Pound chose as his topic "The Future of
the Common Law."

When, a few months after Pound's resignation as dean, Joseph
Beale, Jr., and Samuel Williston, the two Harvard Law professors

most clearly associated with Langdell's philosophy, retired, it was evident that the guard had changed. New Dealer James Landis, who for four years had been on leave from the Law School faculty to serve as a commissioner of the Federal Trade Commission and a commissioner of the Securities and Exchange Commission, was appointed dean. The faculty broadened the curriculum to regularly include seminar courses in topics such as Techniques of Regulating Business Enterprise, Government Litigation, American and English Legal History, and Evidence. Increased opportunities to take courses in Administrative Law and Legislation were made available. Joint seminars with other departments of the School were initiated. Landis initiated a seven-year combined-degree program allowing Harvard University students to enroll in Law School after the third year and pursue advanced courses in history, government, and economics in coordination with their legal studies. But the outbreak of World War II bruskly ended consideration of further curricular change.

4

SYNTHESIS:

Griswold's Deanship

*Rigor, intellectual discipline, training in how to think will remain
as the foundation of the school's legal instruction.*

DEAN ERWIN GRISWOLD, 1949

The selection of James McCauley Landis as dean of the
Harvard Law School in 1937 symbolized the collapse of Langdel-
lian orthodoxy at the Law School. James Landis was its first reform dean and its first professor of Legislation, a personification
of Roosevelt's New Deal liberalism. While a student at the Law
School, Landis had been a protégé of Felix Frankfurter. Under
Frankfurter's tutelage, Landis prepared his doctoral thesis in
1924–1925, and the next year Frankfurter chose Landis to clerk for
Supreme Court Justice Louis Brandeis. With Frankfurter and
Brandeis, Landis imbibed the faith: "The legislature in determining what shall be done, what is reasonable to do, does not divide
its duty with the judges, nor must it conform to their conception
of what is prudent or reasonable legislation. The judicial function
is merely that of fixing the outside border of reasonable legislative
activity . . ." As professor of Legislation, his faith deepened. In
1931 — two years before the coming of the New Deal — Landis
recommended in the *Harvard Graduates' Magazine* a new approach
to legal education in the form of an "imaginary inaugural lecture"
on "the study of legislation in law schools." Sniping at the
overemphasis of case law in the law school curriculum, he
charged, "For a badly reported precedent from the year book of

Henry V there was worship, while for the statute there was scant respect." Three years later Landis published what many scholars believe to be his finest writing, "Statutes and the Sources of Law," which challenged courts not to consider legislation an abnormal intrusion into the framework of judge-made law, but rather as a declaration of a society's general policy applicable by analogy to related legal questions.

What made Professor Landis's views important was that he was given an opportunity to apply them. Early in 1933 he made a celebrated "weekend" train trip to Washington at Felix Frankfurter's request to help Congressman Sam Rayburn draft the first national law to regulate the stock markets. The sophistication of the bill established Professor Landis's reputation in Washington. Shortly after the young professor returned to Cambridge, President Roosevelt invited him to become a member of the Federal Trade Commission. In July 1934, when the Securities and Exchange Commission was created to enforce the new stock-market laws, Landis was named one of the first five commissioners. A year later, replacing Joseph Kennedy, he became the commission's second chairman, at the age of thirty-six. By the time he left the SEC in 1937, the commission's reputation as the ablest of the New Deal's independent regulatory agencies had been secured.

The following year, Landis glorified the work of the New Deal agencies in a series of lectures subsequently published as the book, *The Administrative Process.* His message was clear: We must depend on expert agency officials, not judges, to supervise a national economy. The discretion of this executive department elite should be limited by statutory principles, but within these bounds their authority to investigate facts and formulate policy should be broad. Briefly, in 1938, President Roosevelt considered appointing Landis to succeed Justice Cardozo on the Supreme Court. The appointment went instead to Landis's mentor, Felix Frankfurter.

The major influence of Landis in his two and a half years as dean before World War II was one of style rather than substance. Unlike Pound, Landis was a skillful administrator. He defined the Law School's curricular crisis as a morale problem and set out to resolve it — for example, by supporting a third-year writing requirement to offer to students who were not on *Law Review* research experience and to lessen the tedium of the final law school year.

Such reforms were modest. The real significance of the Landis appointment was that a New Deal insider had been chosen to run Harvard Law School. The deanship of Landis, combined with the influence of Frankfurter, signified to a generation of college students that they could go to Harvard Law School "and help save the country." This mood was short-lived.

An unexpected opponent of the Landis appointment had been Felix Frankfurter. Although Frankfurter retained his high regard for Landis's intellect, he considered Landis temperamentally unsuited to be dean. Frankfurter's judgment ultimately proved correct. Landis's lifelong restlessness and intensity made it impossible for him to preside over the Law School after the United States entered World War II. When France was invaded in 1940, Landis accepted the post of regional director of the United States Office of Civil Defense. In January 1942, he took a leave of absence from Harvard to serve as director of the National Office of Civil Defense and, from 1943–1945, served as director of American Economic Operations and minister to the Middle East.

Landis returned to the Law School in 1945, but his heart was not in it. Until World War II, Landis had been regarded as a boy wonder; an intellectual and political meteorite; a man "on fire." When he came back to Harvard Law School in 1945, he was forty-six years old. Life had begun to pass James Landis by. Nineteen years later he would be eulogized as a man with a brilliant mind — perhaps the most brilliant student ever to study at Harvard Law School — but one who was relentless and did not know how to relax. Shortly after his return, Landis was involved in an unpleasant divorce proceeding, accompanied by circumstances that then were considered sufficiently scandalous to necessitate his leaving Harvard Law School. The last years of his life were largely a waste of his prodigious talents. After briefly serving as chairman of the Civil Aeronautics Board in 1946–1947, he retired to New York City to practice law. In 1960 he prepared a memorable report for President-elect Kennedy on the need for reform of the administrative agencies, suggesting, among other proposals, that Kennedy appoint "an agency czar" to supervise the independent regulatory agencies from the White House. Kennedy did not reward Landis with that or any other important assignment. A few months later the Harvard Law School community was stunned when Landis pleaded guilty to a federal charge of willful failure to pay income taxes for the previous five years. He was sentenced to a month in prison, and a short time later the New York courts suspended his license to practice law for a year. On July 30, 1964, Landis was discovered drowned in his swimming pool.

Federal Court of Appeals Judge Henry Friendly would later mourn the "Greek tragedy of the Landis deanship" as posing a threat to the continued "primacy" of Harvard Law School. The twenty-one-year deanship of Erwin Griswold, who succeeded Landis in 1946, would involve the Law School in a second far more subtle tragedy; a tragedy that because of the commanding influence of Harvard Law School would touch other law schools as well.

By the end of the New Deal, a new type of faculty, a new curriculum, and new methods of teaching were necessary to restore the coherence and purpose of American legal education. The Langdellian curriculum — an effective description of the private-law system of the late nineteenth century — was by then at least two decades out of date. The appending of modern electives alone could no longer restore the accuracy or the utility of the model. Above all else, during Erwin Griswold's deanship, Harvard Law School needed a fresh doctrinal framework for the study of American law. It chose to build buildings instead. By pursuing a conservative course, the Law School was rewarded by its alumni with approximately $40 million in contributions between 1946 and 1977, and it retained its "primacy" as the most prestigious training institution for private law firm attorneys. But the School — with the exception of a few of its professors — failed to play a vital role in the continuing development of American legal doctrine.

The irony of this failure was that Erwin Griswold was the most forceful personality ever to lead Harvard Law School. If anyone could have moved the School back to an important intellectual role, presumably it was he.

Erwin Griswold, as the saying went, "set a high moral tone for the Law School." As distinguished from Dean Landis, Griswold's most serious avocation was philately. His closest brush with personal scandal had occurred in 1926, when his fellow *Harvard Law Review* editors almost refused to elect him president of the *Review* because his temperance lectures so annoyed them. There were no divorces on the Law School faculty after Griswold became dean, professors joked, "because no one would have dared."

Unlike other law professors, Griswold rarely had to "balance factors" or "reason through problems" to differentiate between right and wrong. Griswold always seemed to know the answer to a political question and rarely hesitated to say so. He defended the Supreme Court's school desegregation decision when it was most unpopular to do so not just because it was the law, but also, he would explain, because:

> . . . both by inheritance and training, this concept of equality has been central to my conception of America. My Puritan and Quaker background, the good ladies at the Superior School in East Cleveland, my teachers at Shaw High School, at Oberlin College and the Harvard Law School, my parents, the Windermere Presbyterian Church, my work in the Department of Justice in Washington, where I saw the new Supreme Court Building go up, with "Equal Justice Under Law" inscribed across its pediment — all of these things and more had ingrained into me a belief in the essential dignity of every individual, with equal opportunity for all according to his intrinsic merit, without regard to irrelevant matters such as race, religion or national origin. As I have said, these things to me *are* America. They are our history. They are what we have to offer to the world. They, with their correlative freedoms, are what, in essence, distinguish us from the communists. That Justices of the Supreme Court should reach

conclusions which implement this understanding of our Constitution seems understandable to me.

Such fervor came easily to Griswold. He was equally comfortable defending witnesses who invoked the Fifth Amendment at the height of Senator McCarthy's popularity — even when this divided his own faculty — or scolding local bar associations because lawyers were abusing their "monopoly of the right to practice law" by not providing sufficient legal aid and voluntary defenders to the poor.

Yet the same inner certainty that made Griswold an extraordinarily self-confident man also contributed to his brittleness and impatience. Invariably, faculty members praised Griswold for his sense of fair play: his strong belief in the First Amendment, his eagerness to have all points of view represented on the faculty, his defense of the National Lawyers Guild and the *Nation* magazine when government agencies tried to suppress them. But when assured that their remarks would not be directly attributed, faculty members candidly discussed Griswold's boredom with faculty meetings, his poor attitude in accepting criticism, how often he stared at his antique office clock when professors raised questions he did not care to answer. It wasn't just that "Erwin was no good at small talk"; it was also that his moderate or occasionally liberal political beliefs were at odds with the impatient self-rectitude of a latter-day Puritan.

Students rarely saw him outside the classroom. Griswold often dealt even with the president of the *Harvard Law Review* by mail. But the dean brought his moral sternness to the classes he taught. A student didn't dare admit being "unprepared," for Griswold would respond, "Well, you brought your head along, didn't you?" and then proceed to state enough facts so that he could question the student.

He was a perfectionist. In one of his first speeches as dean, Griswold asserted, "The function of the dean is to do anything about the place that the janitor won't do." Griswold regularly sent letters to the student newspaper about why students must adequately prepare for state bar examinations; how to take law school tests ("Answer the questions in order. Write legibly. Do not write with a pencil. Do not use red, green, orange or other odd colored inks"); even about matters as trivial as lavatory soap ("We have given a great deal of thought and attention to the soap problem. We have tried powdered soap containers. But they can be had only in plastic; and experience shows that they jam, and are promptly broken when men hit them with their hands").

With faculty, Griswold could be an even stricter taskmaster. Individual faculty members bristled as they recalled not receiving salary increases equal to their contemporaries' because Dean Griswold didn't think they deserved them; senior professors being passed over while younger faculty received coveted professorial "chairs"; Griswold's icy insistence that one professor stop teaching at the discretionary retirement age of seventy although a colleague was allowed to teach until seventy-six. At the same time, the dean was protective of his "family." A member of the Harvard University Ad Hoc Committee to review the Law School faculty appointments once observed that the surest way for a young assistant professor to win tenure was for a committee member to suggest that the professor's classroom abilities were not quite good enough.

Despite his forceful personality, the dean entertained few innovative ideas about legal education. Throughout his career, Griswold repeatedly emphasized his desire "to preserve the basic values of a Harvard Law School education, while molding the content and method of our instruction to meet current needs of law and legal practice." To Griswold the "basic values" of legal education were not substantive ideas but, rather, "rigor, intellectual discipline, training in how to think," all of which, he wrote in 1949, "will remain as the foundation of the school's legal instruction."

Never did Griswold's speeches or writings reflect a systematic view of how legal education could be molded "to meet current needs and legal practice" or what role Harvard Law School should play in clarifying or reforming the substance of American law. Unlike Story, Langdell, and Pound, Erwin Griswold was a tax lawyer, not a legal philosopher. In 1952, he summarized his position on the need for legal research by revealing his lack of interest in "broad social questions." Rather, "there is much room for progress in the field of procedure. Criminal law and criminal procedure would be fertile areas for active thoughtful work . . . Another line of activity would be the collection of materials relating to matters which happen in law offices, but never get into courts."

But Erwin Griswold had not been chosen dean because of his theoretical beliefs, but rather because of his administrative talents, and because as Harvard Law Professor Louis Jaffe put it: "Griswold had an air of authority with which he may have been born."

"During the war," Griswold explained in his first dean's report, "the school was little more than a shell, with very few students, a majority of its faculty on leave, and practically all of its classroom and library space turned over to the armed services." The end of the war, rapid demobilization, and the GI Bill changed all that. Where there had been 124 students at Harvard Law School in the spring term of 1945, there were 2131 by fall of 1947, and the Law School briefly employed an accelerated two-and-one-third-year schedule to cope with that many.

In such circumstances, it was natural for Dean Griswold to respond like a quartermaster to the postwar need to rebuild Harvard Law School. In 1948, approximately two years after succeeding James Landis, Erwin Griswold announced his "program" for Harvard Law School. He recognized that, as Roscoe Pound had written in his first dean's report in 1915–1916, "once more there is a call to meet the demands of a new stage of American legal development," yet argued, "The first task that we must undertake has to do with proper housing for our students." Griswold's second priority was to increase scholarship funds.

Only Griswold's final proposal — the expansion of international legal studies — indicated any interest in "meeting the demands of American legal development." In an uncharacteristic, almost quixotic vein, the dean wrote, "We envisage in Cambridge [that] a world school of law would attract young men from all the countries of the world," to study "the rapidly expanding constitutional and administrative law of world organization . . . international trade [and the] common law so that they could properly advise clients in their own countries who might have commercial relations with us. By the same token, American students would come to the school to learn the basic elements of civil law, or other legal systems."

The common need of all points of Griswold's "program" was money. Harvard Law School needed to raise lots of money. This proved to be one of Dean Griswold's special skills. "When I became dean," Griswold later recalled,

> . . . the only fund raising was through the Harvard Fund, and the highest amount received in any year was $5,000. By direction of President Conant, we were not allowed to solicit anyone who was a graduate of Harvard College. We had no complete list of the names and addresses of the graduates of the Law School. The most recent Quinquennial had been put out in 1939. Our chief public relations medium was the student newspaper, the *Harvard Law Record*, and that, I may say, was a slender reed. I remember that when the first issue was mailed out in July, 1946, with such addresses as we had, it took a truck to carry off the copies returned by the post offices for inadequate and incorrect addresses.

In 1950–1951, Griswold regularized fund-collecting by creating a program of annual giving. Every year an alumni "whole area organization" representative approached each of the thousands of Harvard Law School graduate and nongraduate alumni. Next, the alumni would be individually approached by class agents, and sometimes also by representatives of scholarship committees, library committees, the Graduating Class Parents' Committee, and the Twenty-Fifth and Fiftieth Anniversary Gift Committees. In addition there was a Cambridge office of the fund to assist area chairmen and class agents. By 1962 the percentage of graduates contributing had grown from a 1950 total of 13.5 percent to 47 percent — with over 8300 donors participating.

The nub of Griswold's fund-collecting efforts was what former

Associate Dean David Cavers called "alumni cultivation . . . Until Erwin came along no [Harvard Law School] dean ever worked systematically at cultivating the alumni." Every letter (including postcards and reprints), his staff noted, "received an appropriate and considered reply . . . In addition to the mail, he culled the news and other publications and sent an immediate message of congratulation, condolence, agreement, or disagreement when an item concerned an HLS alumnus or friend." Then there were the speeches. Erwin Griswold probably gave as many speeches to local bar groups as anyone has ever been asked to give.

In return for their generosity, the Law School's alumni never requested any formal *quid pro quo.* They didn't have to. On more than one occasion, Griswold observed that he wished he could have had two careers: one as a law firm practitioner in his native city of Cleveland, the second as a law professor and law school dean. In time, he assimilated some of the values of both. Through countless alumni dinners, the dean sat stern but affable as he heard about law practice in La Jolla, Kansas City, or New York City. Meeting after meeting with law firm partners reinforced and colored his outlook. The Law School's mission might have seemed different if he regularly visited inner-city slums or concerned himself with environmental depredations or the annual slaughter on the nation's highways. But that was not Dean Griswold's world. His world revolved around teaching tax law, answering alumni letters, and attending alumni banquets where other men drank and smoked while the dean nursed his glass of nonalcoholic catawba juice and mostly listened.

The fund-raising drives provided a highly visible Griswold legacy. In his twenty-one years as dean, Erwin Griswold collected sufficient funds to double the size of the faculty, extinguish the Law School's pre–World War II debts, quadruple the endowment, and increase student financial aid twenty-three fold. Dormitories to house one fourth of the Law School students were erected in 1950, as were the Harkness Commons cafeteria and meeting rooms; later would come the construction of the International Legal Studies building, a Faculty Office Building, and the neoteric Pound classroom building.

Griswold also had the opportunity to rebuild the faculty of Harvard Law School. But rather than attempting to develop a modern theory of legal education and then seeking a faculty who could teach it, Griswold's faculty selection was rooted in credentialism. Nearly every appointment to a main-subject teaching position had attended Harvard, Yale, or Columbia Law School and either been an officer of the school's law review or first in his class. These potential appointees (and those few who were exceptions to the above rule) then needed the support of senior Harvard Law professors such as Dean Griswold, Henry Hart, and Paul Freund, and influential Law School alumni such as Justice Felix Frankfurter or former Secretary of State Dean Acheson.

Although basing appointments largely on outstanding grades arguably constituted a laudable example of merit-based hiring, the comparative de-emphasizing of outstanding professional achievements and postgraduate writing in favor of influential recommendations tended to encourage potential faculty applicants to be timid in what they wrote or said lest they offend brother *Law Review* members or a pivotal professor or judge. The faculty selected tended to be cautious and atheoretical, its most successful members specialists in narrow fields of law rather than generalists or critics. The byword of the Griswold period was "craft." The New Deal, it was believed, had settled the substantive questions of American law. If one accepted this premise, it followed that the scholarly role of a modern law faculty should be to refine and clarify the post–World War II legal order just as Langdell's progeny had sought to refine and clarify the legal order developed by common-law judges. The seemingly more liberal professors of the Griswold period were just as quiescent in accepting the contours of an existing economy and its laws as Langdell's seemingly more conservative acolytes.

Some of the spirit of faculty selection during the Griswold period was reflected in the most significant constitutional-law debate of the time: Should the Supreme Court decisions be based on "neutral principles"? Throughout the 1950s and 1960s, leading constitutional-law scholars such as Harvard's Henry Hart, Yale's Alexander Bickel, and Columbia's Herbert Wechsler criticized the

Warren Supreme Court when its decisions did not square with their theories of "reasoned elaboration."

The notion was inherently conservative, emphasizing judicial restraints rather than the substantive ends of American law. The advocates of reasoned elaboration sought to protect American society from the excesses of an unbridled judiciary. But in the context of the 1950s, the emphasis on consensual decision making, argued legal historian G. E. White, "was the equivalent of political conservatism, for in emerging areas of social conflict, such as race relations, the executive and legislative branches of government had largely remained indifferent to change." Unlike their intellectual forefathers, Louis Brandeis and Felix Frankfurter, most of the academic champions of reasoned elaboration did not join their commitment to judicial restraint to pleas for legislative reform.

At Harvard Law School, such a faculty temperament cannot be attributed entirely to Griswold. As chairman of the Appointments Committee, he only had one vote. But the force of his personality often enabled him to exercise a "mutual veto" in faculty selection.

Initially, Griswold's recommendations seemed feisty and egalitarian. Before he became dean, virtually every professor appointed to the Harvard Law School faculty had been a Harvard Law graduate. Griswold attempted to diversify the faculty, to bring in new voices that might challenge the "conformity" and parochialism of the School. One of Griswold's first choices was Soia Mentschikoff, the Law School's first female visiting professor. An offer was made to William Coleman, later President Ford's Secretary of Transportation, who would have been the school's first black faculty member. At a law school where the assumption that persons educated in Cambridge are "the best" often seems as natural as breathing, the dean's approach was startling. Some faculty members still shake their heads over the fact that Visiting Professor Clark Byse, a graduate of the University of Wisconsin Law School, was chosen in 1957 for a tenured position over Visiting Professor Phil Neal, a former member of the *Harvard Law Review*. In recruiting visiting professors from the United Kingdom, France, and Germany, the dean made clear his desire to modify the smug belief of some members of the Harvard Law faculty that "all good people come from Cambridge."

But as the faculty grew larger the selection process evolved toward its own set of "neutral principles": Of the seventeen professors hired to teach American law subjects at Harvard Law School during the last decade of Griswold's deanship, thirteen were Harvard Law graduates, all had been members of the *Law Review*, twelve had been officers of the *Review*, nine had clerked for Supreme Court Justices Frankfurter, Harlan, and Brennan — positions typically secured with the recommendation of senior Harvard Law School faculty members.

This was a tragedy of lost opportunities. By largely confining faculty selection to outstanding students, the Law School assured itself of capable classroom instructors but deprived itself of proven scholars and courtroom or government attorneys. The Law School also assured that it would be highly resistant to change, for a faculty selection formula that depended on the good opinion of fellow *Law Review* editors and influential older men was more likely to result in a faculty that valued the quiet virtue of "colleagueship" above the more contentious goal of social reform.

Nowhere was this conservatism clearer than in the Law School's periodic attempts to revise its curriculum. Almost immediately after the end of World War II, Dean Landis appointed Professor Lon Fuller and five other professors to a wide-ranging Committee on Legal Education. Fuller's committee concentrated on the unfinished business of the late 1930s, cognizant, as one committee member stated, that the 1937 Harvard Law School curriculum study "hadn't exactly set the world on fire." Beginning just three years after Yale Law School's Myres McDougal and Harold Lasswell had proposed a total revision of the intellectual premises of American legal education, the Fuller committee focused on the major criticisms made by the Legal Realists — for example, "Instruction centers on the process by which appellate cases are decided rather than on the problems of planning and strategy with which lawyers are chiefly concerned in practice . . . Legal education treats law in isolation from the related social sciences . . . Legal training in American law schools is too restricted in scope and does not give the student a philosophic and historic grounding in the law or an understanding of the broader functions of the legal profession."

But the Fuller committee was unable to develop a consensus as to how these questions should be answered. Although the committee repeatedly asserted that post–World War II legal education must be more "practical," after three years of deliberations its principal achievements were to persuade the full faculty to make mandatory perennially popular elective courses in Administrative, Constitutional, and Tax Law, and require second-year students to take one "perspective" course from an intellectual smorgasbord including Comparative Law, Jurisprudence, Legal History, and Legislation. No first-year courses were changed.

Professor Fuller attributed the modesty of these reforms to the necessity for "democratic compromise." Not only had an entire faculty to be persuaded, but the committee had widely surveyed student and alumni views.

In the Griswold era, the only sustained faculty effort to deal with the obsolescence of the Law School's curriculum focused on the elective system. In 1946–1947, when Griswold became dean, Harvard Law School required all courses in the first and second years and offered only fifteen optional courses in the third year. By 1966–1967, Griswold's last full year as dean, second- and third-year students could choose from over 100 electives, including Islamic Law, seminars in Product and Environmental Hazards, the Legal Status of the Mentally Ill, Land Use Planning, and twenty-two courses in International Law.

But this was not so much curricular reform as a throwing up of hands. Rather than attempt to develop a new intellectual framework for Law School study or to initiate training programs for emerging legal specialties, such as federal government or corporate tax practice, the School chose instead to offer a potpourri of optional second- and third-year classes in the subjects that paralleled the research interests of individual faculty members.

The irony of the Law School's curricular randomness was that Harvard Law School came closer to developing a new philosophical basis for legal education and research than any other American law school but shied away from employing it. Until his death in 1969, Henry Hart was the post–World War II intellectual leader of the Harvard Law School, a Benthamite type of thinker with an extraordinary gift for systematizing solutions to complex legal questions. With Professor Albert Sacks, in 1954–1955 he began transforming a conventional course in Legislation into a much broader second-year elective survey course initially entitled "The American Legal System," later retitled "The Legal Process: Basic Problems in the Making and Application of Law." The course contained the embryo of a modern, albeit conservative, jurisprudence. Students were presented with a series of factual problems and then studied the manner in which private individuals (through contracts, associations, or other devices for private ordering), courts, legislatures, and government agencies would resolve these problems, at all times concerned with the central question: What *should* be the political relationship among private individuals, courts, legislatures, and agencies in a democratic legal system?

The Legal Process course became the most popular second-year "perspective" course at Harvard Law School. Although the Hart-Sacks materials were never formally published, mimeographed versions were used at many other leading law schools. The course's thoughtful use of the "problem method" — as distinguished from Langdell's narrower case method — was widely imitated. The Hart-Sacks approach, however, promised to be more than an alternative technique for teaching law or a second-year elective. In essence, the materials assimilated leading legal questions of the pre–New Deal period and offered a detailed political theory for their resolution. By taking the position that courts were limited in their discretion by the necessity to engage in "reasoned elaboration" and that legislatures and executive agencies were bound by related concepts, Hart-Sacks implied a new doctrinal orthodoxy — what Professor Morton Horwitz aptly calls an institutional formalism — to supplant the discredited logical formalism of Langdell.

This approach was never fully accepted by the Harvard Law

School faculty. During the 1950s a number of Harvard Law School faculty members were persuaded that the curriculum as a whole — and especially the first year — lacked the "breadth" or "depth" to provide Harvard Law students with an understanding of how their legal system worked or what its underlying principles were. In part for this reason, Professor James Casner was appointed in 1959 to chair a Committee on Legal Education to study methods to revive the theoretical framework of the first year. After several months of deliberation, his committee reported that although "development of analytical capacity remains the most important mission of the first year . . . the analysis of cases to test doctrinal generalization or to solve immediate hypothetical problems tends to give a predominantly static view of the law and its work. Opportunities to convey a sense of the evolution and movement of law are at best sporadic. Further, the present courses do not afford an opportunity for any sustained attention to the function of lawyers in society or the purposes of law and lawyers in the embodiment of a society's values or the accomplishment of its objectives . . ."

The committee proposed creating a first-year "perspective" course by presenting one or more traditional first-year courses, such as Criminal or Torts Law, through a historical approach; or by creating a new first-year course built around a historical approach to law; or by transforming the Hart-Sacks Legal Process materials into a first-year course.

Then the Casner committee ran into a stone wall in the form of the more practitioner-oriented members of the faculty.

Shortly after debate began on the Casner report, Dean Griswold circulated a memorandum blandly announcing to the "considerable number of members of the faculty who feel that something should be done in our revision to broaden our legal education, or, to put it in other ways, to give it a greater cultural content, or greater depth in historical perspective [that] the case for the need for this change does not seem to me to have been made." These faculty members, nonetheless, persisted. Four months later, Professor W. Barton Leach circulated a far less deferential memorandum entitled "Culture by Compulsion." Leach wrote that he felt a duty "to do my utmost to prevent this outstanding professional school from being forced into a configuration which, if the trend continues, will resemble a juridical Sarah Lawrence College with slave-drivers."

With neither Hart nor Sacks encouraging the faculty to transform their Legal Process materials into a first-year required course, a compromise was reached whereby a new legal history course entitled Development of Legal Institutions (DLI) would be added to the first year. As was the case in all post–World War II Harvard Law School curricular debates, "no one," in Dean Griswold's view, "was very satisfied with the outcome of the faculty deliberations . . . In committee of the whole, votes such as 21 to 20 or 23 to 19 were rather common." As conceived and taught by Professors Dawson and Howe, the DLI course focused on developments in the history of English and colonial law up to the date that they would have been relevant to the other first-year courses. Even a professor so generously inclined in his judgments as Paul Freund ridiculed the "if-you-were-Henry-II" approach of the course. In 1968 DLI ceased to be a required course, and with its death ended the only serious attempt of Harvard Law School in the post–World War II period to revive the theoretical framework of its curriculum.

Reinforcing the narrowness of the curriculum during Griswold's deanship was a conformity nurtured by Senator Joseph McCarthy's style of investigations. There was a particularly saddening irony in this. Few institutions were as outspokenly hostile to McCarthy as Harvard Law School; few deans as unrelentingly critical as Griswold. But the decade-long struggle to avoid appearing "too controversial" — to be sure, as Griswold once put it, that the Law School's radicals were "sound" — engendered a cautiousness, among other things, that sustained two decades of law school scholarship largely concerned with legal procedures or distant international-law questions rather than more immediate political questions such as poverty, race relations, or corporate power.

From the start, Harvard Law School faculty members publicly opposed the post–World War II Red scare. In 1947, Dean Griswold and three other law professors published a letter in the *New*

York Times protesting President Truman's loyalty oath. Three years later, when the invasion of Korea intensified the vehemence of anti-Communists, the American Bar Association and the Association of American Law Schools respectively supported loyalty oaths for lawyers and law professors. Almost simultaneously Dean Griswold, by publishing a letter reiterating, "I believe in the free commerce of ideas," rejected a demand by Samuel Sears, the president of the Massachusetts Bar Association, that the radical Harvard Lawyers Guild be disbanded.

But in 1953 the Law School lost its nerve when McCarthy-style Senator William Jenner announced field hearings in Boston on communism in education. In mid-March, two second-year Law School students, Jonathan and David Lubell, were subpoenaed to testify before Jenner's roving Senate Subcommittee on Internal Security. Although neither of the twin brothers had been politically active since they arrived at Harvard Law School, both had been organizers for radical organizations while undergraduates at Cornell University.

Both Lubells recall that at the Law School, Dean Griswold was the strongest advocate of their fully cooperating with the Jenner subcommittee. The dean argued that taking the Fifth Amendment was widely regarded as an admission of criminal guilt and would affect their professional careers. To the dean's credit, he later made a complete study of the issue and revised this opinion. But before the hearings, David Lubell recalls Griswold saying "that we were being selfish. We were going to do great harm to the School."

On March 27, the Lubells appeared before the Jenner subcommittee. The senator introduced Jonathan Lubell by stating, "We have evidence that this student is an active Communist organizer." The subcommittee then proceeded to ask a series of questions, such as were the Lubells members of the Communist Party, had they organized for the Communist Party at Cornell University or Harvard Law School, had they distributed the *Daily Worker*, had they written briefs for the National Lawyers Guild. To several questions the Lubells refused to answer, invoking the Fifth Amendment privilege against self-incrimination.

Two days later, Harvard Law School Professor W. Barton Leach circulated a letter to the School's faculty implying that the Lubells had pled the privilege "to the crime of conspiring to overthrow the government of the United States." Leach recommended that the Lubells be expelled: "If we admit a man upon satisfactory intellectual performance and then find him intellectually unqualified, we then exclude him. If we admit a man upon satisfactory character showing and then find his character inadequate, we should also exclude him. We have no hesitancy in doing this upon the basis of property or scholastic crimes; the present instance is much more serious."

Griswold called a special faculty meeting. Pinioned between an enraged minority of his faculty that favored ousting the Lubells, and an equally enraged majority that considered Jenner's hearings to be a witch hunt, Griswold proceeded delicately. By then the dean had already begun research on the Fifth Amendment and no longer subscribed to a position as extreme as that of Professor Leach. But as the dean explained in an interview twenty-three years later, his major concern was to do a "selling job" on the faculty "to put over his conclusion."

The result was a confused, internally contradictory speech. In a typically forthright manner, Griswold began his statement to the faculty by explaining that the statutes of Harvard University permit a faculty to dismiss a student only in cases of serious misconduct. "What is the situation now in the cases of the Lubells? The clear fact, I believe, is that no evidence of any sort is available to us which proves . . . that they have been guilty of misconduct."

Griswold based his conclusion upon a sophisticated interpretation of the Fifth Amendment: "It is not accurate, I believe, to say that the refusal to answer a question on the ground of self-incrimination is sufficient to prove either one of two things, namely, that the person is in fact guilty of a crime, or that he has perjured himself in claiming the privilege. There is clearly an intermediate ground. A person may properly claim the privilege, even though he knows he is not guilty of any crime, if the evidence he would give would help to build up the case for a prosecution against him." But then Griswold hedged. With obvious deference to

Professor Leach, the dean added, "It is clear that no person can now be a Communist, or could have been a Communist in the recent past, without full awareness of the fact that he was engaging in a Communist conspiracy against the United States . . . My present attitude towards [Senator Jenner's] subcommittee is in no sense one of hostility. On the contrary, it is one of entire willingness to cooperate." These could not have been easy statements for Griswold to make. By March 1953, Jenner was known to the American public principally as the senator who had called General George Marshall "a front man for traitors," and "a living lie"; who had stated after General Douglas MacArthur was fired, "This country is in the hands of a secret coterie which is directed by agents of the Soviet Union"; and whom presidential candidate Dwight Eisenhower had refused to embrace in 1952 because "I felt dirty from the touch of the man."

Although recommending that the faculty table the motion to expel the Lubells, Griswold argued, "The fact that the privilege is claimed may justly lead to deep suspicion . . . It is very clear that the Lubells must be watched with extreme care from now on . . ." The Lubells' claim of privilege should "operate as an effective barrier against the admission of the Lubells to the Bar of any state in this country."

A divided faculty voted not to expel the Lubells. But four days later Professor Leach circulated a second memorandum to the faculty explaining how the Law School's admissions policies could be structured "to avoid further Lubell cases." In late April, Leach published in Harvard University's student newspaper a letter he wrote to the Lubells' draft board recommending that both brothers be immediately inducted. The head of the New York City Selective Service publicly refused.

The lack of clear faculty leadership resulted in the Lubells' ostracism at Harvard Law School. Within a week after their appearance before Senator Jenner's subcommittee, the *Harvard Law Record* forced both brothers to resign editorial positions, "consonant," the student-run newspaper explained, "with the necessity for maintaining a well-ordered society." About the same time, the Legal Aid Bureau pressured Jonathan Lubell to quit. Benjamin

Harrison Frankel, Jonathan Lubell's classmate, wrote sixteen years later that "only two persons in the entire bureau defended his right to membership." Other Legal Aid members explained that Boston attorneys had indicated to the bureau that its existence would be jeopardized if they retained Lubell.

In classrooms, both Lubells claimed students refused to sit near them. Their study group disbanded. Friends stopped seeing them or met with them surreptitiously. "In terms of today's atmosphere," David Lubell summarized, it was "unbelievable. It was so bad that when we came into the Harkness cafeteria people would leave the table."

As the months passed, the ostracism did not abate. Early in the summer of 1953, Andrew Kaufman, then the president of the *Harvard Law Review*, today a Harvard Law professor, learned that Jonathan Lubell's grades entitled him to serve on the *Law Review*. Although nearly every member of the *Review* was "totally anti-McCarthy," many believed that the Lubells' activities at Cornell or their refusal to testify candidly constituted improper — if not illegal — conduct.

Under the *Harvard Law Review* constitution, active members "elected" students with sufficiently high grades to qualify for the *Review*. With few if any exceptions, during the previous forty years these students had been elected to the *Review* in midsummer. Jonathan Lubell was asked to wait until all the *Review*'s active members returned in September.

Uncertain of what to do, Kaufman turned to the *Law Review*'s trustees, who included Griswold and Professor Freund. Griswold and the other faculty members "ducked out of the decision," in the dean's words, by informing Kaufman that the decision on Lubell belonged to the students.

A delegation of three *Law Review* members met with Jonathan Lubell in New York City and tried to persuade him to draft a letter that would make his presence on the *Review* palatable to the other editors. Lubell recalled the meeting. "Three-fourths of the interview was a discussion of the Korean War. In some way, this was a qualification for being on the *Law Review* . . . I was unalterably opposed to the War . . . Despite the fact that I was very anxious to be on the *Review*, I didn't pretty it up."

Stuart Land, then a *Law Review* editor, recalls that Lubell's sub-sequent letter to the *Review* "hurt him . . . It was a hostile, argu-mentative document . . . Jonathan said he had a right to be on the *Review* and told us to lump it . . ." After a heated debate, the third-year members of the *Harvard Law Review* voted 16–8 not to elect Jonathan Lubell even if he satisfied certain "conditions." Both Lubells were convinced that the vote was unprincipled. David Lubell charged that the student editors didn't accept his brother "because they thought Jon being on the *Review* would be a professional liability to them," or, as Jonathan phrased it, the edi-tors "feared it would hurt their careers." Most editors of the *Re-view* disagreed. One urged that there were more editors con-cerned about civil liberties than jeopardizing their careers. In his view, the hostility of Lubell's letter undercut the support he might otherwise have received.

Shortly after the *Law Review* vote, Dean Griswold concluded that he had been wrong. He regretted "ducking out" on the *Law Review* decision, and in 1958 wrote a letter of support when the Lubells sought admission to the New York bar. Within a few months of the *Law Review* vote, the dean began publicly speaking out in favor of the propriety of witnesses who invoked "an old and good friend, the Fifth Amendment." These speeches would earn Griswold a citation from the Harvard University faculty and be published in a widely read book. In retrospect, Griswold would recall his irritation that more law professors did not "do anything during the McCarthy period."

As divisive as the McCarthy period could be for the faculty, it was very distant from the experience of most Harvard Law stu-dents. McCarthyism undoubtedly contributed to a widely held desire to be among those students whom Harvard University President Pusey labeled "The Safe." Yet the anti-Communist in-vestigations did not directly affect many students the way the Vietnam War later would. Indeed, the leitmotiv of student life during the Griswold deanship was the extent to which students ignored national politics in favor of an almost exclusive concern with their future careers.

Immediately after World War II, the return of veterans increased qualified applicants to Harvard Law School to about five times the number of men the School could accommodate. By 1950, the GI surge had subsided, but steadily through Griswold's deanship the number of applications increased: from 1265 in 1951 to 3012 in 1966. Griswold exulted, "This has been truly an embarrassment of riches." An upshot of selective admissions was to reduce Harvard Law's failout rate from a prewar level of 30 percent to approximately 1 percent in 1966. As desirable as this was, selective admissions had the reciprocal consequence of stimulating competitiveness within the School. To Griswold, rigorous grading and the private indication to each student of his class rank were the stimuli that "maintained high standards" and sustained Harvard Law School as "a great graduate school." To students, they were what made the School into "a rat race." According to George Spiegel, a first-term student in 1947: "In war, business, or college, I have never seen so many intelligent people so worried as here in Harvard Law School."

The grade-ranking ordeal was also needlessly distracting. Students chained by anxiety to their books had little time to participate in political or cultural events. As the Law School's newspaper editorialized at the height of the civil rights movement, "The Nation Marched; Harvard Law School Talked." The gallows humor of the late 1950s had it that a first-year Harvard Law School student could spend the entire year in classrooms, Harkness cafeteria, Langdell Library, or the tunnels in between.

But the most pervasive influence on student life during the Griswold deanship was the prominence of corporate-law firms. In the absence of a critical theory of law, the influence of these future employers was unrivaled. Harvard Law student Samuel Bleicher explained in 1966:

> Almost from the moment he walks into his first class, the Harvard Law School student is exposed to and encouraged to think in terms of Wall Street corporate-law practice. His professors talk about multi-million dollar cases they handled, his casebooks are filled with familiar business names, and his friends discuss at length the relative merits

of 75- versus 125-man firms. Those who say they are going "back home" to practice feel defensive and are presumed to have some ulterior motive, such as political aspirations. The large-firm lawyer is held out as the ideal career type.

The effect of this one-sided presentation of the lawyer's alternatives is subtly to coerce many students into social, psychological, and political conformity with the image of the "successful" lawyer — the partner in a big firm.

After 1956, relatively few Harvard Law graduates started their own practices. Instead, having listened to their professors recount experiences at leading firms such as the District of Columbia's Covington and Burling or Boston's Ropes and Gray, they signed up at the Placement Office for interviews with representatives of the giant firms. As late as 1949–1950, such interviews had been hard to obtain. That year, only fifty-five firms sent partners to Cambridge; only 232 students were allowed to speak to them. Students with a C average had difficulty finding jobs, sometimes requiring as long as a year to secure one. The postwar economic boom eliminated this problem. By 1956 the School's Placement Office Director Russell Peck proclaimed "jobs for all." Six years later, Eleanor Appel, Peck's harassed successor as placement director, reported that more than 400 firms and corporations would conduct over 6000 interviews in the 1962–1963 school year.

Paradoxically, the creation of a seller's market expanded the influence of the private firms. Between 1950 and 1960, the beginning salary for Harvard Law graduates rose from $3000–$4000 to between $6000 and $7200 in the major firms. Immediately after World War II, a few firms, particularly desirous of hiring Harvard Law graduates, employed students after their second year for summer jobs. By 1957, almost half the second-year class held such jobs; by the end of the Griswold deanship virtually any second-year student who wanted a summer clerkship could secure one, as could many first-year students. This extended consciousness of the link between a Harvard Law School education and corporate-law-firm employment from the third year to the second into the first. Many students took electives such as Business

Planning or Corporate Finance because they assumed such courses would impress future employers.

Leading attorneys regularly traveled to Harvard to conduct panel discussions on topics such as "Corporate Practice in a New York City Firm." How seriously senior law firm partner Richard Nixon took recruiting was well illustrated in October 1965, when he spent a day interviewing in Cambridge for his corporate-law firm but announced he would not have time to publicly address the Law School's Republican Club. By contrast, during the Griswold deanship relatively little recruiting was done on behalf of legal-aid offices or local government jobs. And even when near the end of Griswold's tenure as dean, the Law School helped administer local legal-services programs, few professors gave students the impression that a career in such a field was a respectable alternative.

At the end of the Griswold period, Harvard Law School was regarded as the nation's most prestigious trade school. As with the law school at Columbia, as with the law school at NYU, its primary function was to graduate private law firm attorneys. But the narrowness of faculty selection had limited the contributions that Harvard could make to American law. In the post–World War II period the Law School had never seriously questioned its basic purpose or developed critical studies of American law. In contrast with earlier periods, the central ideas advanced by the School were rarely pathbreaking. The vanguard of legal reform had moved from Cambridge, first to the Warren Supreme Court, then to Congress and liberal state legislatures, and later to a burgeoning public-interest and legal-services movement. Harvard Law School, to paraphrase Roscoe Pound, had begun to lag behind life.

Part II

A MODERN CRITIQUE

5

ADMISSIONS:

A Meritocracy for the Few

Toss a beer can out of any college dormitory in America and chances are you will hit somebody struggling to get into law school. There has been a sad falling off here. A few years ago, when its highest aspiration was to hold the dean for ransom, youth looked as if it might grow up to amount to something. Instead, it wants to be lawyers.

RUSSELL BAKER

Along with 6056 other applicants, Kenneth B. Krohn sought admission to Harvard Law School in September 1975. Nearly a year before he hoped to take his first class, Krohn asked the Law School's Admissions Office to mail him an application. Soon he received a thin brochure entitled "Harvard Law School Applications Materials 1975." A few weeks later a slightly longer pamphlet, describing the Law School in generalized terms ("Harvard Law School is a very different experience for different people . . ."), arrived by third-class mail.

By January Krohn had complied with the formalities of the admissions process, returning to the Admissions Office a two-page application form, an admission file card, and a Harvard Law School data sheet. Most of the information requested was easy to provide, for example, "List all scholastic or academic honors you have received," but Part II of the application was open-ended: "Applicants are encouraged to present themselves and their qualifications as they wish . . ." This was, though not all applicants realized it, the single most important question in the form. It was the applicant's one chance to shape all the numerical and biographical data that would eventually be accumulated into a persuasive, coherent story — to make, as lawyers say, the strongest possible case.

Only when he had completed each of these and other steps did the admissions machinery slowly begin to whir for Kenneth Krohn. "Krohn, Kenneth B." became both a file and a computer entry down at the Educational Testing Service in Princeton. One by one his transcripts arrived from MIT, his undergraduate college, and Harvard University, where he had earned master's and Ph.D. degrees. Most grades were then fed into a computer, and a grade-point average was calculated for each year of college and graduate school the applicant had completed. For Harvard Law School, the Testing Service did this in a somewhat unusual way. The grade-point average was multiplied by a "grade adjustment formula." This formula reflected a conclusion Harvard Law School had drawn earlier in the century: Students from most undergraduate colleges were likely to do less well at Harvard Law School than those from Harvard University and other leading colleges and universities. So the grade-point average of most students was reduced under the adjustment formula. Thus a student from Harvard with a straight A average might receive a grade-point average of 4.0 from the computer; while a student from a little-known state university also carrying a straight A average might receive credit for only a 3.5 average.

Some weeks later the Educational Testing Service received "Krohn, Kenneth B." 's Law School Admission Test (LSAT) score. For most applicants, this score was fed into the computer and an "admissions index" calculated. At Harvard Law School the same formula had long been used: An applicant's LSAT score was recorded in a number between 200 and 800. The cumulative grade-point average similarly was reflected in a number between 0 and 800. The LSAT score and the grade-point average were then added together and divided by two. Ultimately, an applicant's entire record was reduced to a single admissions index number between 100 and 800.

By now there had been an uncompleted "Krohn, Kenneth B." file in Cambridge for several weeks. It had begun when Krohn's two-page application form had been received shortly after January 10, 1975. A secretary had typed a file label on a distinctive form with five boxes. Next to the box labeled "App." she had checked an arrow. In had come Krohn's two letters of recommendation and college questionnaire, and three more arrows had been checked. Finally the report from the Law School Data Assembly Service (LSDAS) had arrived, and the final check was made. "Krohn, Kenneth B." was now a "complete" file.

At this point the admissions index began to exert its powerful influence. The 3000 or so applicant files with the lowest admissions index numbers were routed to June Thompson, the assistant director of admissions. Over the course of seven months she read every word of each application, her basic responsibility was to recommend the rejection of approximately 90 percent of the applicants in the bottom half of the applicant pool. However, if she chanced across something striking in Part II of the application form, or a letter of recommendation — a compelling explanation of a low admissions index number or a stirring presentation of some countervailing virtue — she showed the file to Russell Simpson, then the director of admissions and an assistant dean, or to James Bierman, also an assistant dean.

Krohn was probably in the top half of the applicant pool. These 3000 or so applicants were treated differently. Eighty to 85 percent of the 250–300 applicants with the highest admissions index numbers ultimately would be admitted. Their files were read initially by either Simpson or Bierman. In three out of four cases, the assistant deans voted that these 250 to 300 favored applicants be admitted. If one of the three professors who sat with the assistant deans on the five-member Admissions Committee agreed, a letter of acceptance was sent. On the other hand, if an assistant dean voted to place the applicant on "hold" or if one of the three professors did not agree with an assistant dean's recommendation to accept, the applicant's file was forwarded to the other committee members, and the applicant's fate would be decided at an Admissions Committee meeting.

The next 700 or so applicants ranked by admissions index numbers were treated similarly. For any of them to be admitted, two of the three professors on the committee had to agree. Almost half of these applicants were accepted; most of the rest were placed in the "hold" category.

The final 2000 applicants in the top half of the admission index pool, and the small number of applicants from the bottom half of the class who had received the support of Russell Simpson or James Bierman in addition to that of June Thompson, were treated in yet another fashion. Of these 2000 applicant files, the 1000 ranked lower by the admissions index were read by either Simpson or Bierman. Each had discretion to reject these applicants on his own authority. Most were rejected. The rest were circulated for faculty reading. The higher 1000 files were also reviewed by Simpson or Bierman. For these applicants to be turned down required negative votes from both of them.

By the time "Krohn, Kenneth B." 's file was "complete" it was probably March or April. Harvard Law School, like most law schools that receive the applications of many more students than they can admit, followed a "rolling" admissions process. The assistant deans and June Thompson began reading files in November. They continued taking them home to read as they became "complete" through May. Throughout these months doubtful cases were resolved in meetings of all five members of the Admissions Committee. As the year wore on, the Admissions Committee grew concerned about a different set of numbers: the number of women and minority applicants being admitted to the following year's class. In addition, there would be mention of phone calls or letters received by the Law School's dean from professors, alumni, or other influential persons who had an interest in a particular applicant. But each of the numbers, and certainly the phone calls to the dean, had different meanings to each of the members of the committee. Given virtually no standards by the dean or the faculty, the committee found its meetings slowed into a time-consuming process of re-examining individual applicant files.

Meanwhile, Kenneth Krohn waited. He had always assumed

he would be admitted. Three times since graduating from MIT in 1959 he had taken the LSAT test and on the last occasion had scored a perfect 800; he later would learn that in only 227 of the 128,252 LSAT examinations given from March 1974 to March 1975 had test-takers received a score higher than 774. His grades from MIT were comparatively old and, as it turned out, impossible for the Educational Testing Service to treat under Harvard Law School's grade adjustment formula. Nevertheless, his average of 3.6 or so, back in the days before colleges universally began to "inflate" grades, placed him very high in his class. In addition, he had a Ph.D. from Harvard University and had invented a "new system of general mathematical specifications of computing systems and sequential machines," which had become "the standard classroom material for university courses in the area."

The odds, however, were against Krohn. Of the 6057 applicants, a maximum of 800 could be accepted, of whom about 540 would enroll.

On May 19, Krohn learned that he had been rejected. So were over 5000 others, most of whom were disappointed with what Krohn called "this hurtful practice." But Krohn then did a very unusual thing: He sued Harvard Law School. Charging that the standards used by Harvard Law School's Admissions Office bear "little or no relation to the selection of those applicants most qualified to pursue a legal education and/or the legal profession, or that such standards do not exist at all," Krohn theorized that "Harvard Law School routinely accords preference to members of certain racial minority groups (notably, blacks), women, young applicants, applicants from wealthy families or with personal or political 'connections,' and applicants from less usual geographical locations or those possessing other currently fashionable or exotic characteristics wholly unrelated to academic or professional merit or aptitude; and that, consequently, few if any places are awarded primarily on the basis of academic merit."

To support these claims, Krohn explained: "In its publicly distributed applications material booklet for 1975, Harvard Law School makes the representation that candidates for admissions are to be selected on the basis of their qualifications," and "that the Admissions Committee seeks to select the 'best' applicants . . . on a fair and rational basis." Relying upon these statements, Krohn applied to Harvard Law School. After he was rejected, Krohn claimed that James Bierman refused to explain specifically why or permit him to inspect his application file or general data relative to Harvard Law School's admissions criteria and procedure.*

Frustrated, Krohn wrote the Law School's Dean, Albert Sacks,

> I presented reasonably serious indications of academic competence, having obtained a Ph.D. from Harvard and scored 800 on the LSAT. Whereas, in view of the great number of outstanding candidates for admission, I certainly concede the possibility that I was insufficiently qualified to rank among the top 540 or so who were admitted, I am, I believe legitimately, dissatisfied with the secretive (and, therefore, possibly arbitrary, careless or partial) character of the selection procedure . . . Simply stated, the relief I seek is either to be admitted to the Law School or to be offered convincing proof that I was justly excluded . . .

When these requests and similar ones to the Board of Overseers of Harvard College were denied, Krohn commenced his suit, seeking admission to the class and monetary damages because of claimed violations of his "due process" and "equal protection" rights under the Fourteenth Amendment of the United States Constitution. Noting that he prepared all the legal papers himself, Krohn later joked to a reporter, "One way or another, I'm going to get a legal education from Harvard." It was a hard education. Over the course of a year, Harvard Law School opposed the suit on the ground that Harvard University was neither a "public institution" nor engaged in "state action" and therefore not subject to the requirements of the Fourteenth Amendment. In August 1976, Federal District Court Judge Frank Freedman agreed with

---

* Under the so-called Buckley amendment, applicants to law schools who are admitted and enroll have the right to read recommendations and other materials related to their applications, but applicants who are not admitted have no such rights.

the University and dismissed the case. A federal court of appeals later affirmed the dismissal.

But Krohn's lawsuit does have the enduring value of framing nearly every popular misconception concerning college and graduate school admissions. Contrary to Krohn's principal point, Harvard Law School, like all national law schools, is incapable of acting as a "meritocracy" except for the few. Regardless of the admissions procedures employed, some students cannot afford — or are unwilling to borrow — the funds necessary to pay for four years of college, three years of law school, and seven years of lost or reduced income. Even if all qualified students could afford law school, it is hardly the case that individual admissions offices — or individual law courts — are capable of precisely defining admissions criteria. Properly understood, admissions criteria are political decisions incorporating conflicts of values and conflicts between racial and social groups, which no more reflect objectively "correct" or "just" definitions than the voting preferences of a body politic. But Krohn's suit did make the quite valid point that the ultimate measure of any selective admissions procedure must be the fairness it accords every applicant. So long as law schools collectively serve as the gatekeepers to the legal profession, barring many people competent to become lawyers, even the possibility of "fairness" will seem illusory to some.

A most formidable barrier to admission is money. As of 1975, thirty-eight of the fifty states required, and the laws of the other twelve states encouraged, students to attend a three-year law school in order to become an attorney. At least 137 of the 163 law schools approved by the American Bar Association demanded college degrees. Among the twenty or so "national" law schools, only Boston University, Columbia, and Duke regularly accepted even a fraction of their students after three years of college.

In a nation where only 24 percent of the population in their late teens can be expected to earn a college degree and but 8 percent a graduate degree, the stipulation of seven years of higher education is a rigorous exclusionary device. In 1976–1977, the total cost (tuition, books, room, board, and so forth) per year of attending a full-time undergraduate university or college, according to the College Board, averaged $2790 at public and $4568 at private institutions. In the most academically prestigious public and private schools, costs were considerably higher. These figures can be profitably compared with the totals of a decade ago, when the cost of a year at UCLA was $1850 and a year at Harvard, $3700. By 1980, it is reasonable to assume that the average cost of attending a public university may equal $4500 per year; the average cost of attending a private university, $5800; and the average cost of attending a prestigious university such as Harvard may exceed $9000.

Since 1958, when Congress passed the National Educational Defense Act, the federal government has enacted a series of higher education acts designed to allow students from poor and middle-income families to attend college.

The purpose of these higher education grant and loan programs — equal educational opportunity — clearly has not been achieved. The basic grant figure was set too low; the poor generally are less willing to borrow heavily to attend college than those somewhat better off. Moreover, the soaring costs of attending colleges and universities have far exceeded the grant and loan funds available. Thus there is the paradoxical result that during the same years the federal government was funding higher education as never before, total enrollment at four-year full-time colleges and universities was shrinking, and it was shrinking at the fastest rate among the poor. Between 1969 and 1973, for example, total enrollment at full-time colleges dropped from 42 percent to 36 percent of the eighteen-to-twenty-four-year-old population. In 1969, 16.4 percent of the eighteen-to-twenty-four-year-old dependents of families earning $3000 or less (as expressed in 1973 constant dollars) were enrolled full-time in college. By 1973, this figure had dropped to 12.7 percent, a decrease of nearly 23 percent. At private universities, where financial barriers are greater, the figures are even more exaggerated. Children of parents earning $20,000 or more in 1971 (the upper 15 percent or so of the income strata) were four times more likely to attend a private university than the children of parents earning $8000 or less (the bottom 36 percent of the income strata).

Harvard Law School, however, had advantages that few other law schools enjoy. Its students could borrow $2500 or more each year under federal graduate-student loan programs — as can all law students — and Harvard Law School also is prepared to grant or loan substantial additional funds to needy students from annual alumni gift and endowment funds. In theory, Harvard Law School can realize its objective of making "it possible for any student who is admitted . . . to meet the basic expenses of law school and to complete his or her legal education" — a claim that no more than three or four law schools in the entire country can make.

Nonetheless, Harvard Law School, like other national law schools, has remained a meritocracy for the few. This is illustrated by the parental income levels of students who *do* borrow money through Harvard Law School's Financial Aid Office. In 1972, the parents of fifty-five of the 286 students who received aid had incomes of $21,000 or more. If the reasonable assumption is made that the parents of at least 90 percent of the 277 students who did not receive aid were at least as affluent, it appears that 58 percent of the Law School class come from the upper 13 percent or so of the income strata. In 1976, a like 58 percent of the Law School entering class appeared to come from parents in the upper 15 percent of the income strata; but 16 percent from parents of the lower 50 percent of the income strata. Available data from other national law schools are similar. The inference is unavoidable that attending one of the most prestigious twenty or so national law schools has remained a privilege largely reserved to the children of the upper- and upper-middle-income strata.

Yet money is only the first barrier to admission to law school. Until World War II, state legislatures and state supreme courts, through the administration of bar examinations, determined who would be allowed into the legal profession. These tests are still given but are basically superfluous for graduates of accredited law schools. With nearly every such law student completing both college and law school, at least 95 percent of these students pass a bar exam, albeit some on their second or third try.

In reality, law school admissions committees determine who

will be accepted into the legal profession. In 1975 approximately 85,000 to 90,000 people sought admission to a law school; 39,038 ultimately enrolled as first-year students. Some of the 45,000 to 50,000 not accepted could have become competent lawyers. The law schools of this country decide, among other things, that some qualified people will not be permitted to practice law.

By acting as gatekeepers to the legal profession, American law schools cease to be merely educational institutions. They now are also political institutions, helping determine who can afford to be represented by counsel and who cannot; whose rights will be defended in courts of law and legislatures and whose will not; and, inevitably, which citizens shall receive "equal protection under the laws" and which shall not.

Annually the Educational Testing Service, administrators of the LSAT, and the Law School Data Assembly Service (LSDAS) on request mail to law schools a validity study. In 1972–1973, the results of the validity study conducted for Harvard Law School reported that if Harvard Law School's Admissions Office attempted to predict first-year law school grades on the basis of undergraduate grade-point average alone, there was a positive correlation coefficient of .51; if the first-year grades were predicted on the basis of the LSAT score alone, there was a correlation coefficient of .57; and if the office had attempted to predict first-year grades on the basis of a combination of undergraduate grade-point average and LSAT score, the coefficient was .64 for the 526 Harvard Law School students who had been admitted in September 1972 and completed their first year of law school in June 1973. These were extraordinarily high "numbers." A positive correlation of 1.0 would have meant that the Educational Testing Service's complex multiple-correlation formula accurately predicted first-year grades for every single student.

Rarely do validity studies show a positive correlation of greater than .50 — approximately equal to predicting a person's height by his weight or his weight by his height — for the undergraduate grade-point average and LSAT score combined.

The seeming certainty of such numbers has done much to confuse the purposes of college and university admissions practices generally and to distort rational consideration of "fair" selection principles into hysterical debates concerning the meaning of one factor that should be related to law school admissions: test-taking aptitude. Such numbers have moved some law schools to make admission decisions solely on the basis of grade-point averages and LSAT scores, and many other law schools to over-emphasize these factors. Underlying such law school admissions practices is a philosophical and technical jumble of monumental proportions.

When in the late 1940s admissions offices first began studying LSAT scores and undergraduate grade-point averages for the single purpose of excluding applicants highly likely to fail in law school, there was little argument about the appropriateness of their policies. But by the mid-1950s more qualified applicants were seeking admission to the leading law schools than could be accepted. And by the 1970s there were over twice as many applicants seeking enrollment as *all* 160 or so law schools in the country could admit.

The LSAT was not as much needed to exclude unqualified applicants. But law schools continued to require the test because admissions officers argued that LSAT scores in conjunction with college grade-point averages could be used to help identify the "best qualified" or "most meritorious" applicants. The assumption that high LSAT and grade-point average "numbers" were synonymous with "merit" or "the best qualifications" is demonstrably erroneous. "Merit" is a value judgment, and opinions about what virtues or skills are most essential to a lawyer or a law student are as divided as opinions about any other political question. To say that a law student is "meritorious" because he does well at taking examinations is to offend those who consider a "meritorious" lawyer one who performs community service. To argue that "merit" can be measured in terms of common legal skills such as writing ability, advocacy, or counseling is to denigrate such virtues as imagination, honesty, persistence, or compassion, which are not lesser virtues merely because they are more difficult to quantify.

What the LSAT or undergraduate grade-point average predicts

is part of a reasonable definition of "merit": ability to do well on law school examinations. For technical reasons, neither index measures this aptitude very reliably. There is no uniform national college grading system, and the character of examinations, distribution of high grades, and theory of grading vary not only from college to college but also from teacher to teacher. Christopher Jencks has observed, "Many teachers deliberately try to reward effort rather than ability. Even when grades depend entirely on performance, an able student may do poorly because he has not done the assigned work, while a dull student may do well because he has been unusually diligent." Or consider that a brilliant student in all courses except languages may be denied admission to law school because his grade-point average was 3.6 rather than the 3.9 it would have been if a foreign language were not mandatory. As processed by the Law School Data Assembly Service, students who do well in physical education, ROTC, domestic arts, and "gut" courses such as Cornell University's elective in Wine and Spirits receive as much credit for their efforts as students who earn high grades in academic courses.

Indeed, the greatest tragedy of selective law school admissions is that it may encourage college students to take those courses likely to be most easily graded, rather than more valuable courses (in any reasonable sense). This possibility was recognized by Harvard Law Professor Morton Horwitz when a first-year law student conceded he had never heard of the English philosopher John Stuart Mill, since he had majored in what Horwitz referred to as "rat psychology." Similarly pre–law Adviser D. Grier Stephenson, Jr., reported that an admissions official told a rejected student, "If you had taken more 'cake' courses and had gotten a 3.6, we could overlook your LSAT and let you in." For these kinds of reasons, an oft-cited 1965 report issued by the American College Testing Program, "The Relationship Between College Grades and Adult Achievement," concluded with the assertion that "the practice of basing admission to schools of education, business, engineering, or medicine largely or exclusively on undergraduate grades seems indefensible."

A technical defense of the LSAT also is difficult. The Educational Testing Service acknowledges that "the 'true' score of any given applicant may be within 30 points above or 30 points below the earned score for that applicant." There are substantial reasons to believe that the test may be somewhat less reliable in predicting law school grades at the top law schools than this acknowledgment implies. The Educational Testing Service has found, "As the LSAT score increases beyond 600, the value of the prediction of the LSAT in terms of first year law school success becomes less and less meaningful." For this reason alone, former Harvard Law Dean Erwin Griswold has written, "It is not known whether the Law School Admission Test has any real statistical ability to select accurately from among many applicants, all of whom have the minimum qualifications." If Griswold's suspicion is valid, then the rigid ranking of applicants based on minuscule differences in admission indices is highly arbitrary. It means that an applicant ten to twenty LSAT points below another applicant may be treated differently although ten to twenty LSAT points make no statistical difference.

There is additional evidence that LSAT scores may be culturally biased as well. An Educational Testing Service study in March 1973 found that the mean LSAT scores for black men and women were 400 and 399 respectively, while the mean LSAT scores for white men and women were 533 and 545. These disparities alone do not prove that the LSAT is culturally biased. The test would be biased only if it inaccurately reflected the natural abilities of given social groups. The Educational Testing Service has conducted studies which show that the test is equally valid in predicting minority students' first-year law grades as those of white students. But if minority applicants perform less well on LSAT tests because the vocabulary and concepts tested are less familiar to them than to white applicants, the vocabulary and concepts of the first-year law school examinations are also likely to be less familiar to them. Only recently has the Educational Testing Service begun testing this theory. Harvard's Professor Jencks has estimated on the basis of available data that cognitive test score inequality would fall by 25 to 40 percent if such environmental factors could be equalized. This is only an estimate. But former Supreme Court Justice William O. Douglas has argued that since the LSAT may not reflect the abilities of minority applicants in a racially neutral way, it should be abolished: "The invention of substitute tests might be made to get a measure of an applicant's cultural background, perception, ability to analyze, and his or her relation to groups. They are highly subjective, but unlike the LSAT they are not concealed, but in the open."

The LSAT also may be biased in other ways. Most strikingly, those who can afford to take the test more than once score a mean increase of thirty-one points between the first and second time they take the test and twenty-six points between the second and third times they take the test. Seemingly, this is not a serious matter since any reasonably competent admissions officer should be able to weigh the scores of test-repeaters. But the possibility that the now popular LSAT coaching courses, which generally prepare applicants to take the LSAT by repeated practice examinations, may also increase test scores raises disturbing questions about the integrity of the test. John Sexton, a first-year law student at Harvard in 1975–1976, supervised LSAT centers in New York, Boston, San Francisco, and other cities. After studying the scores of applicants who prepared at such a center, Sexton contends, "Our latest statistics indicate that students who have taken the LSAT once before will show a median improvement of 110 points when they take the test for the second time."

The Educational Testing Service used to respond to such claims by showing critics a College Entrance Examination Board pamphlet entitled *Effects of Coaching on Scholastic Aptitude Test Scores*, which summarized the results of seven studies of coaching. The pamphlet concluded: "Despite variable factors from one study to another, the net result across all studies is that score gains directly attributable to coaching amount, on the average, to fewer than 10 points — a difference of such small magnitude on the SAT score scale of 200 to 800 that it is unreasonable to expect it to affect college admissions decisions." But in most of the seven studies, the word "coaching" referred to attempts "to increase in a relatively short time students' mastery of particular skills . . . tested by the SAT." By "short time," the studies meant, say, four and one-half hours or six hours of coaching. SAT or LSAT preparation courses rarely operate for so short a time. Typically, students will meet for three or four hours a night once a week for six to eight weeks. The one study in the College Entrance Examination Board pamphlet that did measure the effect of intensive coaching over a twelve-week period found scores increased by twenty-six and twenty-one points in two separate pooled control groups. Appreciating this fact, Harvard Law School's former Director of Admissions Russell Simpson acknowledges that such coaching schools may be a serious problem and further noted that the Federal Trade Commission is investigating them. What is unclear is why the Educational Testing Service has not itself seriously studied the issue. For if LSAT scores can be raised by repeated practice examinations or other study techniques, applicants can do this on their own by reading study guides, regardless of the conclusions of the Federal Trade Commission.

Even if college grade-point averages and LSAT examinations were perfectly reliable in identifying "meritcrious" students, there are at least two legitimate competing philosophical principles that law schools might consider when selecting a first-year class.

The first could be termed the "democratic" principle: All social groups should have equal access to social goods. If law schools provided a place for every student with the ability to practice law, there would be relatively little debate about admissions policies. But law schools do not. Like legislatures, they must assume the responsibility of balancing the claims of competing groups in a democratic manner. Democratic balancing usually has been justified on pedagogical rather than philosophical grounds. All law students in a given class, it is argued, will benefit if the diversity of the class resembles that of the country as a whole. "We are," explains the Association of American Law Schools, "a diverse society and our perception of legal problems and our production of solutions will be the better the more comprehensive our perception of the underlying facts becomes. This roundedness of perception can be most effectively done, except for the truly sensitive and empathetic person, by the presence in the classroom and school of different colors and sexes as well as different cultural and economic backgrounds." This pedagogical approach is fraught with obvious constitutional-law dangers. For long periods, leading universities construed "diversity" to mean selecting students from as many different states or foreign countries as possible, excluding blacks, women, and Jews. These prejudices have dissipated, but the inherent subjectivity of applying the principle remains. In the name of diversity an admissions office can justify favoring any social group it believes deserves a preference. To some extent, this may be pedagogically desirable. At the same time, however, such "democratic" practices will always seem unfairly exclusionary to less-favored groups.

Society has a second and very different interest in law school admissions policies. Admissions practices affect the national distribution of attorneys. No matter how "fairly" the opportunity to enroll in law school is distributed to competing applicants, the result will be dysfunctional if graduating law students ignore or under-represent most citizens.

Only within the past decade have American law schools acknowledged a responsibility to structure admissions so that the distribution of graduating attorneys is most likely to approximate the actual social need for them. This has usually been accomplished along purely racial lines, with law schools defending preferential treatment for blacks, Chicanos, native Americans, and other minorities who are under-represented in legal proceedings. To be sure, law schools bear some responsibility for the fact that most American citizens, especially minority groups, cannot afford and do not receive adequate legal representation. But accepting some minority students to law schools will not alone discharge this responsibility. Puerto Ricans, blacks, or native Americans may be more likely to represent their own groups than whites, but the greater probability is that they will be attracted by the same remunerative private law firm jobs as their white classmates are. No law school has yet adopted the more effective and constitutionally permissible approach of dividing its law school classes along the lines of particular programs — for example, general background, preparation for legal-aid or public-interest law, or preparation for government law — which would, without violating the Fourteenth Amendment, better assure that the law school graduated substantial portions of each class likely to serve where they are needed most. A second virtue of this structured approach is that it would provide a clear, measurable standard that faculties and applicants could disscuss and admissions officers openly administer.

As it is, accurately perceived, each law school's admissions policies resemble a moral lottery. "Who gets in" is primarily a function of who reads admissions applications. The crucial variable is not which abstract principles a faculty or dean endorses in the carefully worded admissions policy, but rather who is chosen to serve on the admissions committee. What values these admissions committees act upon and, to a lesser extent, how skilled they are at interpreting applications, transcripts, and LSAT scores determine who will be admitted. No law school validly can represent that it is admitting the "best" students in any meaningful sense. The image of the attributes of a student that emerges from an application is too crude; the definitions of "the best" that admissions personnel have are too various.

Yet given the philosophical and technical shortcomings of the undergraduate grade-point average and LSAT, if admissions committees do not subjectively interpret these numbers, "they are shirking what shold be their prime responsibility. To hide behind the numbers, however sophisticated, allowing them alone to determine who shall attend, is to give neither the law school nor its applicants a fair shake," contends Peter Winograd, the former director of law programs at the Educational Testing Service. The subjectivity of the process is less serious a matter than many suppose. The anomalies of any one law school will be balanced by the reciprocal anomalies of several others. The fundamental defect with present law school admissions policies is not that they are subjective — that is, unavoidable — but that some competent applicants are not given the chance to enter their chosen profession.

By the early 1960s, the civil rights movement had generated at many law schools an awareness of how few attorneys were black.

Although 11 percent of the American population was black in 1964–1965, less than 1 percent of the students enrolled in the 145 predominantly white law schools were black.

At Harvard Law School the figures were even more disproportionate. Although Harvard had been among the first law schools to open its doors to black students, the typical first-year class of 550 students prior to 1963 included few blacks, often only a single one. This was particularly embarrassing to the moderately liberal faculty that had been assembled at the Law School by the time of President Kennedy's "New Frontier."

In the summer of 1965, Harvard Law School began a special summer program for the specific purpose of "attracting Negro students to law study." Aided by a grant of $87,500 from the Rockefeller Foundation, the Law School recruited forty black students predominantly from all-black southern colleges to attend an eight-week introduction to the study of law. Without question, it succeeded as a recruitment effort. Where only a few of the forty students had decided on law as a career before they attended the program, about three-fourths definitely wanted to study law afterward.

The Harvard Law School experiment paralleled similar recruitment efforts throughout the country. In 1966, UCLA Law School, for example, organized the Legal Educational Opportunity Program (LEOP) to increase its black and Chicano enrollment from less than 1 percent of its 1965 entering class to over 23 percent of its entering class in 1970–1971.

Efforts such as these were considerably furthered in 1968 when the Association of American Law Schools, the American Bar Association, the National Bar Association, and the Law School Admissions Test Council joined to form the Council on Legal Educational Opportunity, universally known as CLEO, ". . . to expand and enhance the opportunities to study and practice law for members of disadvantaged groups — chiefly Negroes, American Indians, and Ibiro-Americans — and thus help to remedy the present imbalance of these disadvantaged groups in the legal profession in the United States." The CLEO purposes were, in effect, made national policy by annual grants from the federal government.

Under the CLEO umbrella, virtually every law school soon committed itself to minority recruitment. CLEO's principal vehicle was the funding of pre–law school summer institutes throughout the country. Between 1968 and 1975, 1908 minority students completed six- or eight-week summer sessions, similar to the 1965 program at Harvard.

Many law schools complemented participation in CLEO or similar programs with preferential financial-aid programs. Minority students, responding to questionnaires, had consistently indicated that money was their greatest barrier to attending law school. Most law schools, unlike Harvard, cannot give grant- or loan-aid to every student who needs it. A survey of minority students at ninety-eight law schools in 1968, 1969, and 1970 found that 56 percent of these minority law students were receiving financial aid amounting to two thirds or more of their total expenses.*

Neither of these recruitment approaches would have been fully effective without a third: Beginning in the late 1960s, law schools generally committed themselves to admissions practices that assured that minority students would constitute significant proportions of each entering class. At some schools this was done by formal quotas. At most it was accomplished by weighing the value of LSAT–grade-point average "numbers" with "nonobjective" factors in different ways for minority and nonminority applicants. The Harvard Law School Admissions Committee explained in a written statement dated March 10, 1972:

> The unqualified application of artificially high requirements as to undergraduate academic performance and LSAT scores would have the effect of excluding some minority groups from the Harvard Law School student population because to some extent unusually high achievement

---

* In July 1976, however, a federal district court ruled that Georgetown Law School's policy of allocating 60 percent of its scholarship funds to minority students who constitute only 11 percent of the school's enrollment violated the antidiscrimination provisions of Title VI of the 1964 Civil Rights Act. This decision, although not appealed, will discourage some law schools from allocating financial aid funds to the advantage of minority students.

> is a function of opportunities which have not been equally available to minority groups. This result has seemed to the Admissions Committee to be an unacceptable one. With Faculty support as evidenced by prior Faculty votes, an effort has been made to solicit and accept applications from minority students who will be able to do the work, profit from the experience and contribute something to the school which can be acquired in no other way.

Translated, this meant that the committee recognized the philosophical and technical flaws in admitting students purely on the basis of an admissions index and would temper this "merit"-based criterion with regard for the "diversity" of the class. Russell Simpson, who was then director of admissions, explained that his fear was that unless this was done Harvard Law School would revert to pre-1963 conditions, where very few blacks had been included in each class of 550. To support this policy, the 1972 Admissions Committee statement noted "that the admission of minority students has itself become much more competitive over the last few years. As recently as 1968, we accepted nearly half of the 100 or so known minority candidates who applied. In 1971, the number of identified minority applicants had risen to over 500, and the acceptance rate was about 1 in 5, a rate lower than for the class as a whole just three years earlier."

Opponents of such "preferential admissions" argued that such "lowering of paper standards" amounted to admitting minority students to law school primarily because they were minority students. This emotionally charged debate first welled to a head late in 1973, when the United States Supreme Court met to hear arguments in the *DeFunis* case.*

In 1971, Marco DeFunis, Jr., had applied for admission as a first-year student at the University of Washington Law School. At that time, the University of Washington Law School had not one admissions policy, but two. Most of the 1600 applicants seeking

---

* As this book went to press, the United States Supreme Court had heard oral arguments in the *Bakke* case but had not yet decided it. The case was widely expected to result in a landmark decision concerning "reverse discrimination."

one of the 150 spaces available in the class were judged by the faculty, administration, and student members of the Admissions Committee, predominantly on the basis of an admissions index number similar to that employed at Harvard Law School. One hundred and forty-seven of the 159 applicants with index numbers above 77 were offered admission. Virtually every applicant with an index number below 74.5 was rejected. Applicants with indices between 74.5 and 77.0 were placed in a middle group, where the Admissions Committee considered a variety of subjective factors before making final decisions. Very few applicants in this middle group were accepted. Marco DeFunis, Jr., with an index number of 76.23, was placed on a waiting list and eventually rejected.

If, however, DeFunis had been eligible to answer an optional question indicating that his "dominant" ethnic origin was black, Chicano, American Indian, or Filipino, his application would have been treated differently. Applicants within the Minority Admissions Program were reviewed by a special Admissions Committee subcommittee. Although the minority applicants competed with one another, they were never directly compared to the non-minority applicants. For these minority applicants the committee attached less weight to the admissions index "in making a total judgmental evaluation as to the relative ability of the particular applicant to succeed in law school."

Thirty-seven minority applicants were admitted under this procedure. Of these, thirty-six had index numbers below De-Funis's 76.23, and thirty had numbers below 74.5 and thus ordinarily would have been summarily rejected by the Admissions Committee.

Soon after he was rejected, DeFunis commenced a lawsuit in a Washington trial court, contending that the procedures and criteria employed by the University of Washington Law School's Admissions Committee invidiously discriminated against him on account of his race in violation of the Fourteenth Amendment of the United States Constitution, which provides that "no State shall . . . deny to any person within its jurisdiction the equal protection of the laws." Since the University of Washington Law

School is administered by a state, as distinguished from privately run law schools like Harvard, there was no question that it was bound by the Fourteenth Amendment. The trial court agreed with DeFunis that there had been an unconstitutional denial of his application for admission. An injunction was issued ordering that DeFunis be admitted to the University of Washington Law School in the fall of 1971. The state's supreme court reversed the trial court's decision but DeFunis was allowed to continue in law school while the United States Supreme Court deliberated whether to rule in the case.

By the time the *DeFunis* case was marked up for oral argument before the United States Supreme Court in the fall of 1973, it had become a cause célèbre. The AFL-CIO, the Chamber of Commerce, the American Jewish Congress, and the Anti-Defamation League of the B'nai B'rith requested and received permission to file briefs as "friends of the court" on the side of Marco DeFunis. With extraordinary passion Yale Law Professor Alexander Bickel and University of Chicago Law Professor Philip Kurland framed the argument in favor of DeFunis in their brief on behalf of the Anti-Defamation League of B'nai B'rith:

> For at least a generation the lesson of the great decisions of this Court and the lesson of contemporary history have been the same: discrimination on the basis of race is illegal, immoral, unconstitutional, inherently wrong and destructive of democratic society. Now this is to be unlearned and we are told that this is not a matter of fundamental principle but only a matter of whose ox is gored. Those for whom racial equality was demanded are now to be more equal than others. Having found support in the Constitution for equality, they now claim support for inequality under the same Constitution.

This position was opposed by virtually every law school dean in the country, the Association of American Law Schools, the NAACP, the American Bar Association, Harvard University, and fourteen other organizations. Writing on behalf of Harvard, Law Professor Archibald Cox, University Counsel Daniel Steiner, and

Associate Director of Law School Admissions James Bierman argued that the Supreme Court's 1971 school busing decision, *Swann*
v. *Charlotte-Mecklenburg Board of Education*, allowed school authorities, in the language of Chief Justice Warren Burger, to lawfully
conclude "that in order to prepare students to live in a pluralistic
society each school should have a prescribed ratio of Negro to
white students reflecting the proportion of the district as a whole.
To do this as an educational policy is within the broad discretionary powers of school authorities . . . " The hard question
facing opponents of DeFunis's position was that the Supreme
Court had previously ordered school busing or other compensatory programs only when it had been established that there was a
prior history of discrimination against minorities. This the University of Washington Law School had not established. The Cox
brief confronted this issue by arguing that the Fourteenth
Amendment should permit law schools employing selective admissions policies to make an applicant's probable contribution to
the diversity of the student body the primary standard of selection once there is a promise of satisfactory academic performance.
Thus, Cox argued, it was permissible for an admissions committee to consider the race of all applicants, along with other personal
characteristics, in seeking the best-rounded class. "In this situation no one group, majority or minority, is being preferred to any
other. The objective of improving the education of all is non-dis-
criminatory in every sense of the word. Each special characteristic carries values as a contributor to the diversity of the whole."

But Cox also argued that the "central fallacy" in the opposite
point of view "is the assumption that the academic exclusion or
segregation of minorities has the same psychological, sociological
and political effects as their inclusion."

> In the United States, as a result of the long years of slav-
> ery and Jim Crow policies, any admissions policy that
> denies admission to black students, segregates them or
> limits their number not only carries the vice of exclusion
> but asserts the supremacy of the white race and the inferi-
> ority of others; and for that reason it constitutes "hostile"
> or "invidious" discrimination. On the other hand, there is

no danger of "invidious" or "hostile" implication, whether in purpose or effect, when a predominantly white institution counts membership in disadvantaged racial or other minority groups as a factor favoring selection for admission from otherwise qualified candidates.

A majority of the Supreme Court avoided a substantive decision in the case by ruling that since DeFunis was in his final months in law school and the University of Washington had agreed to allow him to graduate regardless of the Court's holding, the issue was "moot." But Justice Douglas dissented in language that seemed to many to portend the landmark decision the Supreme Court ultimately may issue:

> The educational policy choices confronting a university admissions committee are not ordinarily a subject for judicial oversight; clearly it is not for us but for the law school to decide which tests to employ, how heavily to weigh recommendations from professors or undergraduate grades, and what level of achievement on the chosen criteria are sufficient to demonstrate that the candidate is qualified for admission. What places this case in a special category is the fact that the school did not choose one set of criteria but two, and then determined which to apply to a given applicant on the basis of his race.

Under the Fourteenth Amendment the consideration of each application by a state institution must be conducted, stated Douglas, "in a racially neutral way."

Despite this nondecision, the *DeFunis* case has had a substantial impact. It has spawned a number of court challenges to admissions policies, including that of Kenneth Krohn, which have placed pressure on admissions officers to make decisions purely on the basis of LSAT and grade-point average "numbers" and avoid the possibility of lawsuits. Some state legislatures have enacted statutes that encourage or require this procedure. Admissions officers are fearful that the "next *DeFunis* case" will result in a constitutional-law "straitjacket": This would require admissions offices permanently to employ numerical criteria, which are as biased against minorities as preferential admissions policies seem to some to be biased in favor of them. But since it is unlikely that law school admissions offices can show in a court record the type of deliberate racial exclusion that has been shown in the school busing cases, there is the widespread belief that the "next *DeFunis* case" will require exactly that.

Who then is admitted to law school? In a superficial sense, it is remarkable how little the character of the student body at Harvard Law School and the other "national" law schools has changed with the passage of time. In the Harvard Law class starting in the fall of 1975, for example, 35 percent had attended an Ivy League college. This is somewhat less than in 1957, when 50 percent of the class matriculated in the "Ancient Eight," but more or less consistent with a 1968 Law School survey of 11,600 alumni, which found that 43.58 percent had attended an Ivy League college. It is probable that in every post–World War II year, a minimum of 60 percent of each Harvard Law School entering class has attended one of twenty top private or public universities. Consistency has also characterized the undergraduate careers of students admitted to Harvard Law School, a majority of whom majored in a social science such as political science, history, or economics.

The psychology of entering law students, however, has changed as admissions have become increasingly selective. Only about half of Harvard Law School's alumni in 1968 recalled that they were not in the top 10 percent of their college classes. This is no longer true in any leading law school today. A majority of students admitted — black or white, male or female — rank in the top 10 percent of their undergraduate classes.

Relatedly, the mood of the class has changed. Harvard Law students today — to the extent one can accurately generalize — are more intense, more driven, and more diligent than their predecessors. Many have defined their lives in terms of success in the artificial environment of classroom participation, periodic essays, and final examinations. If they "slip up" at Harvard Law School, they risk the loss of self-respect to a degree that earlier generations of students did not. Duncan Kennedy described these emotions while a student at Yale Law School: "No student intelligent enough to get into this Law School can avoid feeling an odd ambivalence about going through three more years as a peculiar kind of half-man. Yet there are not many students who are really prepared for anything else. 'Success,' which has consumed their energies for years, is their only real connection with adulthood."

For many students, the decision to attend law school often seems ambiguous, muddled, or downright confused. Because students have long given similar explanations of why they came to law school, Felix Frankfurter once concluded that law students "on the whole . . . come by default." Yet underlying students' apparent difficulty in explaining their motivation for coming to law school are two strong and conflicting personal goals that they consistently identify in describing themselves. On the one hand, they seek and see in the law a career that will accord them a solid income, security, and the respect of their contemporaries. On the other, they want the opportunity to help others, to be useful to society, and to participate in politics. Every major survey of law students over the past two decades has underlined this same duality. In 1961, the National Opinion Research Center questioned 33,782 college students during their senior undergraduate year and their first year in graduate school. Specifically, the Research Center found: "Future lawyers consider the following values important: making a lot of money; a chance to help others and to be useful to society; freedom from supervision; and an opportunity to work with people."

Ten years later, a nearly identical survey was conducted among 21,000 college students during their senior year in college and their first year in graduate school. Protest against the Vietnam War and the Cambodian invasion, disorientation because of the assassinations of Robert Kennedy and Martin Luther King, were so marked at some colleges that the chief investigator, Leonard Baird, warned that the class may have been unusual because of the political events of the time. Yet the survey results were virtually identical with those of a decade before. Law students — to a greater extent than their college classmates who had gone to work, medical school, other graduate schools, or into the military — emphasized the importance of high income, status, and prestige in choosing their career. But law students also had a greater than average desire to be of service to others.

In our own survey of students in each of the three classes at Harvard Law School in 1975–1976, there was a similar affirmation of desire to help the underprivileged and restructure society. Nevertheless, in the Placement Office the overwhelming majority of these same students sought interviews with the highest-paying law firms instead of public-interest or public-defender groups.

For many students at Harvard and other national law schools, the experience of law school is essentially a melodrama — a choice between a career promising great financial rewards or a less remunerative and more idealistic life, played out in the minds of extremely bright students particularly eager to be thought of as successful. This conflict underlines the extraordinary capacity to influence law students' career decisions that law schools and their faculties possess.

6

FACULTY SELECTION AND FACULTY ROLE:

The Root of the Problem

Our faculties tend to reproduce themselves; and in the process may by the continual inbreeding that is involved be producing even narrower law students than they were themselves.

ERWIN GRISWOLD

Few decisions are so determinative of the character of a law school as the selection of its faculty. Sociology professor and Harvard Law graduate David Riesman once went so far as to suggest that only at the point of faculty selection is law school reform possible: "Given tenure, academic freedom, the individualism of law professors and the powerlessness of many deans, many of the leading law schools will survive all their reformers."

During Erwin Griswold's twenty-one-year deanship, Harvard Law School's faculty selection largely functioned as a process in which professors were chosen from a pool of individuals who had earned a place and an officership on the *Harvard Law Review* and then secured the recommendations of senior Harvard Law professors such as Henry Hart or Paul Freund or of distinguished former *Law Review* editors such as Justice Felix Frankfurter, Judge Calvert Magruder, Judge Henry Friendly, or Dean Acheson. Putting to one side the international-law scholars and legal historians hired during Griswold's deanship, of the forty-five professors offered tenure between 1945–1946 and 1966–1967, thirty-two had attended Harvard Law School, twenty-nine had served on the *Law Review*, and twenty-three had been officers of the *Review*.

But what was most striking about faculty selection during the Griswold deanship was a loose commonality of values among the senior faculty. Emphasized was not any particular political approach to the law but rather the credentials of one's colleagues. By selecting professors from a small pool of former *Law Review* editors whose subsequent training also tended to be stereotypic — a brief clerkship for a prestigious federal circuit court judge or Supreme Court justice followed by a few years' practice with a leading private law firm or government office — Harvard Law School tended to produce an insular faculty. So confident were professors in each other's certification that they often deprecated the experience — if not the intelligence — of persons with more worldly backgrounds and often were also hostile to the value of rival forms of academic training and research. By the end of his tenure as dean, even Erwin Griswold expressed the fear that the narcissism of the selection process might sustain "a vicious circle, which may be doing a great disservice to legal education and to the contribution which it can make to our society":

> The persons making the selection have come through the traditional law school mill. They had high grades in law school — very high — or they are not likely to be considered by those who are doing the considering. Other qualities are looked for, it is true, and often found, but there is sometimes a sort of atmosphere that one is unintellectual if he feels these qualities can have truly independent significance. Thus our faculties tend to reproduce themselves; and in the process may by the continual inbreeding that is involved be producing even narrower law students than they were themselves.

What was missing was an overall theory of what the purpose of the School should be. Tenure and the widely held belief that law professors should not "tinker" with each other's work deprived the School of the ability to broadly question its research, curriculum, or methods. Since the departure of Griswold, it has become even clearer that professors largely selected on the basis of their student credentials and esteemed recommendations are likely to be theoretically random. The conventional wisdoms reflected by one generation of prestigious alumni are at odds with the conventional wisdoms of the next. Thus, as a faculty grows larger over time, its intellectual character tends to be more disparate. At best, this can be defended as a form of pluralism. But such "pluralism" significantly limits the ability of any faction of law professors to build a consensus for fundamental reform.

Even before Erwin Griswold became dean, Harvard Law School's approach to faculty selection was subject to sharp criticism. Legal Realist Jerome Frank urged that the lack of experienced practitioners on the School's faculty was a grievous deficiency. A medical school dominated by teachers who seldom saw a patient, diagnosed ailments of flesh-and-blood human beings, or actually performed surgery, Frank argued in a 1933 article, ". . . would not be likely to turn out doctors equipped with a fourth part of what doctors ought to know. But our law schools are not doing for their students even the equivalent of that shoddy job. Many of those schools are so staffed that they are best fitted, not to train lawyers, but to graduate men able to become book-law teachers who can educate still other students to become book-law teachers — and so on ad infinitum, world without end."

By contrast, Robert Hutchins believed the greater failing of law school faculties involved their excessive concern with the law as a practical craft. Former law review editors might be well prepared to engage in courtroom argument but did not necessarily have any background in the more speculative realm of legal philosophy. Hutchins scorned the "how-to-do-it law school" because it represented "the degradation of great ideas." In his view, the study appropriate to a university law school is jurisprudence, the intellectual discipline "concerned with the nature of law, its purposes, the means (institutional and conceptual) necessary to alleviate those purposes, the limits of the law's efficacy, the relation of law to justice and morality, and the modes by which law changes and grows historically."

As long as all law professors were selected by a common formula, law schools would be handicapped both in training their students in the practical skills of the legal profession and in hiring professors who could conduct original theoretical or empirical research. Even though professors tended to concentrate on narrow subject fields in their teaching, the common formula by which they were selected, in effect, made each professor responsible for the virtues of Frank's aged practitioners and Hutchins's lofty jurisprudes. In Professor Thomas Bergin's view, this resulted in law professors being "men divided," frustrated because they could not be both:

> The modern law teacher has been suffering from a kind of intellectual schizophrenia for the past twenty-five years — a schizophrenia which has him devoutly believing that he can be, at one and the same time, an authentic academic and a trainer of Hessians. Symptoms of this extraordinary delusion abound. When his academic half is showing, the law teacher finds himself wanting to award the J.D. degree rather than the LL.B. — a desire which garbs itself in innocent concern for the student, but which is really a raw lusting for academic respectability. He also finds himself voting for the abolition of required courses, deploring the case method, establishing research centers, loving the social sciences, teaching the far-out seminars, aching to reform the law, and secretly wishing to be named to a modest federal post such as Secretary of State.
>
> An equally rich variety of symptoms are manifested by the Hessian-trainer side of the law teacher (by Hessian training I mean training for private practice at the Bar). If, like myself, he is a property teacher, he wants to be overheard earnestly discussing such hard-line topics as the recapture provisions of the Internal Revenue Code or the proper formula for avoiding the rule in *Dumpor's Case*. He does not want all the courses to be required — only the grim ones. He believes, to use the felicitous phrase invented by a former colleague of mine, that the proper way to train the beginning law student is "to put his feet to the fire of the cases." He imagines that he was, or surely

would have been, a great trial lawyer. When he fills out a form which requires him to state his business or profession, he inserts the word "lawyer."

During the last years of the Griswold deanship, the School began the first of a series of efforts to find a new basis for reconciling the apparent conflict between theoretical and practical training by hiring a few social scientists to join its faculty. In 1965, the School invited Richard Musgrave, a professor of economics, to teach such courses as Economics for Lawyers and Taxation and Economic Development. Two years later, Lloyd Ohlin, a sociologist with fifteen years' experience studying prison administration, was hired as professor of Criminology. Subsequently, Dr. Alan Stone accepted a joint appointment as professor of Law and Psychiatry at Harvard's Law and Medical Schools.

Derek Bok, who was dean from 1968 to 1971, favored different approaches. Convinced that legal scholarship should be more allied with such emerging fields as public-policy system analysis and welfare economics, Bok encouraged the faculty to appoint professors such as Philip Heymann, Laurence Tribe, Richard Stewart, and Lance Liebman. With the exception of Tribe, each had served on *Law Review* either at Harvard or Yale, but their reputations were associated more with government service or social science–related writing.

At the same time, Bok hardened the tenure writing requirement. Before his deanship, many, but not all, young professors had produced a scholarly article before being granted tenure. But as late as 1969, some professors, such as Charles Nesson, had been granted tenure without writing an article after graduation from law school. Bok "bureaucratized" the writing standard. Not only were all professors thereafter expected to write a tenure piece, but assistant professors' pre-tenure contracts were extended from three to four or five years to underline the significance of the new scholarship requirement.

The Harvard Law School faculty initially was resistant to another Bok proposal, that of offering Gary Bellow, the Law School's first clinical-law professor, an appointment in 1970. As Professor Frank Sander, chairman of the faculty committee seeking to expand the clinical program, so delicately put it, "The faculty had some initial question because Bellow was not well known." Translated, this meant that since Bellow had not clerked in the Supreme Court or a federal circuit court of appeals but had instead become a leading legal services attorney in the District of Columbia and California, he was not "well known" at Harvard.

A few faculty members were more blunt. While a student at Harvard Law School, Bellow had been in Legal Aid, an academic honorary society rated below that of *Law Review*. Since Bellow was among the top fifty students in his first-year class, not the top twenty-five, these professors argued that he did not meet "the necessary academic standards" to teach at the Law School. "But the objection ultimately proved immaterial," according to Sander. It could hardly be suggested that a Supreme Court clerk could better teach a clinical course on poverty law. With students enthusiastically supporting Bellow, he swiftly received tenure.

When Derek Bok left the Law School in 1971 to become president of Harvard University, Albert Sacks assumed the deanship of an increasingly fragmented faculty. Although Sacks supported Bok's reforms, the most distinctive initiative during his first years as dean was his campaign to persuade the faculty to hire the Law School's first tenured woman professor and increase the number of tenured minority faculty members.

It was an ofttimes emotional campaign. As with poverty lawyer Gary Bellow, women and minority lawyers generally were "unknown" at Harvard Law School. Some faculty members argued that requiring women and blacks to be "well known" in a profession that has historically discriminated against them could only result in their virtual exclusion. Other faculty members were unassuaged. Professor Milton Katz characterized the attitude of some of his colleagues: "Of course we want women but our great duty is to never reduce our standard of excellence. It is our conscientious duty never to flinch or falter in pursuing excellence."

What is certain is that until the 1970s women were not being hired by law faculties anywhere. Testimony before the House Subcommittee on Education in June 1970 showed that only 2 percent of the faculty of the leading law schools was female. Shortly afterward, the Women's Law Association began pressing Harvard

Law School to hire a female professor. The association's efforts culminated in a complaint filed in late 1972 with the Office of Civil Rights in the Department of Health, Education, and Welfare, charging that faculty hiring was "done on the basis of an old boy network" and that the School's practice of hiring predominantly Harvard Law School graduates excluded many qualified women from consideration because Harvard did not admit women until 1950, and then only in small numbers. Dean Sacks labeled these charges "groundless," contending that the small pool of women law graduates from all law schools limited the number of women the Law School could consider in choosing its faculty.

But Harvard Law School clearly could do better than it had done. Elizabeth Owens, associated with the Law School for seventeen years as a researcher and lecturer, was suddenly found to be "professorial" material and received a full professorship effective July 1, 1972. At approximately the same time, Diane Lund, an honors graduate in the class of 1961 who had earned a slot on *Law Review*, was hired as an assistant professor with the opportunity to secure tenure, thus becoming the first woman hired at the Law School on the same terms as young male assistant professors. In March 1973, Owens and Lund joined thirty-one other women faculty members and administrators throughout Harvard University urging greater "affirmative action" in hiring women. Elsewhere it had been argued that Harvard University, as a recipient of $60 million in federal funds each year, was bound by the 1964 Civil Rights Act and subsequent executive orders to design an affirmative action program to rectify existing inequalities in its employment. The Owens-Lund letter contended that most university departments had not complied with affirmative action programs, or were "proceeding at a very slow pace."

Shortly thereafter Harvard Law School hired three additional women in non-tenure-track lecturer positions — two to teach in the clinical program and one to teach Copyright Law. When Diane Lund decided not to pursue tenure, a second woman assistant professor, Sally Neely, was hired in 1975.

During the same period, Derrick Bell, the first black professor hired at Harvard Law School, waged an occasionally public campaign to persuade the School to hire additional black professors. Bell, a well-known civil rights attorney, finally sent a letter in November 1974, threatening to resign unless additional blacks were hired. He recalled that when he had been hired in 1969, the faculty had promised to do this. Derek Bok, by then president of Harvard University, denied there was any race or sex bias in recruitment and hiring at the Law School. In Bok's view, Bell's complaint was not "legitimate." The Law School was making "a continuing and intensive effort . . . to identify every minority professor and recent minority law school graduate . . . to see if they would be suitable for an academic position." As the result of efforts initiated prior to Bell's November 1974 letter, Clyde Ferguson, the former dean of Howard Law School, and University of Michigan Law Professor Harry Edwards were invited to Harvard Law School as visiting professors in 1975–1976. Both subsequently were awarded tenure, although Edwards decided to return to Michigan at the end of the 1976–1977 school year.

Simultaneous with his attempts to add to the number of women and minority faculty members at Harvard Law School, Dean Sacks encouraged efforts to build "bridges" between the law and the humanities by supporting tenure for legal historian Morton Horwitz and social theorist Roberto Unger, as well as helping start a fellowship program for young law teachers to study law and the humanities jointly at Harvard Law School and Harvard College.

As a consequence of the Bok and Sacks campaigns to open Harvard Law School's ranks to these new voices, the number of faculty members who were hostile to the Griswold period's more craft-oriented approach to law increased. The schism was reflected in a series of contentious faculty appointment and tenure fights.

The first, in 1973–1974, concerned George Fletcher, a visiting professor from the UCLA Law School. Fletcher had made a serious study of comparative criminal theory. One faculty supporter called Fletcher's approach to law "a more searching European type of scholarship, an attempt to build systems," incompatible with more traditional faculty members' less theoretical approach to legal problems. "He knew the answers. He had an approach.

He set it out very dogmatically," a less sympathetic faculty member added. A third professor claimed that Fletcher personally antagonized a large number of people and that some faculty members opposed his permanent appointment because "they just didn't want to eat lunch with him in the faculty dining room."

After a spirited discussion, Harvard Law School's faculty decided not to offer Fletcher tenure, in part because a number of professors argued that a single footnote in a law review article Fletcher wrote did not stand for the precise principle that Fletcher claimed it did. Regardless of whether Fletcher was rejected because of his scholarly approach or because of his lack of lunchroom panache, the civility of the Law School's appointment process was shattered.

Subsequent faculty-hiring battles resulted in the number of new tenure-track assistant professor appointments slowing in the 1975–1976 and 1976–1977 academic years. Yet the more serious question was could the faculty built up to that time perform the Law School's basic functions.

The School's ability to provide clinical training for its students remained limited. By largely defining leading law practitioners and government attorneys as outside the pool of potential faculty members when they lacked the certification of the *Law Review*, the Law School effectively denied itself the opportunity to hire the most successful specialists in the practical training of future attorneys.

A sense of the magnitude of this omission prompted Erwin Griswold's Harvard Law faculty to hire experienced trial litigator Robert Keeton in 1954 to supervise the School's first elective Trial Practice course. From the start, Keeton arranged for experienced Boston trial attorneys to teach small sections in simulated courtroom exercises, such as cross-examination or argument to a jury. But Griswold did not initially support the innovation. Not only was the course not required but Griswold publicly dismissed the Trial Practice course as a "lark" akin to a college drama course.

After Gary Bellow was hired as the Law School's first full-time clinical-law professor in 1971, such sentiments dissipated. But in the summer of 1977, Bellow and Jeanne Kettleson, the former administrative director of Harvard Law School's Clinical Programs, announced they would leave Cambridge and set up a separate law institute, perhaps under Harvard's aegis. In Bellow's view, no law school can effectively teach students clinical skills in ways that link critical social theory and practice unless it has a core of three or four full-time clinical professors. Were Harvard to pursue these goals, it would have to emulate the staffing pattern of a modern American medical school by hiring leading law practitioners in each of the principal types of law practice as a permanent part-time faculty. In 1977, Harvard Law School received a grant from the Council on Legal Education for Professional Responsibility to experiment with Bellow's approach to a permanent part-time faculty. Dean Sacks is also encouraging an increase in the number of Visiting Professors from Practice as well as encouraging individual professors such as Charles Nesson, Vern Countryman, and David Herwitz to teach some of their courses employing clinical methodology. Even with these advances, Bellow and Kettleson made plain their belief that a more radical shift in the environment in which clinical training is taught was necessary for a Law School effectively to fulfill its responsibilities to provide related theoretical and practical training.

At Harvard Law School, in the post–World War II period, an aversion to original empirical research was a second clear consequence of the *Law Review*-oriented faculty appointments typical of Dean Erwin Griswold's administration. Early in 1947, the Law School's Fuller Committee on Legal Education concluded that empirical studies of the consequences of important national laws are "at least as important to the vitality of the instruction offered in the school as the adoption of any particular instructional method or any particular manner of dividing the subject matters taught." Recognized was the fact that a principal contribution — if not the principal contribution — a national law school faculty could make was in preparing independent critical analyses of important political issues: "In many fields, such as the anti-trust and labor laws, there are crucial public decisions in the air, and little

effort is being made by the universities to secure the facts necessary for an impartial judgment. Except in the field of criminal
law, it is not believed that any research work of this sort is at present actively under way in the school."

In 1950, Professor David Cavers, later named by Dean Griswold to be his associate dean "for research and development,"
organized a series of faculty meetings to study the research needs
of the principal fields of American law, which Cavers defined as:
(1) civil litigation and arbitration, (2) commercial law, (3) corporations, (4) estates, (5) conveyancing and land use, (6) tort liability,
(7) domestic relations, (8) criminal law and criminology, (9) federal and state taxation, (10) labor, (11) regulation of industry, and
(12) governmental structure and processes. At each session,
Cavers described his conception of the type of institutional research that was being proposed, and then endeavored to elicit
from the faculty the ideas they had as to fruitful directions for research in their fields of interest and what, if any, institutional arrangements should be established to carry out research activities.

Better he had been pulling teeth. Few members of the faculty
showed any interest in directing a research project, even if funds
were found for it. There was equally little interest in setting up a
division of research. Indeed, several members of the faculty vehemently opposed establishing any institutional mechanism in
aid of research for fear it might distract from classroom teaching.
Ultimately, Harvard Law School's entire program in American
Legal Studies dwindled into a $5000 survey of Massachusetts dis-
trict courts and a number of ad hoc projects, including a mid-
1950s study of Public Relations and Modern Law Practice.

Only in the field of international legal studies did Cavers' (and
here, also Griswold's) efforts to promote institutional research
make any significant headway. Troubled even by Cavers' modest
successes, in the mid-1950s Professor Lon Fuller orchestrated a
vehement protest to Cavers' concept of "group research" which,
in part, led to Cavers' resignation as associate dean.

To the credit of the Law School, it did continue to fund research in juvenile and adult delinquency, supervised by Eleanor
and Sheldon Glueck, after Roscoe Pound's more expansive Insti-

tute of Criminal Justice failed in the 1930s for lack of students. But it was only in 1969 when The Ford Foundation provided a grant for the Law School to fund a new Center for the Advancement of Criminal Justice that Harvard Law School again housed any enduring institutional program for the field study of American law.

For many law students the most painful aspect of the modern law professor's role is students' lack of personal contact with their teachers. This is a consequence of law professors' self-image as a select class which makes them reluctant to delegate responsibilities. Where most graduate school professors aspire to be research moguls, or at any rate "nonteachers," under the rule that "the higher a professor's standing the less he or she has to do with students," law professors have reversed this "flight from teaching" with an equally conspicuous "flight to teach." Law professors grade their students' examinations, seek to teach first-year classes, and some average as much as five to ten hours' preparation for each classroom hour. In the abstract, such loyalty to teaching can only be commended.

But the size of law schools significantly handicaps the effectiveness of professorial classroom efforts. At Harvard, many law classes average 120–160 students.* Faculty members are scarcely accessible to students. An April 1975 survey of 214 Harvard Law School students found, for example, that 86 percent rarely or never spoke to a professor outside of class. Eleven percent "occasionally" did; only 3 percent often did so.

Students believe such inaccessibility handicaps their education. In April 1975, Harvard University's Visiting Committee found: "There is a profound sense among the students present of a lack of sufficient contact and rapport with the faculty, which was reflected specifically in concerns expressed about the supervision of the third year written work requirement, faculty participation in

---

* Our survey of Harvard Law School student opinion in 1975–1976 corroborated the findings of a 1968 Harvard Law School survey of 11,600 alumni, and those of Yale Law Professor Robert Stevens's survey of eight law schools, that students considered large classes among the "most harmful" or "least popular" aspects of legal education.

the first year's [moot court] Competition, and a perceived need for a Dean of Students." The Educational Testing Service's nation-wide survey of graduate students' perceptions of their professors was less specific but equally telling. Only 23 percent of the law students polled felt their professors "give helpful feedback on tests, papers, and reports." This compared with the favorable view of 60 percent of the students in schools of education, 59 percent of the graduate social scientists, and 52 percent of the graduate biology students. It is no mystery why Yale Law School, with classes averaging twenty students or less, is often imagined in near mystical terms by Harvard Law students. As the *Harvard Law Record* editorialized in October 1968: "That many students graduate from this school without one faculty member knowing them well enough to write a recommendation is a lamentable commentary on the deficiencies in faculty-student relations."

Historically, Harvard Law School has responded to this complaint like a transportation consultant before the invention of the wheel. Derek Bok's Committee on Legal Education in 1967 proposed instituting a system of faculty advisers to meet once during the first year "at the average rate of one half-hour per student" to satisfy the students' "desire for more personal contact with members of the faculty." During the meeting the faculty member was expected to help the student plan the student's entire second- and third-year program. But Bok added: "An important by-product of such a measure would be to give every student the feeling that there is at least one member of the faculty with whom he may meet, if he wishes, and whose advice he might even seek on other questions." An equally felicitous view of emotional social engineering was taken by Dean Sacks in 1975 when he wrote to the faculty: "I suggest that any faculty member who has fewer than two consultations with a student before the [required third-year] paper is completed should consider carefully whether this results from the student's free choice, or means rather that the faculty member is subtly communicating to students a low receptivity to consultation."

The marvel of it all is that Harvard Law School's faculty did invent the wheel; they just don't seem to have any faith in it. In 1949–1950 Harvard Law School followed the University of Chicago and Columbia Law Schools in hiring recently graduated students to meet with first-year students in groups of twenty "to help relieve the confusion of the first year." Originally, these "teaching fellows" taught a year-long course called Group Work (later renamed Legal Practice and Method, then Legal Methods) to introduce the student to legal research, brief writing, and courtroom argument. However, for years only six teaching fellows were hired; in 1961, the course was reduced from a full year to half a year; it was never given for credit.

The faculty was always aware that the fellows were useful surrogates in discharging what Professor Charles Nesson termed "the faculty's duties of intimacy." But the belief that the fellows could not be trusted to grade examinations or to lead sections of beginning classes, as is typically done in other university departments, made the faculty reluctant to expand the fellows' responsibilities.*

In 1976–1977, the Law School began an experiment that may lead to the total elimination of the fellows. With Dean Sacks's support, Professor Charles Fried hired ten second- and third-year students to supervise weekly small section meetings in his first-year Contracts class. By limiting each section to thirteen first-year students, the upper-class section leaders had time to criticize a variety of beginning writing exercises, as well as to preside over informal gatherings where students could "speak and participate without anxiety or concern about being embarrassed," according to the Law School's official report concerning the experiment. Both Dean Sacks and Professor Fried were sufficiently enthusiastic about the upper-class students' performance that in 1977–1978 Professor David Shapiro supervised a second round of first-year small sections.

Presently, there is little indication that the Law School either

* Recently, other law schools have employed alternative approaches to the problem of large class size. Stanford Law School, for example, employs a sufficient number of professors so that it can teach some first-year classes with fewer than thirty students. Columbia Law Professor Harvey Goldschmid urges, "It is possible to provide a mix of large classes, taught by unusually gifted professors such as Harvard Law's Paul Freund, and small classes in all three years of Law School. This allows for greater individual student attention, has proven to be economically practicable at Columbia and recognizes that not all law professors are as gifted as Paul Freund."

will employ graduate fellows or upper-class students to lead sections in second- and third-year lecture classes. The prevailing beliefs that professors must be responsible for all grading — to preserve the integrity of the grading system — and all teaching, seriously affect the use of faculty time. More than one law professor has responded bitterly to the suggestion that a professor only works "nine [classroom] hours a week." In reality, course preparation time, teaching, committee work, "colleagueship," grading, and meeting with students leave comparatively little time for anything else. When Harvard's legendarily prodigious Archibald Cox was asked how he managed to meet all of these responsibilities and also publish and speak frequently, he replied with tongue barely in cheek, "I neglect my family."

7

CURRICULA:

Beyond the Hairy Hand

One can hardly escape the conclusion that a lawyer who has not studied economics and sociology is very apt to become a public enemy.

LOUIS BRANDEIS

For decades students at Harvard Law School have begun their legal education with five first-year courses that Dean Langdell first prescribed in 1871: Contracts, Criminal Law, Procedure, Property, and Torts. Although the substance of these five courses has almost entirely changed in the past century, the learning experience has not. Plunged into what Justice Holmes aptly termed a "fog of details," students begin their legal education with the methodic study of leading or typical cases. For several class hours, Contracts students, for example, might debate the alternative measures of damages suggested by *Hawkins* v. *McGee*, the legendary "hairy hand" case. Closely questioned by experienced professors, first-year students find that class discussion, and ultimately reading, often becomes a treasure hunt for the precise meaning of a judge's rule and the legal arguments used to sustain it.

This rapid immersion in the detail of existing legal rules is symbolic of the fundamental intellectual failing of American legal education. In the effort to make students "sharp by making them narrow," to paraphrase Burke, the curricula of modern law schools poorly relate the study of law as a social theory to its actual practice. The jarring novelty of first-year classes is a powerful signal to beginning students that law schools have little, if any, interest in their previous four years of undergraduate education. The tendency of law schools to continue classroom discussion of legal rules for a full three years signifies an almost equal disdain for such practical skills as drafting, counseling, negotiation, or fact investigation. Such an education encourages quiescence. Not only are students not presented a coherent social theory with which to challenge existing legal rules, but their lack of skills training increases their dependency on initial employers.

The unevenness of American law schools' integration of social theory and practice is well illustrated if one views legal education as part of seven years of university learning. With the exception of Canada (where standards are similar to the United States), no other industrialized democratic nation requires law students to spend so much time receiving academic training, yet offers so little clinical training in the practice of law. In England and Wales, for example, most aspiring solicitors and barristers receive three years of academic training at a university and then two years of apprenticeship under the tutelage of experienced practitioners. Other European nations follow the West German model of legal education. After studying law at a university for about four years and then spending an additional six months or so preparing for a state bar examination, students rotate among positions in the court hierarchy, a district attorney's office, and a practicing attorney's office during a two-and-a-half- to three-year apprenticeship.

By contrast, in the United States there is virtually no relation between the first four years of a law student's university-level education and the three graduate years spent in law school. Nearly every student completes an undergraduate major in a field like political science, typically spending the equivalent of about one year studying courses required in the major field, one year studying other required courses, leaving approximately two years to survey unspecified elective courses. In 1955, Harvard Law School Dean Griswold offered one criticism of such a structure of undergraduate education when he complained that "whole transcripts may be made up of courses like Topography, Principles of Advertising, Reporting, Advertising Copy and Layout, Advertising Media, Salesmanship, and Press Photography . . . or Scene Design, Acting, Stage Costume Design, Stage Lighting, Producing, Advanced Acting and Playwrighting . . ."

More recently, a number of legal educators have concurred with the view of former Yale University President Kingman Brewster that for many students "education takes too long." Herbert Packer and Thomas Ehrlich of Stanford Law School, for example, argued in a 1972 report prepared for the Carnegie Commission on Higher Education:

> At the present time, most students take four academic years for their baccalaureate degrees and three academic years for their law degrees . . . We have had some experience with undergraduates who came to law school after three years. Our experience leads us to believe that three years of college are enough for many students . . . This means that the present practice observed in some universities of permitting undergraduates from one's own university to enter after three years should be extended to all undergraduates.

Similarly, Professor Paul Carrington of the University of Michigan proposed to the Association of American Law Schools in 1971 that the *standard* time of admission to law school should be after three college years.

In view of the substantial financial barrier to all but the children of upper and upper-middle income levels earlier described, a case might be made against requiring every American law student to complete four years of undergraduate education. As recently as 1951, only 16 percent of the law schools approved by the American Bar Association required four years of college. In 1948 only 37 percent of this nation's lawyers had earned college degrees. Alexander Hamilton, Abraham Lincoln, Clarence Darrow, and thousands of other American attorneys historically have performed satisfactorily within the legal profession without completing college. For this reason the American Bar Association does not absolutely require in its recommended standards that all law students complete an undergraduate education. Only ten states require attorneys to do so. The requirement primarily exists because a college degree is demanded by the overwhelming majority of approved law schools.

More effective structures of legal education seem possible. In 1936, University of Chicago President Robert Hutchins proposed that students complete a two-year undergraduate liberal arts education before beginning graduate school. Implicit in such a proposal is that law school studies could be lengthened to four years to frame the study of law in a broader context of history, philosophy, sociology, and economics. Harvard Law School employed a variant of this scheme beginning in the late 1930s when it admitted some Harvard undergraduates after three years who then spent four years studying law and advanced university courses in history, government, and economics. According to former Dean Griswold, this program was continued until the 1950s, when "the draft killed it." Alternatively, for that small number of students who early are certain that they wish to become lawyers, universities might design integrated five- or six-year undergraduate and law school programs — a concept recently considered by Claremont College and City College of New York.

As it is, the failure of American law schools effectively to integrate prelegal education affects the three law school years. The law school's function is confused: Should law schools attempt to provide students the broad training in politics, history, and ethics that many students do not receive in college, or should they offer training in the skills of the practicing lawyer?

This confusion is compounded by the obsoleteness of first-year curricula in most law schools, where the same five first-year courses that Dean Langdell initially required over one hundred years ago continue to be taught.

When Dean Langdell designed this first-year curriculum, it provided a comprehensive introduction to American civil and criminal law. These courses allowed Langdell and his colleagues the opportunity to describe the historical development of the American legal system, and also presented a conservative political theory of the purposes of law and the appropriate roles of the legislature and the judiciary. To this date, these five courses provide a partial description of the American legal system and are essential conceptual building blocks to understanding such advanced law school courses, as Commercial Transactions and Estate Planning.

But no more than that. As federal and state post–New Deal legislation has brought American law into a legal jet age, the five courses resemble the equivalent of a horse-and-buggy-age introduction. At Harvard, and at most other leading law schools, no introductory course clearly explains to students how the American legal system, in fact, works; what are its underlying theoretical ideas; how the system developed historically; what are its most important enduring controversies.

Only in the past few years have American law schools and scholars begun to outgrow the rigidity of Langdell's first-year curriculum. The Association of American Law School's 1971 Carrington Report recommended that the significance of the five traditional first-year courses be drastically reduced so that students could also study "law and the legal process in its broader setting." Specifically, first-year students could study "the techniques of other disciplines in the solution of legal problems," aspects of constitutional theory, administrative, corporate, and tax law.

Although Harvard Law School through 1976–1977 had barely modified its traditional first-year requirements to permit students to take one half-year elective course in subjects ranging from Administrative and Constitutional Law to Environmental Law and Theories of Violence, a 1975–1976 catalog survey of twenty leading American law schools found substantial variations developing elsewhere.

Twelve of these twenty law schools had made Constitutional Law a first-year requisite. The University of Southern California required not only Constitutional Law, but also a theoretical property course entitled The Institution of Land Ownership, which analyzed "the development of legal rules dealing with land, water, and other natural resources as attempts to serve the social functions of allocating wealth and power," and Law, Language, and

Ethics, a jurisprudence course drawing on learning from episte-
mology, ethics, semantic analysis, aesthetics, sociology, psycho-
analysis, and other disciplines to "introduce students to the function of legal rules and concepts in the organizing of society."
Georgetown Law Center required courses in the Federal System
and Legislation; the University of Pennsylvania Law School in Income Security and Labor; Antioch in Administrative Law and
Evidence; Northeastern in Federal Income Taxation.

Each of these innovations represented an attempt to adjust the
introductory law school curricula to the growing significance of
public-law or legislative topics, or to give first-year students a
clearer political or philosophical framework for the study of law.

Professors at Harvard Law School are quick to describe how
traditional first-year courses have been modernized. Criminal
Law, for instance, no longer ignores criminal procedure. Property
Law, which used to emphasize the feudal origins of land law, now
devotes greater attention to landlord and tenant problems.

But the Law School has been too little conscious of the extent to
which the first year can be a powerful acculturating experience.
Initially, the study of law is like the study of a foreign language.
Many students experience an understandable desire to make as
much of the new language as simple and definite as possible.
Confronted by first-year professors who immediately demand
that they employ this language, the students may find the political
substance of rules studied to be far less significant than the implied lesson that their success or failure largely turns on swiftly
learning to use the new language, which, more precisely means,
learning to manipulate legal rules regardless of their political
significance.

So powerful is the first-year emphasis on rule manipulation
that the casebook materials or teachings of professors describing
the conflicts underlying existing legal rules tend to be ignored as
first-year examinations approach. In my own first year at Harvard
Law School, Torts Professor Morton Horwitz was one of the most
popular of the five main-subject instructors because Horwitz
"played Hamlet with the policy issues." But when the final examination approached, his popularity waned as my classmates became edgy that "they didn't really know torts law" since Horwitz

taught so differently from the other four instructors. An extraordinarily large number of them bought commercial outlines or treatises to be sure that they had not misunderstood issues that might be tested.

A similar dynamic occurred in the study group I knew best during the first year. In the fall, their concern had been to understand the broad implications of each case. As the year progressed, the group became increasingly concerned with briefing cases and writing outlines that summarized the hard-and-fast legal rules that might be tested. In the final weeks before exams, the only time I recall a student broadly generalizing about law was when one wag subsumed the cases involving livestock that we had studied in Contracts, Torts, and Property Law under a novel legal rubric he called "The Law of Cows."

Only if the psychological dynamics of the first year are substantially changed is it likely that law study can be released from "the fog of details." One way this might be done is by presenting novitiate law students courses in legal history or legal philosophy simultaneous with, or before their initial contact with, such categories of law as contracts, to underline that the rival social visions that legal rules exemplify are far more important than any particular rule itself.

Such integration might be especially effective if achieved within a school that presented a coherent view of law throughout the entire length of a legal education. But state bar requirements pose a further obstacle to theoretical variation among law schools. Most states employ a two-part examination, joining to the Educational Testing Service's Multi-State Examination in Constitutional, Contracts, Criminal, Evidence, Property, and Torts Law additional essay questions in Wills, Trusts, or Estates; Business Associations; Commercial Transactions; Tax Law; and similar subjects.

Largely consistent with such rules, over 90 percent of Harvard second- and third-year students in 1973–1975 enrolled in courses in Corporations, Tax, Constitutional, Evidence, and Commercial Transactions Law; over 70 percent studied Business Planning or Corporate Finance, Antitrust, or Administrative Law; 60 percent, Federal Courts, Labor, and Estate Planning.

As distinguished from bar examiners, the Harvard Law faculty requires virtually no second- and third-year courses. In 1976–1977, students could choose from over 150 elective courses. As has happened with undergraduate curricula, the Law School has adopted a Disneyland approach, substituting a breadth of tantalizing academic subjects for a consistent point of view. The question endures whether a seven-year university-level education that may be devoid of any course that effectively relates the technical doctrines of law to legal history, legal philosophy, American sociology, or American political theory is adequate preparation for the enlightened practice of law.

This is hardly an abstract question. A telling recent illustration of Brandeis's observation that "a lawyer who has not studied economics and sociology is very apt to become a public enemy" concerns the teaching of legal ethics. Historically, Harvard, like most law schools, did not teach courses in legal ethics, believing that students were either innately honest or they were not, and that courses in such topics as fiduciary relations and trusts were "permeated by ethical presuppositions and assumptions and standards." The double shock of Watergate and a 1970 ABA study of disciplinary enforcement, chaired by retired Supreme Court Justice Tom Clark, challenged these assumptions.

Effective February 1975, the ABA amended its standards for the approval of law schools to require that each school provide its students "instruction in the duties and responsibilities of the legal profession." In October 1974, Professor Andrew Kaufman, Professor Robert Keeton, and Teaching Fellow David Rosenberg circulated a memorandum conceding that Harvard Law School had "not been doing its job":

> It is too bad that we are graduating students who do not know who Eldon, Mansfield, Maitland, Kant, Bentham, Kent and Shaw are. But how do we justify graduating practitioners who do not recognize a conflict of interest, do not understand the obligation of confidentiality, do not know an open panel from a closed panel, and have never been told of any of the problems related to the distribution of legal services? . . . As far as questions of law reform are concerned, how can we expect young lawyers to take

an active interest in problems they don't know exist or whose ramifications they don't understand?

So prodded, the Harvard Law School faculty approved the requirement of a course in Professional Responsibility. Rather than merely asking students to memorize ABA ethical strictures, the Harvard course also exposed students to issues such as the inequality in the availability of legal services, the need to reduce the cost of legal services, and the attorney's responsibility to represent unpopular clients.

Although legal ethics courses are a constructive first step in introducing students to the character of the American legal profession and their ethical responsibilities, a legal ethics course alone cannot provide students with a sufficient background in American legal history, the sociology of the profession, or jurisprudence for them to fully appreciate the need for law reform.

The intellectual character of legal education remains too diffuse. As long as most courses involve the detailed study of a category of law and are taught by professors hostile to studying law within the framework of a more general social theory, students are likely to retain a minute knowledge of existing legal rules and consider the occasional critical course to be little more than an interesting but soon forgotten embellishment.

So far it has been the practicing bar rather than law faculties that has raised the sharpest questions about the overemphasis of the classroom study of rules in law school. In recent years, judges and attorneys have questioned whether Harvard and other American law schools can effectively train students in the skills necessary for particular fields of law.

Take litigation for one example. For 160 years Harvard Law School has offered its students the opportunity to practice courtroom argument in moot and club court programs. Since Langdell's deanship courses in court procedure have been required. In the post–World War II period, a mandatory first-year course in Legal Methods has taught students brief-writing and library research skills; popular electives have been offered in the law of Evidence and Trial Practice. A 1975–1976 catalog survey of twenty leading law schools found that most of these courses were widely replicated.

Nonetheless, Chief Justice Warren Burger concluded after discussions with several judges that in some general jurisdiction trial courts fewer than 25 percent of the attorneys are genuinely qualified to appear in court. His opinion is shared by Chief Judge David Bazelon of the District of Columbia Court of Appeals, who has characterized some attorneys as "walking violations of the Sixth Amendment," and by the influential Second Circuit Court of Appeals, which found that from 15 to 75 percent of the attorneys appearing in some district courts lacked adequate training. In 1975 the Second Circuit proposed minimum educational requirements for attorneys appearing in its courts.

Although the proposal later was withdrawn, the judges' initial recommendations amounted to an indictment of many law schools' teaching techniques. As federal litigation has grown more complex, effective representation not only requires doctrinal reasoning and brief-writing abilities, which can be taught well in law schools, but also sophisticated fact-gathering and trial strategy skills, which probably are best learned in practice. Accordingly, the Second Circuit's most stinging proposal was that students be trained in trial advocacy, not by law professors but by "lawyers who are familiar with litigation." This recommendation underscored a final principal curricular weakness of American legal education: By fully excluding practical training from the formal education of their students, American law schools employ the least-direct methods for training students in much of what lawyers actually do.

This is not a problem limited to potential litigators. By necessity, most large corporate-law firms provide their new lawyers a one- to two-year training period. Recently graduated lawyers rarely have adequate preparation in drafting, client counseling, or negotiation. Future law teachers usually spend one or two years clerking for a federal or state judge to hone their legal writing skills and develop a sense of reality about judicial decision making.

Harvard Law School Professor Gary Bellow and Assistant Dean

Jeanne Kettleson have done preliminary research on the effect on poverty-law practice when attorneys do not receive specialized skills and ethics training. In "The Trouble Within: Bureaucratization in Legal Services Representation," Bellow and Kettleson, in cooperation with Carl Hosticka and Michael Lipsky, found that poverty attorneys tend swiftly to "routinize" their clients' grievances into case types. "Few lawyers engage in or rely on extensive legal research, fact investigation or strategic planning." Attorneys often seem unable to discover what a client's actual legal problems are or how the client might be most effectively served. "Many outcomes seem to be significantly influenced by the values, attitudes and needs of the lawyers rather than the clients." To some degree, Bellow attributes these results to formal legal education, emphasizing the need for the appreciation of the difference in social class between most attorneys and their poverty clients, and the importance of understanding the client's problems as the client perceives them.

By contrast, the few law school experiments in specialized legal education have focused on more abstract academic concerns. For example, Yale Law School's now abandoned Divisional Program required each student to write a thesis concerning a specialized field of law rather than providing interested students specialized practice experience. Harvard Law School's third-year writing requirement reflects a similar approach.

The widely held belief that law schools offer students broad opportunities to survey elective subjects of trivial value and fail to provide them with effective skills training has fueled a movement for two-year law schools. In recent years, two-year law school plans have been endorsed by Chief Justice Burger; 1976–1977 ABA President Justin Stanley; former Congressman Roman Pucinski; William Pincus, president of the Council of Legal Education for Professional Responsibility; former Stanford Law School Dean Bayless Manning; the Association of American Law School's Carrington Report; and Harvard Law Professor David Cavers —among many others. Most proposals include the option or requirement of third-year specialized training obtained directly from practicing lawyers or in new training institutions devoted to preparing students for specific fields of law.

Advocates argue that for the same reasons that one would not expect doctors to perform surgery until completing internship, lawyers should not be considered trained until they have finished a vocational or apprenticeship year. Additionally, a practice-oriented third year would reduce the tedium of that year in law school.

The Harvard Law School type of education, in effect, is in a vise. On the one hand, the overemphasis on rules study is criticized as leading to student quiescence. Largely deprived of a broader knowledge of rival political or economic theories, students have little intellectual basis with which to criticize existing rules. On the other hand, this same overemphasis on rules study equally deprives students of the time to study such practical skills as courtroom argument. Within the law school community, both pressures have heightened a long-standing clash over teaching methods. It is to this clash we turn in the next chapter.

8

TEACHING METHODS:

Birds Sing Better Than
Books Know How

If the question whether English law can be taught at the Universities could be submitted in the form of a case to a body of eminent counsel, there is no doubt whatever as to what would be their answer. They would reply with unanimity and without hesitation that English law must be learned and cannot be taught, and that the only places where it can be learned are the law courts and chambers.

A. H. DICEY, introductory lecture as
Vinerian Professor at Oxford, 1883

When a client or an acquaintance admires a lawyer, the lawyer is often praised for his or her reasoning ability. "Lawyers," it is said, "cut through to the heart of the matter . . . They ask the right questions . . . They know how to solve problems."

One of the most proficient teachers of legal reasoning at Harvard Law School is Clark Byse. Like many of his colleagues, Byse relies on the distinctive interrogative approach popularly known as the Socratic method to question students on their understanding of actual law cases, a technique known since the time Langdell initiated it as the case method.

Before class, seated in his book-lined Langdell Hall office, Byse often seems to possess a languid air. Slightly hunched behind his massive wooden desk, the sixty-six-year-old professor regards visitors with doleful eyes. "Well, Mr. _____," he begins answers to questions almost shyly, warming to his subject as he speaks. A similar change comes over Byse as the time for a class session draws near. Visibly his posture stiffens as he reviews his notes. "I can't see you now," he says firmly. "I've got a class in ten minutes." Slipping on an impeccably tailored dark suit-jacket, Byse impatiently flicks lint off it. By the time he arrives in his cavernous Langdell North classroom, there is a buoyancy to his manner. He chats whimsically with a number of students near the lectern, his eyes playful now, his manner exuberant. A firm hand reaches out and grasps a student's shoulder, an unmistakable gesture of friendship or support. Moments later, Byse grins and mischievously pats a second student on the cheek. But this is prelude. Forcefully he plants his book and seating chart on the standing lectern.

At precisely 10:10 A.M., virtually every student is in an assigned seat, notebook out, casebook open, pen poised. Clark Byse at this point is unmistakably *Professor Byse*: mercurial; authoritarian; his jests biting now; his energy like that of a coiled spring.

Above the professor's Langdell Hall office desk is a gift from an earlier class, a papier-mâché rabbit popping out of a papier-mâché hat. The figure has a single-word caption: "Why." In Professor Byse's classroom this word is seldom spoken; it is usually roared. "Why, Mr. _____ ?" or "Why, Miss _____ ?" Byse starts hundreds of questions during a school year. Sometimes the vehemence of Byse's "Why" causes him to rise up on his toes like a carnival-goer trying to gain leverage before slamming the weighted hammer down and ringing the far-off bell. "Why" is the concept that trails the students home after class; "Why" surfaces in their minds as they read cases alone; and as examinations approach, "Why" nags at their sleep. In Professor Byse's control, "Why" is the essence of legal reasoning, the force that pushes a class from comprehending law as particular rules applied to particular facts to a glimpse of an entire social order. "Why" is skepticism, "Why" is argument, "Why" is doubt, and ultimately "Why" is the basis of courtroom logic: comparison and generalization.

"Miss _____ ," Byse begins this session, "what was the promise in *Hamer versus Sidway?*"

Like many cases in first-year law casebooks, the facts in *Hamer* v. *Sidway* seem slightly ridiculous. At a family gathering in 1869, an uncle promised his nephew that if he refrained from drinking, using tobacco, swearing, and playing cards or billiards for money until he turned twenty-one the uncle would pay him $5000. The nephew agreed and six years later wrote to his uncle that he had lived up to his promise. "Dear Nephew," the uncle replied, "I have no doubt but you have, for which you shall have $5000, as I promised you." But before the nephew collected the money, the uncle died. The almost comic-opera question of the lawsuit was: Can the virtuous nephew collect the $5000 from the recalcitrant executor of his uncle's estate? The case is included in virtually every modern American contracts casebook because it illustrates some of the most fundamental principles of contracts law.

Miss _____ answers Professor Byse's question, "An uncle promised his nephew $5000 if he wouldn't commit any vices until he was twenty-one."

"Well Miss _____ ," Byse retorts, "the imagination runs rampant. State the facts clearly. Why editorialize?"

She does so.

"How old was the nephew?"

"Hmmm . . ."

"Anybody know?"

A second student shouts, "Fifteen or sixteen."

"Was the contract enforced?"

"Yes, the court did."

It comes out softly this time, "Why?"

The student doesn't answer.

Byse offers, "Because it was supported by consideration." Miss _____ starts to nod as Byse ridicules his own answer, "Or do we say there was consideration because it was enforced?" A brief pause. Like a referee in a sporting event, Byse construes part of his task to keep the game alive yet limited to a specific field. After thirty-three years of teaching law, he is a master at this. He tosses out a fresh question. "What was the argument of the defendant?"

Miss _____ answers, "There was no benefit to the uncle."

"What did the plaintiff argue was the benefit to the uncle?"

Miss _____ sees the trap. "He didn't," and correctly circumvents it. "The plaintiff argued that the consideration was the detriment he suffered by not drinking, smoking, and so on."

Now the game has picked up. Byse plays with the student's answer. "How could it be a detriment not to indulge in bad habits? That is no detriment, is it?"

The student stumbles. "Some people will think it is," and another student, startled, loudly exclaims, "Huh!"

Byse slaps that down. "Is someone here a moose hunter?" Then quickly reiterates the question, "How could this be a detriment?"

"Because the plaintiff had a legal right to drink, smoke, swear, and play cards."

Byse holds up the answer so everyone in the class will precisely understand it. "Recall the editor's note on the meanings of the word 'right.' *Plaintiff was legally privileged to drink and smoke. That is a right.*" He briefly pauses for dramatic effect. "All right then," Byse continues, reading from a page he has just picked up from the lectern, "I promise you $5000 if you do not (a) commit murder, (b) commit suicide, (c) get arrested, (d) drive faster than the legal speed limit, (e) bother me, or (f) refuse to accept a gift of $5000 from me. Consideration in all of these cases?"

A new student answers, "None except bothering. Other cases involve illegal activities or gross disparity."

Shrilly in Professor Byse's mind a cacophonic alarm goes off. Red flags wave. His body visibly stiffens. "Gross disparity," he roars with painful disdain. "What is gross disparity?" The student isn't expected to respond. With six thunderous words of formal legal logic, Clark Byse has eviscerated two words of frothy layperson fudge talk. Somewhere in the back of the room the phrase "gross disparity" collapses to the floor. The two words have been annihilated. They are absolutely dead. Briskly Byse presses on, "Miss _____ just said a detriment was a sufficient consideration. Now, murder is wrong — there is no privilege to murder, therefore no detriment. The same with suicide. But not get arrested. What about that?"

Ten years ago, a student would have argued at this point that there was a legal privilege to commit civil disobedience if one was willing to accept the consequences. References might have been made to Martin Luther King, Jr., and Gandhi, or draft resisters. There would have been a heated student debate; a useful release from the tension of trying to phrase every argument in the language of formal legal doctrines.

But this class occurred in January 1977, and no one was quite sure why Byse had asked the question.

A student responded dully, "There is no legal right to be arrested."

Byse's forehead furrowed slightly. "Anybody disagree?"

Another student answers, "No law makes it illegal to get arrested."

The class is thoroughly confused; someone hisses.

"Is it consideration?"

"I am not sure."

Byse struggles with the hypothetical question and a related one for ten minutes until yet another student stammers to silence. He then starts the reasoning process over again. "We have an eminent killer shooting people. He says to the uncle: 'Give me $5000 and I won't shoot people.' Better yet, $50,000 — make it worth his while. Is there consideration?"

Mr. _____ answers, "There is no legal right, but look at the legal benefit . . ."

"The killer wasn't going to shoot the uncle."

"But other people . . ."

Byse cuts in sharply, "You can't do this by magic. You can't justify everything by a vague notion of public policy. We are trying to develop an organized society, one in which there will be a general rule that the full power of the state will only be invoked to enforce certain contracts . . ." And for a full forty-eight minutes the colloquy concerning a trivial one-and-one-half-page 1891 case goes on, with Byse rapidly shifting hypothetical variations on the case, prodding students to vocalize alternative legal arguments and debate directly with each other, and, at one point, chewing out the class for not seeing obvious relationships between his hypothetical questions and earlier cases the class had discussed.

Only in the very last few minutes of the class, when Byse had moved on to another case, does a student vocalize what the doctrine of legal consideration is really about.

"The courts don't want to turn gifts into enforceable promises."

"Aha!" exclaimed Byse. "The courts do not enforce gift promises. Gifts are one category of promises different from others. But why?" And this "Why," though not a roar, felt like one. For weeks the class had been absorbing the notion that contracts was the category of law that made a market economy possible. By allowing persons to enforce their private bargains with each other, theoretically the most efficient allocation of resources will be realized. But to make this possible, proclaimed a prominently situated case holding in the students' text, "the law will not enter into an inquiry as to the adequacy of the consideration." Now the rug was being pulled out from under the absoluteness of this principle. Plainly the law sometimes will inquire.

"Why?" Byse asks. "What are the functions this doctrine performs?"

With astonishing coolness, a student raises his hand and answers, "Cautionary and evidentiary. It is easier to prove a contract if there is evidence of it. Parties are less likely to enter contracts lightly if each must give up something."

For Byse, the answer is almost too good to be true. To highlight its importance, he writes on the blackboard, "Form and Substance." Pointing to the word "Form," he writes, "Form — evidence of a contract." Pointing to the word "Substance," he explains, "Substantive Rule: Parties are discouraged from making rash enforceable promises. You should see page 118 where Von Mehren summarizes these ideas for you." He continues for a few minutes relating this point to the next case, but the dénouement has been reached. For Byse, a successful class hour has been taught.

After a lengthy World War II study of the place of skills in legal education, Columbia Law School's Karl Llewellyn concluded: "Case instruction is not only the most significant American contribution to legal education, but is unrivalled as a machinery for basic training in analysis of holdings and in application of doctrine." The learning principle might be called vicarious participation. Even when not called upon in class, students try to answer the question in their own minds. The reasoning process guided by the professor can be internalized so that students consciously attempt to compare or distinguish case holdings as they read on their own. The contrast with classroom lectures is impressive: Using a Socratic approach, students develop a habit of mind with which to examine any legal issue; hearing a lecture, a student memorizes certain facts that may or may not thereafter be forgotten.

Despite this advantage, the case method is one of the most controversial aspects of American legal education. Sustaining the effectiveness of a large class often involves considerable student tension, particularly during the first year of law school. Students realize they may be called upon at any time and questioned by a professor who can run logical circles around them, on material that is still confusing to them. Since this embarrassment occurs in front of 140 other students, many first-year students come to dread attending class. On occasion some law school professors have been insensitive to the emotional vulnerability of their students.

This was vividly illustrated in October 1975, by Harvard Law Professor Arthur R. Miller. By any standards, Professor Miller is an especially quick-witted and brilliant instructor. He is also exacting. On the first day of each year's course, he makes a statement of procedure: Students must be prepared for each session; if they must for any reason come to class unprepared, then they are expected to indicate to Miller's secretary that they would prefer not to be called on. They need not give any reason. But Miller believes that unprepared students interrupt the classroom dialogue, so it is important that he know in advance which students not to call on. The professor explains that there are no negative consequences from asking not be called upon.

Nonetheless, when a few months into his 1975–1976 first year Civil Procedure class, a student unexpectedly answered a question by saying "unprepared," Miller chided him.

"Why not?" the professor demanded. The student explained that he had been up all night preparing for a moot court oral argument. Sternly, Miller replied, "That's not good enough." The student, Miller explained, should have allocated his time better and at the very least should have handed in a note indicating that he was unprepared. Miller's tone was alleged to be so derisive that the class, in the words of one student present, "just sat there . . . The next person who was called on was so scared that it sounded like he wasn't prepared either." When a second student asked him to speak louder, Miller quipped, "Nothing has been said anyway."

After class, nearly the whole section remained in the lecture hall to discuss the incident. There was another meeting of over 100 students the following day. Individual students recalled, "I was just scared to death in that class" and "It was almost like Daddy had just spanked someone." The anger soon dissipated. *
Several students felt their reactions had been blown out of proportion. But others feared Miller's reaction: They were very scared about their grades. One student recalled his initial response: "I won't make *Law Review,* I won't get to work on Wall Street. I was afraid of Miller's hatred. " Eventually thirty students signed a mildly worded protest letter ("We cannot by our silence tacitly condone the treatment to which one of us was, we think, needlessly subjected . . ."), then, after two students removed their names, a meeting was held to decide the least offensive way of delivering the letter.

Nearly a decade ago Yale Law student Duncan Kennedy characterized in an oft-cited "Polemic" the emotional dependency some first-year students feel toward their professors:

> It is not the work load which is being challenged. It is the underlying relationship of teacher to student. Is it acceptable at 22 or 23 or 24 to let oneself be publicly insulted, day after day, by another man no matter how brilliant? . . . Is

* Miller believes the long-term effects of his "tough" teaching are small. He is proud of how much civil procedure law his students learn and that student year-end evaluations of him are consistently high.

it acceptable, after years spent dealing with the complicated emotions inevitably involved in the relations of intelligent and aggressive young men with their fathers, to
plunge oneself into an essentially paternalistic community
where the route to success is to establish yourself firmly in
the affections of powerful older men?

As a description of student sentiment at most law schools at
most times, Kennedy's *cri du coeur* would be an overstatement. But
the articulation of such student views during the past decade has
undoubtedly influenced law professors' sensitivity to student
feelings. Many follow the lead of Duncan Kennedy, now a Harvard Law professor, by allowing students "to pass" if they are unprepared, or by calling on a lot of students to eliminate the sense
that any single student is being "picked on." Other professors
notify students ahead of time that they will be called upon. Many
professors believe that for additional reasons the case method is
in decline. It takes such extraordinary skill to employ it effectively that many teachers have reverted to simpler lecture types of
formats.

In part, this also reflects intellectual dissatisfaction with the
method. Two generations of legal scholars have joined Jerome
Frank in arguing that case instruction, by focusing on the abstract
legal principles propounded by the highest courts, "distorts and
falsifies what it teaches" by ignoring the significance of the facts
of a particular case to lower courts, and the role of trial courts, administrative agencies, and legislatures. Harvard Law School's Lon
Fuller in 1948 went so far as to write that "traditional" legal education therefore "is not merely defective in detail, but in basic ori-
entation . . ." In his leading casebook, Fuller tried to reorient
contracts law by joining to his selection of leading cases background material as varied as excerpts from Aristotle's *Nichomachean Ethics* and continental legal history. Younger law professors, such as Harvard's Richard Parker, are doubtful that this
makes much difference. In Parker's view, case instruction can be
"the worst method to convey critical material." When the theoretical materials are used largely as embellishment, students tend

to focus on case holdings that will be tested on final examinations rather than the more speculative background materials, with the result that the seeming firmness of the cases becomes "a powerful tool with which to dismiss a critical approach." In his courses, Parker emphasizes rival views of politics and society, showing how the tensions underlie the cases. "Unless students understand these tensions," Parker doubts that they even can make a meaningful study of leading cases. Other professors such as Stanford Law School's Richard Danzig have prepared student casebooks from the point of view of legislatures rather than private litigants. Structured throughout his text is a wide-ranging critique of the fact, value, and capability assumptions underlying the American law of private agreement.

Without question, opportunities to work directly with legal factual records and court proceedings have increased in the post–World War II period. At Harvard Law School in 1976–1977, every first-year student participated in an introductory Legal Methods course that includes a detailed factual record of a single case as well as mock appellate court advocacy. Approximately 20 percent of the second-year class receive further simulated appellate court experience in an optional second-year moot court competition. Over 20 percent of second- and third-year students are trained in courtroom argument in an elective course, Trial Practice, taught by prominent Boston litigators, including President Nixon's former defense counsel, James St. Clair. Another two hundred second- and third-year students receive actual litigation experience by working for one of four legal-aid or voluntary-defender organizations. After completing the second year, almost every student spends two or three months during summer vacation working in a law office; about 50 percent of first-year students do so as well.

But a common criticism of the Harvard Law School model of legal education is that the emphasis on classroom discussion is still excessive. Although the Socratic method is useful for learning to reason like a lawyer, it is undoubtedly among the slowest methods for learning the substance of law. Even so devoted a defender of classroom colloquy as Columbia Law School's Karl

Llewellyn wrote: "It is obvious that man could hardly devise a more wasteful method of imparting *information about subject matter* than the case class. Certainly man never has." Llewellyn's vehemence was shared by Yale Law School's late Alexander Bickel who explained, "If you have something to say, the Socratic method is time-wasting beyond belief"; and by Stanford Law Professors Herbert Packer and Thomas Ehrlich who concluded, "Large classes after the first year (and sometimes even then) tend to be an academic wasteland."

Frequently the tension of first-year classes is succeeded by apathy or sullenness in second- and third-year courses. As Harvard Law Professor David Herwitz found in a recent second- and third-year Corporations class, classroom dynamics also can change. Calling on a student to answer a question, Herwitz was informed that the student would volunteer when he had something to say. A second student replied that he didn't care to comment. A third said, "I pass." Exasperated, Herwitz asked, "Pass what?" Replied the student, "Pass everything. I haven't read the case." Warily, Herwitz remarked, "Well, we can go on like this all day." Allegedly the student responded, "Yes, if we are lucky." Variations of this story can be heard at almost any law school. One 1976–1977 Georgetown Law student rebuffed her instructor with the startling exclamation, "I pay good money to attend this law school. I'll raise my hand when I have something to say." It's not for nothing that so many law professors prefer to teach first-year classes.

Others offer a different criticism of the excessive use of classroom instruction. Emphasis on legal reasoning ability comes at the expense of training in other relevant legal skills. A revealing survey of 1960 and 1970 alumni opinion at six American law schools published by Yale Law Professor Robert Stevens found that where substantial majorities of law school graduates (61 to 96 percent of the sample groups at the six schools) believed that their schools had placed great emphasis on learning to "think like a lawyer," only 0–27 percent felt similar emphasis was placed on developing "proficiency at legal writing," 0–5 percent on "the ability to counsel and interview clients," and 0–6 percent on "the ability to negotiate and arbitrate." It is primarily the failure of American law schools to graduate attorneys competent in lawyering skills that has buoyed the movement for clinical law school training.

High above New York City's Park Avenue works the sugar daddy of the clinical legal education movement. His name is William Pincus and for the past twenty years he has worked as hard as any other person to alter the character of American legal education.

As long ago as 1921, the Carnegie Corporation's A. Z. Reed concluded his eight-year study of American law schools with the uncharacteristically blunt generalization: "The failure of the modern American law school to make any adequate provision in its curriculum for practical training constitutes a remarkable educational anomaly." Legal Realist Jerome Frank concurred in that judgment, and throughout the 1930s and 1940s Frank excoriated Langdell's "library" law schools, calling instead for "clinical lawyer schools." Frank's slashing attack was renewed in 1952 when practicing attorney Arch Cantrall published a controversial article arguing that law schools almost totally failed to teach their students the most basic skills of law practice.

But it was not until William Pincus joined The Ford Foundation in 1957 that these disparate complaints found an effective champion. Yet when Pincus first became interested in clinical training his motive was strikingly different from that of Reed, Frank, or Cantrall. Fourteen years later Pincus would explain: "After about a year's experience in philanthropy, I began to have doubts about providing unquestioning support to the existing structure of legal education. My uneasiness did not extend to legal education alone. My questions were about the American system of justice."

Persuaded that only if law schools established free legal clinics for the poor could this "imbalance" be alleviated, Pincus soon convinced The Ford Foundation to make an $800,000 grant for experimental programs in selected law schools, and in 1965, the foundation appropriated another $950,000.

In 1968, Pincus's enthusiasm for clinical training induced him to leave The Ford Foundation and accept the presidency of the Ford-funded Council on Legal Education for Professional Responsibility (popularly known as CLEPR). By then, Pincus's case for clinical legal education had broadened into a vast panoply of arguments.

At a personal level, Pincus reasoned, clinical education ameliorated a principal defect of the modern law school, "the fact that our present prolonged system of higher education, coming on top of a lengthy primary and secondary school experience, retards the emotional development of the individual." As he observed in an interview, "From kindergarten on up you learn how to get along with teachers. Clinical teaches you how to cope with clients, judges, other lawyers, families of clients, et cetera. It prepares you to function once you get out of the cocoon."

". . . Without robbing one of the pleasure of enjoyment, it helps one to penetrate facades; it helps to get at the real nature of persons and issues. Even oneself. Hitherto in the law student's education there has been tremendous concentration on obtaining credentials for the purpose 'of cashing in on the marketplace.' Clinical helps to diminish this self-centered outlook by placing the professional in a helping relationship to another . . . It is like what marriages and their children do to reduce self-centeredness."

Pincus also adopted Frank and Cantrall's view: "Clinical legal education introduces the law student to a number of legal skills which go beyond analysis of written materials, library research, and writing. These skills range from fact-gathering, to interviewing, counseling, drafting, trial strategy and trial and appellate advocacy . . ." By learning these skills under trained instructors with sufficient time to provide careful supervision, the student is exposed "to a standard of performance which can serve as an example for his future professional life."

This is important, Pincus theorized, not only because practice is the best of all instructors, but because legal ethics cannot be learned in a classroom, only in a real-life situation. ". . . No one can learn to be controlled by ethical principles by standing outside a problem and commenting on it, looking in at a situation which does not involve him personally. Only in the clinic, where the teacher and the student are personally involved; where they have to take action and face the consequences; where they undergo tensions which upset their emotions and take away their peace of mind, is there opportunity to develop the moral fiber and the proper instincts for dealing with ethical problems in a professionally responsible way."

Ultimately Pincus envisioned a complete transformation of the law school's curriculum:

> Academic work should constitute 80 percent of the first year curriculum; 50 percent of the second year curriculum; and a very small percentage, no more than 20 percent, of the third year curriculum. In all three years, clinical work, in a sequence which gives the law student increasing responsibility, should take up the remainder of the time. The academic method, carried over from college and before, should predominate at the beginning of law school but gradually taper off. And, it should be devoted mainly to subject matter and theory which is fundamental: torts, contracts, property, criminal law, constitutional law, and administrative law. Clinical work should progress from research and writing on legal problems (first year), to investigation, interviewing, and counseling (second year), to taking full responsibility for a client (third year).

In his initial years as head of CLEPR, it appeared as if Pincus's logic alone might spur this transformation. By the 1970–1971 school year, 100 law schools were administering 204 clinical programs in fourteen different fields of law. In the next five years the clinical movement swelled so that by 1975–1976, CLEPR could "conservatively" estimate "that slightly more than 90% of the American Bar Association–approved law schools provided some form of credit-granting clinical education." "Overall," Pincus calculated in 1975, "24 percent of all the full-time students in the second and third year of law school are benefiting from clinical legal education."

Impressive as these figures were, it was also clear that the future of the clinical education movement was very much in doubt. Clinical courses are significantly more expensive than law school large lecture courses. For clinical programs to retain their present position within the law school budget requires schools to either make fundamental changes in their curricula or receive considerable outside financial help. With the CLEPR cornucopia due to dry up in 1979 and other substantial foundation support unlikely, the pressure is on the law school clinicians to develop a source of government funding.

In addition, for clinical courses to be effectively taught, Pincus believes, they need to be conducted "in-house" under the tutelage of clinical faculty members. Two thirds of existing clinical courses are taught outside law schools, without any faculty supervision. This was the price CLEPR paid for trying to start a national clinical movement "on the cheap with as few intra-faculty political problems as possible." But these "farm-out" courses are handicapped by the inability of most practicing lawyers to provide students sufficient feedback about their work. And Pincus grumbles about the unfairness of asking law students to pay tuition while they work in an off-campus law office.

Reliance upon farm-out courses or in-house poverty-law clinics has had the further consequence of limiting most clinical courses to legal-aid work. Since relatively few law students graduate to work in these fields, the practical value of clinical training to most law students continues to be underestimated.

Yet the most formidable obstacle to the growth of clinical legal education remains the hostility of established law school faculties. If American law schools wanted to sustain the clinical movement, it is within their power to expand the credit hours accorded these courses, remove credit hour restrictions, enhance the clinical experience by permitting full clinical semesters, encourage the development of new courses in such fields as corporate law or estate planning, and reduce funding problems by abandoning the more esoteric second- and third-year seminar courses in favor of mandatory clinical experience. But many law teachers do not support the clinical movement. They regard clinical training as a threat to their jobs or academic integrity. As late as 1975–1976, clinical supervisors remained second-class citizens on most law school faculties, with such denigrating titles as "instructor," "lecturer," "adjunct professor," or "staff attorney." Only 15 percent were hired under contracts that could lead to tenured positions. Although clinical supervisors often worked longer hours, they were typically paid less than academic professors.

In 1977, CLEPR announced a new grant policy to promote parity between clinical and academic law professor salaries. But the policy merely underlined the obvious. Clinical legal education had not been fully accepted in American law schools, and in the eyes of most senior faculty members had yet to prove itself. Since students continued to support the courses — or, as some law professors snidely suggested, anything else that got them out of the classroom during the second and third years of law school — law faculties were willing to tolerate some elective clinical courses, especially if they were subsidized. But most faculties were not sympathetic to the fundamental criticism of American legal education that the clinical movement implied. In this sense, William Pincus had begun a revolution but had not been able to complete it. The battle to win clinical training an essential place in each law school's curriculum, however, was far from over.

Perhaps the individual most likely to affect the immediate future of clinical law training is Gary Bellow. Bellow, formerly at the University of Southern California Law School, now at Harvard, is a law professor particularly concerned with providing a more effective integration of legal skills training and social theory. In Bellow's view, the seeming conflict between theory and practice in law schools is misplaced. "Clinical education," he urges, "properly understood is not an additional course added to an already overburdened curriculum but a way of going about learning which can be applied to the whole curriculum, or to any course or courses within it." When effectively taught, clinical training can respond to three basic needs that traditional legal education ignores.

Foremost is the need to redefine the lawyer's role. To increase legal services, Bellow argues, requires lawyers trained in a new type of general practice, which he calls "primary legal care." "As the profession specializes," he suggests, "there is greater need for generalists . . . Someone must retain a unitary vision of the client, see the person as a whole, be able to respond to all of his or her problems, not just the housing problem that the client first brought in." Thus, to increase the delivery of legal services to the poor and to the middle class, there may be a need for paralegals to specialize, but not attorneys. In an illustrative series of articles, Bellow faulted most legal-services programs for their inability "to appreciate the complexity of their own practice." Typically, attorneys accept without question the premise of law schools such as Harvard "that legal doctrines are complex, working with clients is simple." Bellow disputes this. "Working with clients is also complex because of the large number of institutions and regulations which affect poor people's lives. When a legal service lawyer describes work as routine and boring what he often is saying is that he hasn't taken the time to master a number of laws such as Social Security, Housing or Garnishment, as they relate to the clients' problems. The problems seem simple because the lawyer often has chosen to focus on the most routine aspects." Law students, taught to narrow clients' problems into established doctrinal pigeonholes, are not encouraged to appreciate what is most important to the client, to guide the client to nonlawyers who can help with nonlegal problems, to discuss the relationship between legal rules and how government agencies actually work or how lawyers sometimes can best represent their clients through legislative lobbying or community organizing. Since most practicing attorneys never receive this type of sophisticated skills training, most clients, believes Bellow, receive "mediocre" representation.

In part, this is the result of the way in which students learn. "All education must focus on developing the students' capacity for self-learning," Bellow advocates, "not merely the level of information they receive." He faults law schools for instilling in their students fear of making mistakes. This invites attorneys — particularly attorneys with heavy case loads — to imitate uncritically established modes of practice and be unduly accommodating to courts and opposing counsel at the expense of their clients. By contrast, the one-to-one teacher-student relationship in clinical training "unfreezes" the student's resistance to self-criticism. As a result:

> Few who have done clinical teaching are not struck by the extent to which they are continually challenged by their students to justify their actions and statements, and to relate their insights and ideas to the students' perceptions of the reality of the legal order. Despite the deep commitment of legal education to the development of skepticism and caution in the handling of authoritative pronouncement, we do not often bring the law professor's views, ideas, and modes of inquiry within this prescription. The sense of confidence, knowledge, and introspection generated by the performance of lawyer-role functions in clinical programs offer the possibility of redressing the balance of authority in the present teacher-student relationship in the direction of greater student-initiated speculation, criticism, and thought.

Finally, Bellow describes "the need for reconstruction." He sees "shocking gaps between America's traditional pluralistic ideals and what is going on in the legal system." Merely by identifying these gaps, he contends, law teachers can produce some change. But Bellow expects more than that.

He urges each law school to act as a social critic, each clinical-law student as a participant observer. "We want students to build an alternative vision of the society that will be needed to nurture ideal professional and non-professional roles; an alternative perception of a legal system and lawyers more responsive to primary care and reflective learning." For Bellow such an order would be more democratic, more humanistic, and more socialistic. "How do you begin to involve lawyers in questions of real wealth and income re-distribution? How do you use lawyers to imagine a social order in which lawyers would have a lessened role? We need to create a learning environment where all courses are concerned with reconstruction . . ."

For six years at Harvard Law School, Bellow has directed a second- and third-year elective program, the Lawyering Process.

As structured in 1976–1977, the course began with a three-week Trial Advocacy Workshop. Modeled after a similar course developed by Harvard Law Professor Robert Keeton for the National Institute for Trial Advocacy, the workshop functions like an adrenalin rush. The seventy-five to ninety students enrolled in the course are assigned to sections of twenty to twenty-four students. Daily, the section meets for two hours with a faculty team leader such as Professor Keeton, a teaching-fellow assistant team leader, and three practicing trial lawyers and judges who serve one-week stints as visiting instructors. In each session the visiting attorneys present a courtroom argument or witness-examination that the students had been assigned to study the evening before. Then three or four of the students present the argument or examination and receive detailed criticism of their performance.

After that the section is separated into subgroups of five or six students so that each student can make a presentation before one of the members of the teaching team. During this time the students are as free to criticize the teacher-expert or each other as a faculty member was to criticize them, illustrating Keeton's teaching approach, which is memorialized in his only known attempt at blank verse: "Tell me and I will forget. Show me and I will remember. Involve me and I will understand."

Following dinner, the students meet with the teaching team and review student performances on video tape or engage in more role-playing. At the end of the evening, all students gather to watch the visiting attorneys and judges present a performance of the next day's lesson. In this fashion, students gain experience in each of the principal aspects of a courtroom trial: summation, direct and cross-examination, presenting evidence, opening statements, and examining expert witnesses. During Thursday and Friday of the last two weeks, students participate in two full simulated trials.

The thirty-to-forty-hour weekly schedule on top of other class work is demanding, but most students find the course exhilarating. The mad-dog pace of the course alone acts as an emotional "upper" for many students, an especially welcome relief from the wearisome slowness of most second- and third-year courses. But the principal advantage of the workshop is an atmosphere significantly different from that of the average law school class. There is no penalty for not doing well. Indeed, it is assumed that students won't do well at first but if given sufficient feedback and opportunity to practice, they will improve. Since the experienced attorneys have different styles, the students are given the further security of knowing that there are no absolute right and wrong answers in trial practice; it is all right for each student to develop a personal style. According to Professor Keeton, since the visiting lawyers and judges are reimbursed only for their travel and hotel expenses, the workshop program costs no more to operate than conventional second- and third-year law school seminars.

In conjunction with the Trial Advocacy Workshop, students attend a related ethics course in Professional Responsibility. In the spring of 1977, the course was taught by Gary Bellow. He begins one class session by explaining that the purpose of the course is to relate moral or ethical concerns to the lawyering skills the students learn in the other segments of the Lawyering Process Program.

The class session is a Bellow tour de force. It's Friday afternoon — the worst time to start any law school class. Before Bellow arrives, a student loudly announces to a friend, "This is going to be boring."

It's not. When Bellow is in control of his material, he is one of the few charismatic professors at Harvard Law School. Alternately relaxed, joking, slouching, then intense, personal, demanding, this day he leads his class in an emotional odyssey designed to vivify the ethical problems of the legal aid attorney. "The ethical mandates of the Code of Professional Responsibility do not resolve the moral issues involved in 'zealously representing a client' or 'being a minister of justice.' The code won't help you with the feelings involved."

To illustrate, he has the class read a 1971 *Life* magazine article about a talented but cynical New York City legal aid lawyer named Martin Erdmann. By the strictures of the code, Erdmann is an incompetent lawyer. The code demands that no attorney accept a case unless he or she is fully prepared, yet Erdmann handles thirty cases a day, often with no more preparation than a glance at a file. Nearly every attorney would argue that Erdmann's approach is justified. Only one in a thousand of his cases went to trial. Erdmann usually secured for his clients the lightest sentences available.

But Bellow wasn't satisfied. "This whole course is about seeing alternatives, discovering what more you could do. What more could Erdmann do?" Pushed, the students grope for answers. "Erdmann did not read a grand jury transcript and blew a case." "He never got clients out on bail." "He doesn't bring *habeas corpus* . . ."

Bellow interjects, "Did you ever read *One Just Man?* It is about everyone in The Tombs demanding a trial and the whole New York City criminal justice system coming to an end. What the author graphically illustrates is the degree to which unjust legal institutions depend on clients' acquiescence to them." He elaborates: "The ethical mandate of canon 6 results emotionally and practically in feelings of control for the lawyer. These feelings are confirmed and accepted by judges and other lawyers. That is why Erdmann feels competent. But it's a competence within limits — attorneys stop experiencing the need for alternatives and see what they do as inevitable and right . . . You need a reference group to resist this type of pressure." For Bellow's students, this class is their first such reference group.

Bellow poses another dilemma. "Did Erdmann act ethically in resisting the prosecutor's demand for a three-year sentence for a child molester . . . Look at Disciplinary Rule Number 7: A lawyer may not intentionally fail to seek the lawful interests of a client. Erdmann knows his client is guilty as hell. Can he say to the court, it's really better if the client gets a long term? Absolutely not. There are many ambiguities in this class but not on this issue. The question for you is whether such partisanship is justified."

A student shakes his head. "I had trouble with what the prosecutor did [accepting Erdmann's proposal of a one-year plea]."

Briefly, Bellow explores what the prosecutor could have done.

Then he returns to his main point: "Erdmann is bound by canon 7 to disregard the consequences of his own acts. He is not allowed to take into account that what he does may be a bad result from society's point of view. Now how is that going to make you feel?"

No one answers.

"I don't have any professional answers to this except to share my own feelings. I am not sure canon 7 is a bad rule . . . we could debate that. But it is extremely hard to live a full life and feel that cynical . . ." The class is still very quiet. "You are going to have to work out your own norms — your own justifications of the role you'll play. I do not want you to forget it is an emotional context . . . There's an endless tension between being committed to a legal system you know is not entirely just and loyalty to a client who you know is not always going to be fairly treated. You're going to have to struggle for a long time with this one . . ."

The third component of the Lawyering Process Program is a large weekly class also taught by Bellow or the second primary instructor in the clinical program, Assistant Dean Jeanne Kettleson.* Beginning three weeks into the semester after the Trial Advocacy Workshop ends, classes in the Civil or Criminal Lawyering Process are primarily devoted to a sociological and psychological description of the lawyer's role. Although formally considering such skills as interviewing, negotiation, counseling, and cross-examination. Bellow maintains in his book, *The Lawyering Process*, "The issue is *us*, and what we have become." In a typical session on client interviewing, Kettleson lectures on the personality structure, aspirations, and expectations of both lawyer and client.

Both Bellow's book and this type of lecture initially confuse many students. But after viewing a video tape that illustrated several "interpersonality" problems, an increased number of students seemed comfortable with the social science vocabulary. As

---

* In 1976–1977, a third section in Prison Advocacy was led by Lecturer on Law Michele Hermann, who later left Harvard Law School to become an assistant professor at the University of New Mexico Law School.

Kettleson wrote in a 1975 memorandum, when the course is successful it provides "more general frameworks and explanations — what amounts to a sort of cognitive map — of lawyer work that students can use to assess past performances and as a guide in planning and preparing future ones":

> For example, we can tell a student how to cross-examine a particular witness and rehearse and coach him or her through an acceptable, even good, performance, but we probably haven't taught much that the student can use the next time he or she has to cross-examine a witness. On the other hand, if the students learn about a general framework or map that provides: some categories for identifying and generating sources of material for use in cross-examination; five or six steps to be followed in constructing a particular cross once the material is known; and some criteria that would help the students choose among alternatives at each stage, students could use such a framework or map to prepare an effective cross-examination in almost any case.

The combination of the Trial Advocacy Workshop and the Professional Responsibility and Lawyering Process classes provides a general "cognitive map" to civil and criminal legal-aid work, but the essence of the clinical program remains field work. For twelve weeks, each student works twenty to thirty hours a week in a legal-aid or voluntary-defender office or in a public-interest setting such as the Consumer Protection Division of the Department of the Massachusetts Attorney General.

The success of student field work usually turns on the quality of the field supervisor. In Bellow's program, where teaching fellows supervise no more than eight students (after having themselves received a rudimentary one-month training), the quality is generally high. Susan Kupfer, who oversaw field work at a suburban office of Greater Boston Legal Services, for example, spent up to sixty hours a week at her "half-time" job. Such dedication means she can personally read nearly every student's initial client interviews, discuss the interview in detail with the student afterward, review weekly each student's case file, read and criticize each student's legal papers, as well as lead a weekly seminar. Frequently her small, glass-enclosed office witnessed a succession of mini–law classes in which she riffled through student papers and snapped questions as if at a Ph.D. defense. Compared to Professor Byse, Kupfer's questions are far more pointed, but since she works one-to-one with her students, she is able to build a rapport that makes it possible for her students to accept demanding criticism without the anxiety of the large school classroom. Where field supervisors have been less conscientious, law faculty critics have scathingly identified "mass produced mediocrity," "inadequate legal research," and "tolerance of sloppy work habits."

Gary Bellow's Lawyering Process course is undoubtedly the most popular student elective at Harvard Law School. As a result of persistent student demands, the course will be expanded in 1977–1978 to accommodate 300 students, with new sections offered in Bankruptcy, Torts, and Government Service.

Yet Bellow is not satisfied. After taking his course, relatively few Harvard Law students choose a legal-services or public-interest career. "I've been increasingly aware," he explains, "that the way students are dealing with substantive doctrines and the policy questions they reflect is not adequate for the kind of lawyers we want them to be. To be a good poverty lawyer requires understanding market structures, the bureaucratic institutions which affect them and the actual working of the American welfare state. A young lawyer learning legal-aid practice needs an integrated environment in which theory ranges from doctrine to social analysis, and practice confronts day-to-day problems and the practical uses of theory. That is, we need clinical education at both the macro and micro levels."

In 1977, Bellow announced plans to establish a Legal Services Institute in a low-income area in Boston, specifically organized to provide legal service to indigent clients. Although an enduring affiliation with Harvard Law School is being considered, Bellow emphasizes the physical separateness of the institute. If practical problems are resolved on schedule, Bellow envisions that early in

1979, a faculty will have been assembled. "At stage one, the faculty of the [institute] would themselves practice in the best form they know how, trying to give reality to the kind of learning, feedback and self-review that we would want in all legal services programs in the United States." About a year later, the institute would bring third-year students from conventional law schools and integrate them into an educational process in which the faculty also are practicing, learning, and studying. The curriculum would emphasize courses such as the legal, political, and economic aspects of low-income and low-wage markets; taxation and distribution programs; and the bureaucratiziation of social services to the poor. "No student could come who did not make a five year commitment to legal aid work. The students would practice and study in ways which connected theoretical analyses and practical work. The notion would be to create a curriculum which permitted students to both use what they were learning day-to-day and yet constantly force them to examine the values and assumptions they were adopting and advancing."

Ultimately, Bellow would like to bring lawyers from the legal-services system to the institute for six months to a year for advanced training and to develop a research program. "I know this is a big undertaking, but I think it is possible . . . What I have in mind is an 'alternative school' which affords the sort of education which those lawyers who want to work with the poor really need."

By the time Bellow's institute welcomes its first students, the two most innovative law schools of the post–World War II period will each be nearing teenage.

Down in Washington, D.C., halfway between the Capitol's riot-torn 14th Street corridor and 1960s radical chic, is Antioch Law School, the nation's first combination law school–public-interest law firm. A highly personalized expression of the educational theories of its founding co-deans, Edgar and Jean Cahn, Antioch was originally funded in 1968 as the Urban Law Institute, an OEO research and development project, officially beginning as a law school in 1972 when the institute was affiliated with Antioch College. The structure of the school reads like a William Pincus dream come true.

In 1976–1977, each student spent the first two weeks of law school living with a ghetto family to develop some understanding of the impoverished clients they would soon represent. Culture shock was succeeded by "boot camp," sixty hours of intensive training in legal ethics, interviewing, negotiation, and legal analysis. Then, during their first weeks of law school, students were assigned to one of three clinics: Private Law (representing housing-, consumer-, and family-law clients), Public Law (including labor-, sex discrimination-, and constitutional-law problems), or Criminal Law. Simultaneously, they began a highly traditional first-year classroom curriculum. But the emphasis of the school is on learning from clinical experience. After five months, students rotate to the second of the three clinics and, at the start of the second year, to the third. The balance of the second and third years provides students with advanced clinical experience, including a two-month internship in the federal government or the District of Columbia municipal government. To satisfy ABA standards, Antioch students attend law school on a year-round basis, and throughout the second and third years also complete a conventional classroom core-and-elective curriculum. To an unfortunate extent, the first five years of clinical-law training at Antioch have been marred by recurring internecine squabbles. Although such discord has sullied the reputation of the school, the Antioch concept has not been emulated for a more fundamental reason: money. To administer the law school's ambitious in-house clinics has required substantial public and private financial aid.

By contrast, Boston's Northeastern University Law School is a bargain. The law school operates its own variant of the cooperative (or co-op) plan. After students complete their first year, they alternate in the second and third years between three-month quarters of full-time academic work and full-time employment in law offices. Since students are paid for their law office work and second- and third-year tuition is reduced, the effect is to cut the average cost of law school to students to about one-half to two-thirds that of Harvard.*

Because Northeastern Law students work in four different law jobs, the possibility that any student will receive inadequately supervised practical training is significantly lessened. Indeed, the co-op rotations directly contribute to the law school's striking buoyancy. By the time Northeastern Law students graduate, they have already been paid for a full year of law work. The resulting sense of maturity is buttressed by the law school's pass-fail grading system. While most law students suffer from second- and third-year "blahs," Northeastern Law students tend to speed through their academic quarters with relative enthusiasm. In effect, Northeastern is the country's first two-year law school, having effectively compressed a standard three-year curriculum into seven three-month quarters.

Nevertheless, former Assistant Dean Molly Geraghty, who supervised Northeastern's co-op program from 1974 to 1977, was skeptical that the law school can be replicated. In her view, the transitional problems in converting from a traditional to a cooperative curriculum alone may be "insurmountable." Even if conventional schools could be converted or new schools created, she fears that cooperative training may be a "slightly fragile idea." Although in 1976–1977 she was able to place all Northeastern Law students in jobs ranging from prestigious Boston law firms Hale and Dorr, and Ropes and Gray, to the United Farm Workers and Children's Defense Fund, Geraghty wondered whether, if there were several Northeastern Law Schools, the co-op job market might be saturated.

---

* Currently, two thirds of all clinical programs employ Northeastern types of "farm-out" programs. A number of California law schools, including Stanford and the University of California's Hastings College of Law, have developed optional "extern" semesters with field placements ranging from Washington, D.C.'s Center of Law and Social Policy to clerkships with the state's judiciary.

9

GRADES, LAW REVIEW, AND PLACEMENT:

The Rewards System

We can hardly deny the omnipresence of the question, "Was he on Review?"

Report of the Special Committee on Examinations, Grading, and Related Matters, Harvard Law School, June 4, 1969

Imagine this scene. Jack is twenty-two, a magna cum laude graduate of a leading university, recipient of a Law School Admission Test score in the upper 2 percent, a former high-school student-body officer, and a lettered athlete. Jill is twenty-four and a summa cum laude graduate of her college. Although her LSAT score lagged a few points behind Jack's, she has published two articles in nationally circulated magazines and helped establish a community organization while in college. At Harvard Law School in a typical year, there are about 300 students similar to Jack and 100 similar to Jill.

Soon after arriving, they learn that virtually the only honor for distinguished first-year performance is a place on the *Harvard Law Review* and that *Law Review* editors are chosen for the ultimate law school rewards: a chance to clerk for a Supreme Court Justice in the first or second year after graduation, teaching positions, opportunities to work in the most prestigious government and private law firms. They soon discover that most of their professors are former *Law Review* members and that *Review* editors have ac-

cess to the offices of professors whom students generally otherwise can expect to see only in class.

As with Gatsby's distant dim green light, for many, earning
grades high enough to qualify for *Law Review* becomes an idée
fixe. Night after night will be spent studying until 10 P.M., 12 P.M.,
2 A.M. Many will join study groups to discuss cases and jointly
take practice exams. In the final weeks before January and June
final exams, the study schedule accelerates. There just isn't time
to speak to parents; strained personal relationships will have to be
repaired later; non–Law School interests are completely ignored.
In the last days before exams, the collective irritability of the class
is palpable. Deprived of sleep, feeling the full measure of competitive pressure, students come to believe: "Everything is riding
on these seven days. Everything in the world."

Then the first-year exam results are computed in July, and 525
of each class of 550 students lose.*

It is difficult to imagine a rewards system more demeaning,
distorting of values, or arbitrary. Unlike medical schools, where
incentives primarily are designed to insure that each student will
be a competent practitioner, the law review system exaggerates
the worth of a tiny minority of students, lessens respect for all
non–law review related activities, and encourages students to
value self-aggrandizement more than service to others.

Not that law students should not be graded. Grades serve as a
powerful tool with which women and racial minorities can dis-
solve or challenge historic patterns of discrimination. As Harvard
Law Professor Archibald Cox has insisted:

> . . . One great, practical accomplishment of the Harvard
> Law School over the years has been taking young men
> from many different, social, economic, and geographic
> backgrounds, giving them truly equal opportunities for
> accomplishment, judging them solely upon intellectual
> promise and performance as measured by the examina-
> tions, and thus opening doors to them in the legal pro-

* Another ten students qualify for the *Review* in a second-year writing competition
and eight more qualify at the beginning of the third year on the basis of first- and
second-year grades.

fession and, through it, still more doors into universities, business, government, and other institutions that they would otherwise have found closed. Unless one denies the validity of distinctions in intellectual performance in the law, I think of no system that is fairer to the individual or more beneficial for society than this.

There is some evidence that students study more conscientiously under a competitive grade system than a pass-fail one.*

But employing any grading system to single out a tiny fraction of a large and talented class is an entirely different matter. For final examinations at Harvard Law School, students must write detailed essays analyzing complex legal questions. To suggest — as some faculty members have — that professors can apply objective standards to grade exams with mathematical precision is quixotic. Law is not mathematics. Law is not pure craft. Standards of quality are invariably subjective. One professor's A may equal a second professor's B+ or B. Indeed, since professors often must grade 200 to 400 examinations a semester, spending as few as five or ten minutes on each, it is unreasonable to assume that any professor can apply a grading standard with perfect consistency.

Nor is a law review–related grading system pedagogically sound. Most schools encourage students to work hard throughout their entire stay, or they emphasize the final year's grades, in order to encourage students to experiment until they learn the most effective approach to their field. At Harvard Law School, the fate of a student's law school career is largely determined during two weeks in the first year. Although second- and third-year grades are important to potential employers, their value is diminished by the omnipresence of the *Law Review*.

This is a highly unfair result. It takes some students longer to adjust to the intellectual demands of the law than others. To judge students irrevocably before they have "caught on" is to

---

* But not very persuasive evidence. Since reopening in 1968, Northeastern University Law School has administered a pass-fail grading system. Student enthusiasm to master the skills of their chosen profession and to pass required state bar examinations apparently provides as effective a motivation as a more conventional grading system.

mock the concept of merit-related rewards. Derek Bok, the president of Harvard University, earned sufficiently high first-year grades to qualify for the *Harvard Law Review*. But he almost dropped out of law school after receiving a C− ("or was it a D+?") on a midyear practice exam. If he had attended Harvard Law School after 1972, when midyear examinations were first counted in the *Law Review* competition, he would not have earned a place on the *Review* and probably not been hired as a Harvard Law professor and presumably today would not be president of Harvard University. His legal talents, however, would have been exactly the same.

Many gifted students whose talents are as great or nearly as great as those of Derek Bok are never rewarded at Harvard Law School. These students excel in long-term writing projects, courtroom argument, or client counseling — skills that simply are not measured on first-year examinations. Indeed, all that is measured is an ability to describe the elements of a legal problem under time-pressure — an important ability, to be sure, but only a small part of what law work actually requires.

The grading system is unfortunate in another sense as well. Since so much turns on the results of examinations, it has become customary for law professors to grade all of their students' examinations. This may involve one to two weeks of work each year — time that arguably could be better spent in legal research, meeting with students, or class preparation. As a Harvard Law School faculty report recognized in 1969: "Teachers in other disciplines would surely say — have said — that it is 'unthinkable' personally to grade 200 to 400 handwritten bluebooks of four-hour examinations."

Yet law professors are unable to spend sufficient time evaluating student work to give each student more than a letter grade. For students in the class of 1971, this was "The Trouble with Grades":

> The present system never gives the student any feedback about how well or poorly he is doing until it is too late to respond. Apart from the practice exam, there are no points along the way where the student is challenged by quizzes,

written work, or group projects. At no point, even after his
grades are handed to him, does he receive any constructive
guidance about how well he is absorbing the law and what
his relative strengths and weaknesses are. A student
whose basic problem is that he does not understand how to
study law generally is not likely to find any assistance
under the present system. In fact, under this system he
may not even realize he has a problem until he receives his
grades. It is disheartening for a student to go through a
year of hard work only to be told by a letter grade that he
approached the law incorrectly.

The cost law schools pay for first-year students' unnecessary
emotional isolation and frustration is an often noted lessening of
student enthusiasm in the second and third years. Harvard Law
School's Dr. Alan Stone argues:

> The crucial human attribute which the law school ig-
> nores, and indeed in many cases defeats, is the student's
> sense of self-esteem. The problem can be seen by carica-
> turing the typical emotional pattern of the not fabulously
> successful law student: intense effort and anxiety during
> the first year; withdrawal, depression, and disengagement
> from classroom involvement during the second year; re-
> newed anxiety and concern about occupational opportu-
> nity and ability during the third year. This pattern of ever
> increasing disengagement from the formal educational
> process is to be contrasted with the experience of the medi-
> cal student who, during his last two years, is given increas-
> ing professional responsibility in the clinic and ward. Al-
> though his class time decreases, his total hours increase
> until they approach those of the intern, for whom a twelve
> hour day is a luxury.

A further cost to students is in the distortion of their values.
How much different would be the history of the law if leading
law schools acted upon the belief that the most honorable career
for an attorney was to serve those too poor to hire representation

before courts or government? Imagine a very different novitiate year. On the first day the dean informs the entering class: "You are about to enter a profession considered noble because under the United States Constitution and the traditions of the common law, it has an ideal of providing equal representation for all. No matter how great the disparities in wealth or talents elsewhere in society, both the adversary system and democratic practice demand formal equality before the law. Accordingly, we expect you to spend some of your time working in a free legal clinic for the poor. This will not only be a good practical education for you but will also illustrate your most basic ethical responsibility. For the practice of law in this country, we must never forget, is a monopoly. We deserve the security and dignity of our profession only if we satisfy the public's needs of adequate legal representation. If each of you works throughout your career to achieve that goal, you can personally contribute to the increasing justness of our society . . ."

Instead, American law schools immediately toss students into the cauldron of a grade competition whose principal utility is identifying a few outstanding law school students to future employers. The time demands of the grade competition are so intense that few students are able to read broadly in the law, visit law courts and offices, or become acquainted with the attempts of other professions to solve social problems. And law schools do not encourage them to do so. Rather, this narrowing process is justified as necessary to the "professionalization" of lawyers.

Students disagree. A 1973 survey of graduate students conducted by the Educational Testing Service found that whereas 69 to 84 percent of students in humanities, biological science, physical science, social science, education, and medicine felt their "grading system is fair," only 38 percent of law students could agree. The Harvard Law School Visiting Committee was informed in 1975 that Harvard Law students favored the institution of an optional pass-fail grading system by a vote of 984 to 383, with ninety-seven students undecided. Our own survey of Harvard Law students found that 61.3 percent of second-year students and 78.3 percent of third-year students favored the *Law Review* "admitting anyone who wants to write."

Under student pressure Harvard Law School modified the rigor of its traditional grading system in the late 1960s to permit some students to qualify for *Law Review* on the basis of a second-year writing competition, and then modified it again in 1972 to require midyear final examinations to give students earlier feedback. Other law schools have done considerably more. Stanford and Rutgers (Newark) Law Schools allow students to choose between competitive grading (A, B, C, etc.) and pass-fail grades for all courses. Yale, the University of Michigan, and Duke Law Schools have instituted more limited pass-fail plans. Both the Yale and Stanford *Law Review*s are open to volunteers. Generally, however, grading reforms in other law schools have been as limited as those at Harvard Law School.

Overwhelming all other extracurricular activities at the Law School, the *Harvard Law Review* influences students not only because of its selection competition, but also because of its character.

Within twenty years of its formation in 1886, the *Law Review* evolved into the most prestigious legal journal in the country. It endures as virtually the only journal that is financially self-sufficient among the better than 180 university law reviews. But the utility of the *Review* and its tens of imitators is seriously compromised by the conflicting nature of its two basic functions.

At its best, the *Harvard Law Review* is a prominent technical journal that has been successful in publishing such pathbreaking articles as "The Right to Privacy," an 1890 polemic co-authored by future Supreme Court Justice Louis Brandeis that spurred the emergence of an important doctrine of law.

Greater praise, though, is usually accorded the *Review*'s second function: training its student members in legal research, criticism, and writing. In 1956, Northwestern's Dean Havighurst explained: ". . . Law reviews are unique among publications in that they do not exist because of any large demand on the part of a reading public. Whereas most periodicals are published primarily in order that they may be read, the law reviews are published primarily in order that they may be written . . . Large subsidies are therefore provided. The number of self-supporting student-edited reviews could probably be counted on one finger."

Annually, *Harvard Law Review* editors return to campus a month early to work sixty-hour weeks reading recent court decisions and doing preliminary research for future student articles (typically, notes on individual law cases). Student editors also "subcite" (substantively edit), "techcite" (technically edit — that is, correct the footnotes), and "collate" (rewrite with the author) each article, whether authored by students or legal scholars. During the school year many student editors spend fifty hours a week on the *Review* in addition to their class work. Impressed, Columbia Law Professor Karl Llewellyn once termed the reviews "One of the most satisfactory educational tools in existence . . . The student-run law review is a unique American achievement . . . Here is the only known group of first-rate professional periodicals responsibly edited and partly written by *undergraduates* in the discipline. The importance of those reviews here lies in the fact that they are themselves also educational machinery with cleanly developed techniques for rapid and amazingly effective training, machinery recognized by faculties as having peculiar value in supplementation of the standard curriculum."

The fact that law reviews generally are student-run also constitutes their fundamental weakness. No matter how carefully chosen, law review editors usually lack the knowledge or practical experience to write probing legal analyses or studies of the empirical consequences of law. In a word, they tend to hide behind their footnotes, substituting a forest of annotations and the most "neutral" or "reasonable" synthesis of formal legal doctrines for original examination of what the law actually is or ought to be. Yale Law School's iconoclastic Fred Rodell once marveled how "the average law review writer is peculiarly able to say nothing with an air of great importance."*

Besides inexperience, law review editors are handicapped by

---

* Professor Rodell sweepingly added: "There are two things wrong with almost all legal writing. One is its style. The other is its content." Since this, alas, is a legal writing, it is assumedly equally condemned by Rodell. Grieved Thucydides: "There are no safe havens."

other limitations. Most student-written articles are prepared with unnecessary haste. Typically, the first draft of a student-written case note is produced in two to three weeks. That is insufficient time for anyone to explore the background of a legal rule, assimilate related social science literature, and examine its practical consequences with original field research. So law review editors almost never do any original field research and rarely make a careful study of relevant social science literature. What often passes for legal scholarship is in reality no more scholarly than a beginning lawyer's courtroom brief.

Further, at a typical law review, elaborate layers of editors and editorial committees rewrite each student-author's work to an extent that would make *Time* magazine's Ivory Tower blush. Although the initial legal research may remain untouched, the conclusion or theme of the article will be argued, often at great length, with the result that novel thoughts are frequently washed out in a compromise solution. In this way, explained one *Harvard Law Review* editor, you lose "wild, original ideas." A colleague rather bitterly informed us that his proposal for a student note was rejected not because it was an inappropriate topic but because members of an editorial committee believed it would take "a political point of view we'd rather not publish." Another editor generalized: "There is no ideological consensus that can develop because of the way people are selected, but I don't know if that's bad. What's amazing is that despite the ideological differences, most articles come out so incredibly neutral." *

* A few law reviews have adopted expedients that result in student contributions being less timid. Duke University's pioneering journal, *Law and Contemporary Problems,* employs a faculty editor to supervise symposium issues on a single topic of current interest. This allows student editorial assistants to participate in an interdisciplinary approach that integrates contributions from economists, social scientists, and public officials, as well as legal scholars. Harvard Law School's *Civil Rights-Civil Liberties Review,* like other recently created reviews, has limited its focus to a few areas of law, and by tradition has attracted students with activist enthusiasms.

Most reviews, however, continue to follow the *Harvard Law Review* model. The cumulative result is that the reviews, besides being narrow in intellectual focus and timid in style, often are redundant as well. The Supreme Court's recent "death penalty" decision, *Furman* v. *Georgia,* for one example, was the topic of 37 separate law review articles.

Yet as long as law reviews are viewed primarily as training vehicles, their editorial timidity is not their most fundamental problem. Granted it is wasteful to have so many reviews publishing so much that is banal, and it is unfortunate that youthful law scholars are not given a more effective training in social science research, the fact remains that the intensive two-year training of law review members in research and writing may be the most effective training presently offered in American law schools. All students deserve a comparable education. For law schools to accord frequent faculty contact and intensive research and training only to a chosen few is a fundamental failing of Amercian legal education. Law schools provide the most attention to students who presumably need the least extra help. With practitioners criticizing law schools for failing to provide skills training to their graduates, this approach is not so much callous as misdirected. By subsidizing the reviews, law schools support a pedagogical strategy whereby a minority of their students are given an intensive training in some practical skills while the vast majority are inadequately trained.

For years the popular television series "Mission Impossible" began each episode with a secret agent locating a hidden tape recorder. Activated, the machine solemnly intoned, "Your mission, Mr. Phelps, if you choose to accept it . . ." and then described some improbable feat of derring-do.

One can only speculate what Harvard Law School Dean Albert Sacks told Doug Phelps in January 1977, when he hired Doug to be the Law School's first Alternative Careers Administrator. But in the Winter 1976 issue of the *Harvard Law School Bulletin,* the dean observed, "He confronts a most interesting and difficult set of challenges."

That was to put it mildly. A 1970 survey of the 15,750 Harvard Law School alumni then practicing law found that 74 percent worked for law firms, 12 percent for private industry, and most of the rest for the federal government or for a state or local government. Since 1970, the number of public-interest law jobs has more than doubled, so that by 1977, at least 7500 of the country's 450,000 practicing attorneys worked full-time for the federal Legal Services Corporation, a local legal-aid or public-defender office, a government consumers' advocate or ombudsman office, a public-interest group, or related employment.* With 5.5 percent of the country's 1975 law school graduates locating public-interest jobs, Harvard Law School's long-time Director of Placement Eleanor Appel stated in an interview that there are sufficient public-interest jobs available "to place half" of each Harvard Law School class of 540 graduates.

Yet since 1970, the number of Harvard Law students accepting public-interest jobs has decreased. In the class graduating in 1976, only five students joined programs funded by the federal Legal Services Corporation; only two, a public-interest group. In part, because so few Harvard Law students seemed interested in their work, relatively few public interest firms attempt to recruit in Cambridge. Of the 703 separate employers scheduled to interview at the Law School in 1976–1977, 614 were representatives of private law firms (representing, however, only 545 separate firms since some multi-city firms sent multiple representatives) and forty-nine corporations and accounting firms. Only twenty public-interest and legal-services organizations were scheduled to interview. Of these, three canceled for lack of student interest.

To some degree, of course, Harvard Law students prefer Wall Street firms for the same reason Willie Sutton robbed banks. With leading corporate-law firms offering starting salaries of $25,000 or more, and few public-interest jobs paying more than

---

* Data on the number of attorneys employed in public-services fields are difficult to ascertain. As near as could be determined, in 1977, the federal Legal Services Corporation employed or helped fund 3200 attorneys working full-time in civil legal-services work. The National Legal Aid and Defender Association estimates there are approximately 3100–3300 attorneys working full-time in public-defender agencies. In its study, *Balancing the Scales of Justice: Financing Public Interest Law in America*, the Council of Public Interest Law calculated that there were 600 public-interest lawyers practicing in the 92 tax-exempt public-interest law centers they surveyed. At least 500 additional attorneys work in legal aid offices not funded by the Legal Services Corporation, as grassroots organizers in various environmental, consumer, and civil rights groups not included in the Council for Public Interest Law's survey, or for private law firms that devote the majority of their efforts to labor, employment discrimination, poverty, tenants' rights, or similar legal problems.

$10,000–$15,000, young lawyers, in public-interest attorney Mark Green's view, may "talk like Danny the Red," but they "go the way of Oliver Barrett IV." Considering that 214 students in the 1976 class graduated with $5000 or more in law school debts, it is at least understandable that a fair number of law students have little enthusiasm for living in the red.

But few people seriously maintain that money alone explains why so many Harvard Law students arrive with idealistic ambitions of public service and so few graduate and act upon them. Harvard Law Professor Abram Chayes, for one, has theorized that the expense and timing of law student recruitment works to the disadvantage of all employers but the major law firms. As he explained in a 1974 address to the New York University *Law Review*:

> I think the important feature of the placement process as it has developed is that it increased both the timing and the leverage of the major metropolitan law firms. Why is that? First of all, they are the ones that can interview. If you look at the people interviewing at Harvard or any other major law school, they are largely representatives of major metropolitan firms. They have the personnel to send out; they have the means because they have a regular turnover; and they are the ones who are there. Secondly they are the only ones who can make offers early enough — that is, because they have a regular demand, they make offers in early fall. We've managed, by some sort of cartel among the law schools, to require that those offers remain open until December 15. But on December 15 the offers close — you must accept or not, there you are. So the person who holds an offer from one of those firms is under enormous pressure not to wait until the spring when some other opportunities may be open . . .
>
> This phenomenon cuts against not only government and public service-type opportunities. It cuts against smaller firms and smaller places in the country, where very often a young lawyer can make a large contribution as a lawyer

and as a citizen. So it's not only that this is a juxtaposition of private versus public. It's a juxtaposition of major law firms in major metropolitan centers against all other kinds of opportunities both public and private.

By 1976 views like Chayes's had become the conventional wisdom. While government and public-interest employers often could not afford to send representatives, it had become common for partners in major firms to travel to Harvard for preliminary interviews and then invite favored students to make all-expense-paid visits to their cities for final interviews. There, students would be accommodated in first-class hotels, and wined and dined at plush restaurants or country clubs. After two and a half years of near anonymity in law school classes of 100–150, the effects of this earnest and personal attention from a distinguished law firm partner could be, well, bracing. Throughout October and November, blue-jeaned second- and third-year students periodically disappeared, to reappear with Brooks Brothers suits, suntans, and accounts of "the best French restaurant in Beaumont, Texas." The effect on students holding out for public-interest jobs was somewhat less bracing. Complained Placement Director Eleanor Appel, "Students looking for those jobs feel they're getting absolutely nothing from this office because they see their classmates getting wined and dined and traveled and all they get is a legal service organization which is planning to come in and then cancels."

For these reasons, many students enthusiastically concurred with Professor Chayes's view that the law schools have an "affirmative duty . . . to correct some of these rigidities and structural disadvantages of our present placement system." Chayes proposed charging each private law firm a fee for the privilege of interviewing at Harvard Law School. "The proceeds could be used to finance interviewing from other organizations that are not as well fixed as the large law firms, or do not interview because they simply cannot afford to send a lawyer to Harvard or Yale or N.Y.U."

Instead Dean Sacks appointed Doug Phelps. The appointment

was notable because it was accompanied by Dean Sacks's conces-
sion that "legal aid and public defender offices, most government
offices, and some private offices cannot compete effectively
. . . If the school is to be neutral as to job choice, it must act to
make available public service jobs to interested students." A
measure of determination to re-establish the Law School's "neutrality as to job choice" was the Harvard Law School Fund's an-
nouncement in the summer of 1976 of its intention to raise $100,-
000 from alumni "in order to provide more help to students interested in alternatives to the traditional law career."

Phelps's nomination — although made with some reluctance — also symbolized a willingness to open the administration
to a different kind of voice. For not only was Phelps the most
qualified person available for the job, he was also a bona fide political activist. In a Law School administration most remarkable
for its conciliatory character, Phelps fit in about as naturally as
what Anais Nin once termed a spy in the house of love.

Eight years ago, Phelps began his circuitous path to the administration of Harvard Law School by being elected student government president of Colorado State University. At that time CSU
had outgrown its "cow college" origins, but a statute still on the
books technically required each student to work two hours a day
on an agricultural project, and the school was governed by the
state board of agriculture. Phelps soon proved to be about as
much of a Patrick Henry as either the board or the student body
could stand. When the board of agriculture proposed increasing
student fees to help pay for a new football stadium, Phelps had
the temerity to suggest that this was a peculiar way to reward a
team that had recently lost twenty-six consecutive games. The
issue of "student control over student activities" escalated until
Phelps led an occupation of the student center. For this he was
duly incarcerated, but the case was hurriedly dropped. How,
even the conservative *Denver Post* asked, can students illegally oc-
cupy the one building on campus that they, in fact, own? The university administration wasn't quite sure how to answer that question, but they placed Phelps on disciplinary probation for a year
anyway. At about the same time, he became, in a referendum that

Phelps initiated himself, the first CSU student government president ever voted out of office. "[The students] approved of my goals," recalls Phelps, "but not my tactics."

He accepted his defeat philosophically and spent much of the next year working as Rocky Mountain regional coordinator for the Vietnam Moratorium and on the National Supervisory Board of the National Student Association, formerly a CIA-funded organization, which had renounced its past with sufficiently vigorous opposition to the Vietnam War to earn a place on Nixon's enemy list.

In 1970, Phelps was a "risk admission" to Harvard Law School because of a lowly C average, achieved by earning A's in classes he had attended and F's in courses he had skipped to participate in activist politics.

His devotion to scholarship proved no greater at Harvard Law School. Near the end of his second year, he dropped out of school to run for Congress in Colorado against Wayne Aspinall, one of the Environmental Action's "dirty dozen." Shortly thereafter, he withdrew to support another environmentally concerned candidate and become New England coordinator of McGovern's Get-Out-the-Vote campaign.

His next move was to Amherst, Massachusetts. Hired by the Student Association at the University of Massachusetts to be its first full-time staff organizer and research coordinator, Phelps, in turn, asked prominent activist attorney Leonard Boudin to help students win the right to sue the university whenever necessary to represent student clients effectively. The university backed down and soon the student Legal Services Office was expanded to four full-time attorneys funded by the student body to represent students in all civil and criminal matters. Phelps himself became the staff coordinator of six full-time organizers grouped together in a separate Student Organizing Project. Among other things, it lobbied the state legislature to oppose cuts in the university's budget, sought passage of a student collective-bargaining bill, and helped establish the first student federal credit union in the country. By 1977, Phelps was hired by neighboring Hampshire College to teach a course called Community Organizing and Citizen Action.

But by then Phelps had been arrested twice more, been vindicated both times, and had filed suit against the Justice Department and the Federal Bureau of Investigation.

Shortly after the federal government cordoned off the town of Wounded Knee in South Dakota's Pine Ridge Indian Reservation on February 27, 1973, Phelps attended a meeting in Amherst sponsored by the Committee to Support Wounded Knee. Impressed, Phelps agreed to address the student body at Colorado State in late April. Before he arrived in Colorado, Frank Clearwater, an Indian supporter of the American Indian Movement, was fatally shot by federal agents during an exchange of gunfire at Wounded Knee. Phelps invited a gathering of 350 students at CSU to accompany him to Clearwater's funeral on the Rosebud Reservation, approximately 90 miles east of Wounded Knee.

The next day, when Phelps and several others crossed the Colorado border into Nebraska, they were arrested under the Federal Anti-Riot Act. On September 15, a grand jury refused to indict Phelps or eighteen other students. But a U.S. Attorney went before a second grand jury in Cheyenne, Wyoming, and secured an indictment against Phelps and two leaders of the American Indian Movement, alleging a conspiracy to aid and abet a riot and interfere with federal officers. A few months later the indictment was dismissed.

Phelps was not assuaged. Alleging that he had been illegally spied upon, harassed, intimidated, arrested, searched, and prosecuted as part of a Justice Department campaign to neutralize support for the American Indian Movement, he filed a $100,000 damages action against Attorney General William Saxbe and over one hundred other policy-making Justice Department officials and FBI agents.

Soon after being absolved of the Anti-Riot Act indictments, Phelps returned to Harvard Law School. He was graduated in November 1975. Even so, he was startled when Harvard Law School called him "out of the blue" to interview him for the post of Alternative Careers administrator. He hardly regarded himself as the traditional Harvard Law School type. Nor apparently did some of the faculty who attempted to block his appointment, allegedly because Phelps had been delinquent in handing in a written-work requirement.

But Phelps was impressed by the candor of Dean Sacks and Al Daniels, the recently appointed director of the Office of Placement and Counseling. Both acknowledged they had no fixed ideas about what an Alternative Careers administrator should do, and encouraged Phelps to design his own job.

Phelps proposed that he must be more than a job broker. As he put it in an interview, he had to "wage a crusade to educate and inform students that public interest work can be done, is being done, is vital." If students were not going to be "cowed" by their classmates "running around with suits and ties to talk to corporate-law firms," the Alternative Careers Office had to create sufficiently persuasive noncredit courses, symposia, guest luncheons, and interview opportunities to better educate students about the alternatives. "The Harvard Law School should encourage its students to begin from the premise that one's career is not the mere result of an effort to discover the future and find a place in it, but rather the product of one's effort to create the future," explained Phelps.

He is not sanguine that he will be able to persuade students to do so. In many respects, Phelps believes, the climate at the Harvard Law School militates against his work. "The missing ingredient is commitment. What can we do," he asks, "to get students to act on ideals?" If the type of "neutrality as to job choice" that Dean Sacks identified as the Law School's placement goal is to become a reality, Phelps believes that there must be a willingness to re-examine the total environment created by the Law School's academic program.

To support this contention, Phelps noted in his April 1977 remarks to the Law School's Visiting Committee that past surveys of first-year students suggest that as many as 50 percent hope for future careers in public-interest law, legal services, and government. In 1976–1977, 600 students registered their support of public-interest and law reform work by pledging $13,000 from their summer earnings to make it possible for other students to afford to take jobs in public-interest fields. Yet virtually none of these students was willing to take the risks of beginning a life-long career in public-interest work.

Phelps's argument is amplified by Mark Byers, Harvard Law School's first full-time vocational counselor. The Law School largely lacks the curriculum or faculty role models that instill students with a sense of choice about their careers. The size of the classes, the initially confusing nature of law, the intensity of the grading competition tend to disperse the students' sense of self-worth. "People," Byers elaborates, "come to grad schools with identities made up of new and tender tissue. It's all there, it's formed, but it is uncalloused, the hide hasn't toughened. Partly because that identity is still conditional on being in school . . . They still see a large part of their self-worth tied to how schools judge them.

"For a while there is this mystification. It's very hard to talk about law when you don't know about law . . . The content of the cases is about the real world but it's being discussed in an alien language . . . It's a regressive experience for a lot of competent people." For some, "participation in class becomes a problem. Unless you can somehow become involved, there's a slow wearing away of self-esteem." And then "like death and taxes, it all gets back to the *Law Review* competition. Only twenty-five can be 'the best there is.' People look a little askance at you if you try to fulfill any individualistic or humanistic goal. They say that's very nice, but there is still the final judgment."

During job interview season, Byers says, second- and third-year students come to him, saying, " 'I'm not on *Law Review* and I got mostly B's. What do I do? How do I differentiate myself?' There're no easy answers. You can assure them they're going to get jobs. But they want jobs with the leading firms . . . Their express values are anti-elitist, but they'd like to have that choice."

With few professors arguing otherwise, it's easy for law students to believe that legal-services work "isn't intellectually satisfying" and that the prestige and financial enticement of the larger firms are particularly ego-gratifying. "To the extent," Byers adds, "people feel guilty about being with corporate law firms they make an adjustment in their feelings about it . . . They worry that their suspicion of power or success is sour grapes, based on an incapacity to succeed. By reverse logic they tell themselves they have to function in a traditional setting so that they can then make a decision of free choice."

In such a psychological climate, can Doug Phelps's mission succeed? Certainly yes, to the extent that his enthusiasm and perseverance will undoubtedly increase the number of Harvard Law students attracted to public-service jobs. But it is equally certain that such a reform will be minimized unless the Law School makes a broader institutional commitment to public-service–oriented legal education.

For blacks and women the pressures of job interviewing at Harvard Law School are compounded by the difficulties of breaking down historic patterns of race and sex discrimination. Although Harvard Law School administers a compensatory admissions program for minority students, the School has yet to make a comparable moral commitment to helping these students in job placement. In 1976, 490 of the 545 private law firms that interviewed at Harvard Law School completed a voluntary employment questionnaire. These 490 firms included most of the giant city law firms in the country, the crème de la crème of the "Wall Street" or corporate-law bar. But only 27 of these firms had even one black as a partner; only 116, even one woman. Although women have begun to make significant inroads at the associate- or junior-lawyer level, over half the firms interviewing at Harvard Law School employed no blacks even as beginning attorneys.

In some regions of the country, exclusionary practices were particularly apparent. Among the forty-five firms interviewing from the southern states of Alabama, Florida, Georgia, North Carolina, South Carolina, Texas, and Virginia only 1 of the 986 partners employed by these firms was black; only 7, female. The twelve firms interviewing from Dallas, Texas, employed 402 attorneys as partners and associates — none was black. Nor were any of the 487 partners and associates employed by the ten Minneapolis–St. Paul firms interviewing at Harvard Law School. Nor any of the 247 attorneys employed by six firms from Cincinnati; nor of the 241 attorneys employed by seven firms from Oregon. In such major metropolitan areas as Los Angeles, only 16 of the

1739 attorneys from the thirty-seven interviewing firms were black. In Chicago, discrimination was especially virulent, with twenty-six of the forty interviewing firms employing no blacks, although the city itself in 1970 was 33 percent black.

If such historic patterns of race and sex exclusion are to be ended, presumably the largest, most prosperous firms would be best able to lead the way. However, an analysis of the hiring practices of the forty-eight firms interviewing at Harvard Law School that employed 100 or more attorneys reveals employment patterns nearly identical to the 442 smaller firms.*

Few problems so squarely illustrate the conflict between Harvard Law School's liberal institutional values and the School's powerful and generally conservative alumni. Prominently printed on the Placement Office's stationery is the caption: "The Harvard Law School has long been committed to a policy against discrimination in employment based on race, color, religious creed, sex or national origin. Accordingly, the School's facilities are available

* NUMBER OF WOMEN AND BLACKS EMPLOYED BY PRIVATE LAW FIRMS
INTERVIEWING AT HARVARD LAW SCHOOL, FALL 1976

	48 Firms Employing 100 or More Attorneys	442 Smaller Firms	All 490 Firms
Employed no black partners	39	434	463
Employed no women partners	23	351	374
Employed no black associates	9	238	247
Employed no women associates	0	85	85
Total number of partners	2789	8581	11,370
Number of black partners	9	18	27
Percentage of black partners	.32	.21	.24
Number of women partners	38	113	151
Percentage of women partners	1.4	1.3	1.3
Total number of associates	4150	8379	12,529
Number of black associates	95	154	249
Percentage of black associates	2.3	1.8	1.9
Number of women associates	565	1020	1585
Percentage of women associates	13.6	12.2	12.7

only to employers whose practices are consistent with this policy." In capital letters in the rules for using Placement Office services is the same requisite: "NO EMPLOYER MAY PRACTICE DISCRIMINATION IN ANY FORM BASED UPON SEX, RACE, COLOR, RELIGIOUS CREED OR NATIONAL ORIGIN." The Law School has had difficulties enforcing these standards.

Gail Bowman's was a well-known case in point.* When her travail began in October 1975, Gail was a second-year student at Harvard Law School seeking a job for the following summer in Chicago. An average student in Law School, Gail had been elected to the Law School Council as well as appointed as a member of the Student-Faculty Committee on Legal Education.

But Gail was a black and a woman. And that didn't seem to sit well with the hiring partners of the Chicago bar. Gail alleged that one pointedly inquired, "What conceivable purpose the Harvard Black Law Students Association could have besides social?" Gail recalled that a second exclaimed, "How come black students can't write?" Finally, in an October 8 interview with the prominent Chicago firm Kirkland and Ellis, something in Gail snapped. Questioned by John Morrison, a distinguished Harvard Law alumnus, Gail soon was convinced a job offer would not be forthcoming. Morrison said, reviewing Bowman's résumé, "Oh you did marvelously in high school [where Gail's grade-point average had been 3.98 on a 4.00 scale], you did very well in college [where Gail earned several scholarship awards], it is a pity you couldn't have done so well here . . ."

A few minutes later Gail explained to Morrison that she had been reluctant to interview with his firm because Placement Office statistics revealed that none of the firm's 133 attorneys was

---

* At the time the interview in question occurred, Ms. Bowman was one of several students helping research this book. The decision to file a complaint was purely her own. Her case is recounted because the facts concerning this incident were more ascertainable than in any other similar incident.

According to Professor Victor Brudney, chairman of the Law School's Placement Committee, there were approximately ten other formal complaints filed between 1971 and 1976 alleging race or sex discrimination. In each of these instances, the law firm subsequently either was excluded from using the Law School's placement facilities or was required "to alter its behavior" in a manner satisfactory to the Placement Committee.

black. Morrison quickly noted that the firm had until recently employed three black attorneys but each had left to take a position with a business corporation. Gail alleged that in the course of a subsequent detailed explanation, Morrison made three offensive remarks:

"The corporations just keep hiring our blacks out from under us. We just can't keep them. Well, you know the corporations have to meet their quotas just like we do."

"We once had a black gal working for us. She was just like you only she was short."

"In fact, you'll appreciate this, this is funny. The last black to leave our firm went to work for Clorox . . . you know. Now, isn't that funny, a black man working for a bleach company?"

Startled by Morrison's jocular manner, Gail was unsure how to respond. In an interview she recalled: "If I'd heard this on TV, I'd have forgotten it. But a job interview is special. My career is at stake. When he made the Clorox remark, I remember turning away and looking at the floor, thinking I really should say something."

It was a feeling that intensified. The next day Gail told Assistant Dean Russell Simpson that she'd felt insulted. Simpson explained to Bowman how difficult it was to demonstrate that such comments constituted a sufficient ground for a finding of discrimination. Simpson also discussed with her the most appropriate way to respond. If she wanted to put her thoughts in writing in the form of an informal complaint, Simpson urged Gail to come back and talk about it.

But neither Simpson nor any other official of the Law School in the ensuing eleven months of the controversy thought to ask Kirkland and Ellis why it was that a firm with over 130 attorneys in Chicago and another 40 in the District of Columbia had apparently employed only 3 black associates in its entire history. In light of the fact that all 3 had recently left, the Law School reasonably might have wondered whether the firm in fact was complying with its requirement of equal employment opportunity. Instead the Law School narrowed the broad question of Kirkland and Ellis's compliance with its employment rule to the consideration of who-said-what-to-whom in Gail Bowman's interview with John Morrison.

Initially dissatisfied with Simpson's reasoning, Gail met with Meldon Hollis, a friend who is also black and was president of the Law School's Council. Hollis, in turn, wrote to Kirkland and Ellis complaining of remarks by a representative of the firm that a "student found paternalistic and racially offensive." Replying for the firm, John Morrison vigorously denied that he or his firm had been "at all insensitive to the feelings of minority students . . . We believe that the facts relating to the interview disclose nothing more than an innocent misunderstanding." Before Hollis received Morrison's letter, both he and Gail heard rumors that a Kirkland and Ellis partner had telephoned the Law School and threatened to stop making contributions. A subsequent *Harvard Crimson* article quoted Wesley E. Bevins, Jr., the director of the Law School Fund, as stating that Morrison had expressed disappointment that Law School officials did not trust his word against Bowman's. Both Morrison and Bevins denied that any threat had been made to reduce contributions from Kirkland and Ellis attorneys. But Bevins acknowledged that Morrison was a Harvard Law School fund-raiser in the Chicago area and that Bevins on his own initiative had gone to Professor Victor Brudney, chairman of the Law School's Placement Committee, to attempt to work out a settlement of the dispute.

The Bevins-Brudney effort came to naught, but knowledge that the Alumni Fund Office had taken an interest in the case persuaded Bowman that the Law School was unsympathetic. On October 22, she filed an informal complaint with the Placement Office that not only described her interview with Morrison but also referred to the similar experiences of two other students who had interviewed with Kirkland and Ellis. Two weeks later Dean Simpson sent Gail a note inviting her to examine a letter he had prepared to mail to Kirkland and Ellis, urging the firm to take steps so that incidents similar to those charged in Gail's complaint would not recur.

Although Bowman was impressed by Simpson's personal concern, she felt this resolution of the case was far too "casual" and not sufficiently protective of the interest of students. She informed the assistant dean of her intention to file a formal complaint and completed the appropriate papers in early December.

In due course, the Law School's Placement Committee met to consider Bowman's complaint and Kirkland and Ellis's denials of her specific charges. The committee then voted to ask Dean Sacks to appoint an independent fact-finder to investigate the complaint. The dean subsequently persuaded University of Pennsylvania Law Professor Robert Gorman to act as fact-finder.

Gorman's charge was not clearly explained to Gail Bowman. Early in his research, Gorman acknowledged to Bowman that it would be difficult to prove one way or another who-said-what-to-whom in a one-on-one interview. He suggested his report could usefully deal as well with "the larger questions of sex and race discrimination in the interviewing and hiring process at Harvard." By this Gorman meant that he would generally explore the "overt and covert" signals that some employers give to minority students to persuade them to go away, and that he would try to make suggestions as to how the Law School could deal with such signals.

At the same time, Gorman viewed his "charge" from the Law School's Placement Committee to include an effort to mediate the dispute between Bowman and Kirkland and Ellis. After Gorman persuaded Morrison to prepare an apologetic letter, Gail became convinced that the professor did not intend to make a serious study of the firm's allegedly discriminatory employment practices — which she believed was the purpose of a formal complaint investigation. Her frustration mounted when Gorman filed a report in early September finding no violations of the rules of the Placement Office and recommending that no sanctions be imposed on either Morrison or Kirkland and Ellis. Not only did the report not consider Kirkland and Ellis's overall compliance with the Law School's standard of equal employment opportunity but the report's analysis of the three allegedly offensive remarks seemed to Gail one-sided. Gorman did not decide whether or not Morrison had said: "The corporations just keep hiring our blacks out from under us. We just can't keep them. Well, you know the corporations have to meet their quotas just like we do." Although Morrison originally denied having made such a statement, he subsequently acknowledged that he might indeed have made a comment similar to that which Gail alleged. But Gorman argued that it would have been all right had Morrison used the term "quota" since "that term was not used, and was not reasonably to be understood, to mean a ceiling upon employment of blacks but rather a floor, a minimum." The fact that Gail Bowman could find offensive a hiring law partner's assertion that his firm only hired blacks as a form of tokenism was not even considered.

The Harvard Law School Placement Committee later in September decided to thank Professor Gorman for his "efforts to conciliate" and mail Bowman a letter informing her that "several members of the Committee believe that you reasonably construed Mr. Morrison's behavior to give offense," and otherwise agreed with Gorman's conclusion that no sanctions should be imposed.

The Law School also instituted several reforms in its complaint procedures. But the School has not committed itself to a job placement affirmative action program comparable to its admissions affirmative action program. Rather, Alfred Daniels, the director of the Law School's expanded placement and counseling operations, referred to unpublicized meetings that he and Dean Sacks were holding with leading law firms to suggest steps that these firms could take to increase the hiring of minority students and women. More emphatically, Dean Sacks argues that Harvard Law School is doing more than any other law school of which he is aware to encourage affirmative action in employment. But he agreed that the Law School's efforts were limited to asking firms to disclose the number of minority and female attorneys they employ, administering complaint procedures, and holding the unpublicized meetings to which Daniels alluded. The Law School has not committed itself to programs to limit use of its placement facilities to firms that establish affirmative action goals nor to act in unison with other law schools to withdraw interview privileges from firms that unfairly have excluded minority students or women.

10

TOWARD A NEW MODEL FOR AMERICAN LEGAL EDUCATION

Blessed be the amending hand.

SIR EDWARD COKE

Like John Winthrop's characterization of the Massachusetts Bay Colony as "a City upon a Hill," Harvard Law School has dominated American legal education for close to one hundred years by the visibility of its example. So vast an improvement were Langdell's reforms over the earlier Litchfield type of school that early in the twentieth century Harvard emerged as a model for virtually every American law school.

It is the extent to which other law schools continue to emulate Harvard that constitutes the School's most significant influence and, paradoxically, the most significant weakness in American legal education. The near-universal emulation of Harvard Law School has limited the emergence of rival theories of legal education. This is dangerous to American law. No institutions endowed with the resources of a major law school exist that conduct critical studies of the American legal profession and the nation's laws and each year graduate students prepared for a career in law reform. Such reform-minded law schools could provide a wide-ranging challenge to the existing legal system. They could better insure that all economic interests are represented in adversarial and legislative proceedings. Today, isolated critical law professors only occasionally can perform this role.

Yet there is reason to believe that the homogeneity of American legal education will lessen.

The manifold complaints of law practitioners and law students — that legal education takes too long; that law graduates lack essential skills of their profession; that law faculties are hostile both to social science research and clinical training — reflect a more basic problem: The structure of American legal education is no longer adequate to prepare attorneys for an increasingly specialized profession.

In the century since Langdell first assumed his duties as dean of Harvard Law School, the character of the American legal profession has changed. Underlying Langdell's model was the assumption that all attorneys, whether in solo practice or in the large Wall Street type of firm, could be trained by a general legal education emphasizing the laws important to business associations and wealthy private clients. As late as World War II, this assumption remained valid. Fully 92 percent of attorneys practicing in 1948 worked in private law firms.

But by 1970, the percentage of practicing attorneys working in private law firms had shrunk to 77 percent, with 15 percent of the profession working full- or part-time for government and 13 percent for private industry. In 1977, the number of attorneys working for legal-services or public-interest organizations had increased to at least 7500, with Thomas Ehrlich, president of the federal Legal Services Corporation, projecting that his legal-services program alone would employ 6000 lawyers by the year 1979.

Accompanying the growth of poverty legal services were the beginnings of potentially far-reaching changes in the delivery of legal services to the middle-income classes. A recent study by the American Bar Association found that each year about 23 percent of adult Americans need legal advice, yet one of three adults had *never* consulted an attorney, and close to two-thirds have sought legal help only once or twice in their entire lives. For this reason, many thoughtful observers of the American legal profession predict that high-volume group-service mechanisms for providing legal representation to the middle class will constitute the most significant reform in the profession in the next quarter century. With the Supreme Court in the *Goldfarb* case having ruled that bar association minimum-fee schedules are a violation of the antitrust laws and subsequently having prohibited states from banning all advertising by attorneys, soon there may be significantly increased use of employee-group legal plans and firms specializing in high-volume, low-cost services for the middle-income range.

Simultaneous with the growing specialization of attorneys in private, government, poverty, and corporate employment sectors has been a parallel specialization within private practice. The post–World War II multiplication of laws and the increased complexity of legal practice has led to a growing tendency for private attorneys — whether in practice alone or in large law firms — to limit themselves to specific types of legal practice such as litigation, corporate, estate planning, copyright, or tax.

American law schools today fail to prepare attorneys for practice in any legal specialty. The current model of legal education is comparable to a system of medical education that prepares only general practitioners, leaving surgeons, psychiatrists, and medical researchers to gain the most important aspects of their training during their first jobs or by reading on the side.

Thomas Ehrlich and Jane Lakes Frank, deputy secretary of the cabinet, contend that this is a direct consequence of the outdated methodology employed by law schools:

> Few law schools, for example, offer more than an occasional course on legislation. Yet in recent decades statutory law has increased far more rapidly than judicial law. Law schools have not adapted their curricula to that reality.
>
> Until recently, the teaching of administrative law was almost a caricature of the problem. Judicial review of administrative action rather than the action itself was the exclusive focus of attention. One result is the absence of any conceptual framework for weighing the merits of rulemaking by administrative agencies or even by legislatures.
>
> Moves to correct the exclusive focus on individual con-

troversies are now occurring in many law schools. But we need a much larger effort along the lines of schools of public health. At least some law schools should be concerned with minimizing common legal problems of the public through aggregation.

Professor Louis Brown of the University of Southern California Law School has made a similar point. By focusing on law cases rather than on the prevention of litigation through legal planning, most law school courses misrepresent what private practitioners, in fact, do.

But improving the practical training of law students will be of small consequence unless it is accompanied by corresponding reforms in the doctrinal framework of individual law schools. In the same sense that public health schools represent a fundamental departure from medical schools, what is needed are public-law programs that define their purpose in fundamentally different terms from Harvard Law School's.

Few principles are more basic to American law than that of equal representation. Without access to legal processes, citizens' rights can neither be vindicated nor defended. Yet to this date only 7500 of the country's 450,000 lawyers serve the needs of the nation's 29 million poorest citizens, while another 140 million citizens generally are priced out of the market for legal services. Providing effective representation for the 80 to 85 percent of the nation's population that usually cannot afford a private attorney should be the basic ambition of public-law programs.

As Ehrlich and Frank suggest, radically different approaches to the delivery of legal services may be essential. Many legal problems such as divorce, probate, or real estate transfers might best be addressed by creating simpler procedures that do not require lawyers. With respect to such problems, the aim of a School of Public Law might be to persuade legislatures to favor "de-lawyerization" and provide shortened training programs for non-lawyer administrators of the new streamlined procedures. Other problems of the poor and middle-income classes might best be addressed by training attorneys expert in supervising class actions, where a single attorney makes a consolidated legal presentation on behalf of hundreds or thousands of accident victims or consumers. Still others might best be pursued by training attorneys to lobby at the legislative or administrative agency level. There, presently, the law profession has tolerated an imbalance in legal strength approximately equal, claims Federal Trade Commission Chairman Michael Pertschuk, to a baseball contest between the world series champions and the Bushwick Little League Irregulars. For other legal problems, the most difficult task of a School of Public Law might be to train attorneys to deal with clients and life circumstances highly different from those they have, themselves, experienced.

Some professors at existing law schools have addressed such questions. But the study of alternative systems for the delivery of legal services is unlikely to have a significant impact on a law student's overall education unless it is presented as a prominent aspect of a coherent theoretical and clinical training program. For example, besides emphasizing the importance of contact with future clients during legal training, Gary Bellow's proposed Law Institute will replace existing law courses with novel subjects such as "Law and the Market" (a study of inequality in American employment and consumption markets and the limits of current regulatory responses) and "Law and the Distributive System" (which will focus on the policies underlying the Internal Revenue Code and transfer-payment programs such as Social Security and Medicare). Only by training students to represent poverty and middle-income clients with a curriculum that highlights their position in American society is the importance of alternative legal delivery systems likely to be appreciated fully.

In the broadest sense, the most serious failings of American legal education are little divisible from larger questions of distributive justice. In aggregate, the greater than 160 American law schools serve as the gatekeeper to the nation's legal profession, helping shape its overall size, role, and ethics. For this reason, the most effective route to the reform of legal education is at the national level. When the issue is the character of the profession as a whole, the ameliorative efforts of any single school, or, for that matter, any single state, in the long run are unlikely to be significant.

Ultimately, to create schools of public law will necessitate loosening the pinions that state bar associations and the American Bar Association Standards for the Approval of Law Schools place on legal education. In a legal profession as large and diverse as that in the United States, it is absurd that few law schools specialize in training government, legal-services, or public-interest attorneys; that all leading law schools employ identical four-year college–three-year law school structures; that only 2 of 162 law schools could reasonably be defined as "clinical."

The research of curricular critic Jane Kelso suggests that one reason differentiation does not occur is that over 80 percent of the courses studied by law students are "bar or bar related." Current ABA Standards for the Approval of Law Schools further inhibit differentiation by specifying that law schools must require "either a bachelor's degree from a qualified institution or successful completion of three fourths of the work acceptable for a bachelor's degree," must offer "those subjects generally regarded as the core of the law school's curriculum," and "shall require" at least 1200 class hours, no more than 300 of which may be in field work.

As with medical licensing, the legal profession would benefit by creating different standards for attorneys preparing to practice in different fields such as poverty services. These standards should test clinical abilities as well as substantive knowledge. But they need not be measured outside the law schools. It is sufficient for a national conference of state and federal bar examiners to design national standards and to police the integrity of accredited law schools' course requirements and examinations.*

Creating new schools of public law probably would also require amendment of the ABA Standards for the Approval of Law

---

* Such a new licensing system for public lawyers, however, should occur simultaneously with reform in the bar exam standards for all attorneys. To assure the effectiveness of public attorneys they must receive a license of equal dignity to that received by private attorneys. Until such a time as all bar examination standards are revised, public lawyers will best be served by passing existing state bar examinations.

Schools. As with the concept of national bar standards for new types of law practice, one ambition should be to permit the most effective preparation for emerging fields within the law profession. But there are other considerations that also must be accommodated. Soaring tuition and living costs in recent years have re-emphasized the extent to which the length and expense of legal education largely limits the profession to the children of parents in the upper-income strata. The movement for clinical legal education has unsettled conventional wisdoms about adequate law training. Given the uncertainties about innovative law schools such as Antioch and the failure of curricular innovations such as Yale Law School's much-heralded Divisional Program, it would be unfortunate to replace the rigidities of the current ABA standards with standards equally rigid, however well intended.

Preferable would be a period of experimentation. In recent years there has been much discussion about two-year legal education. If the two-year structure means merely covering two thirds of present law school curricula in two-thirds the time, this is arguably among the worst possible alternatives to the present structure of legal education. Without improving the competence or education of graduating students, such a plan would press law schools back toward a generalized core curriculum. Assuming that such a two-year structure was begun as an alternative to present three-year law schools, financial pressures would likely drive most law schools toward a two-year format, with the unfortunate result that other alternative structures of legal education would become less feasible. Two-year legal education should only be encouraged within one of two possible contexts. National bar standards could formally recognize the difference between a two-year general law school education and three-year specialized training, so that attorneys entering the most complex legal fields would be required to receive more rigorous preparation. Or alternatively, a two-year course could be taught on an accelerated year-round basis rather than with the current eight-and-a-half- or nine-month academic calendar. Year-round training is already being employed by such innovative law schools as Antioch and Northeastern. A two-year program conducted in twenty-four consecutive months probably could cover the equivalent of 90 percent or more of present law school curricula. Additionally, students would save a year's living expense and be able to earn a living one year earlier, a monetary saving of as much as $7500 to $10,000 per student, even taking into account necessarily higher tuition charges and loss of summer earnings.

But neither variant of a two-year legal education alone is as promising as it might be if joined to other structural reforms. Columbia, Stanford, Duke, and other law schools have experimented with the option of admitting undergraduates after three years of college. Although such experiments have usually been adopted for the primary purpose of attracting talented college students before they are admitted to Harvard or Yale Law School, they do suggest that law schools might profitably experiment with two or three years of required undergraduate education succeeded by four-year law schools that provide students greater opportunity to study the law as a social theory and greater clinical experience.

The initial efforts of Gary Bellow to provide coordinated theoretical-fieldwork–ethics training is instructive. Arguably, if law schools were designed to prepare legal specialists rather than offer a Disneyland of second- and third-year elective courses and extracurricular activities, nearly any legal field could be taught more effectively. As a counterexample, consider the field of corporate law. Typically, a Harvard Law student interested in working for a private law firm will study seven separate corporate law–related courses in the last two years of law school, graduating with little training in such practical skills as memoranda drafting, no class that places the plethora of corporate laws in a more general political and economic framework, little background in the ethical problems typically confronted by corporate attorneys, and little or no sense of the business realities that accompany corporate practice.

Within the context of a specialized corporate law–related program, more illuminating approaches could be designed. Introductory courses could study the role of business firms in the American economy and the clash of political theories underlying our complex web of corporate-related laws. After accelerated classroom instruction in the rudiments of relevant corporations, accounting, tax, antitrust, and securities law, students could participate in simulated clinical exercises focusing on the transactions most characteristic of corporate-law practice. As in actual practice, students would approach a business problem such as incorporation, capital formation, or merger by simultaneously researching all relevant formal categories of law. Thus, instead of examining the law pertaining to a merger in separate courses in Antitrust, Corporations, Tax, Accounting, and Securities Regulation, the students could study an actual merger in detail, seeing how these various fields of law interact and jointly shape the wisest legal action. Initial steps toward this transactional approach have been taken by Harvard Law School's David Herwitz in his Business Planning course, and by Harvard Law Professor Victor Brudney and Yale Law Professor Marvin Chirelstein in their course on corporate finance, among others.

But the success of these efforts has been limited by the omission of related theoretical and ethical training and by high classroom faculty-student ratios. To deepen students' sense of the ethical and practical realities of corporate law, simulated transactions should be supervised by teams of law faculty and practicing attorneys, as in the National Institute for Trial Advocacy Program adopted by Professors Bellow and Keeton for use at Harvard Law School. Crucial would be the opportunity for each student to receive detailed criticism of written work. By careful selection of model transactions and visiting attorneys, the training most lawyers receive in the first year or two of corporate practice could be replicated during law school.

The corporate-law counterexample illustrates how great would be the need to develop new pedagogical materials and decrease faculty-student ratios before initiating schools of public law. Undoubtedly this will require new sources of funding.

Historians usually describe Abraham Flexner's 1910 report criticizing proprietary medical schools as the decisive event in twentieth-century medical education. It was an important report. But far more important to the reform of medical education was the subsequent decision of the Rockefeller Foundation to invest approximately $100 million — equivalent to more than one billion dollars in 1977 — to transform the standard medical school curriculum from four years of classroom work to two years of classroom and two years of clinical education.

Five decades of philanthropic support have been supplemented by larger federal programs. In 1975–1976, the federal government contributed $25,024,386 (52.5 percent) of the Harvard Medical School's $47,606,969 budget; private donors contributed $10,803,-953 (18.2 percent) — enabling the school to spend approximately $70,000 for each of its 664 students.

By contrast, in 1974–1975 Harvard Law School averaged expenditures of about $5500 for each of its 1600 students. That year federal contributions totaled $119,000 (1.4 percent) of the Law School's $8,718,000 budget.

For an American law school to adopt a novel program, let alone enable its students to afford soaring tuition and living costs, will require increased federal support. Current grant and loan programs patently are inadequate. After decades of seeming indifference to the financial facts of life, legal educators are now debating new proposals for federal loan assistance to graduate- and professional-school students. The most widely discussed of the contemplated alternatives is outlined in a 1976 memoradum prepared for the Law School Admission Council Committee on Student Aid, then chaired by Harvard Law School's Director of Financial Aid, Russell Simpson. The Simpson memo recommended nationalizing the tuition deferment plan then employed by Yale University. Students would be enabled to borrow up to 80 percent of total tuition and living expenses in the form of a federally guaranteed insured loan. Repayment would be made directly to the federal government after graduation through withholding of a portion of annual salary, similar to the withholding of income tax payments. Income levels would be taken into account by requiring "a progressive percentage of adjusted gross income and would be established to require no repayment at the [Bureau of Labor Statistics] low budget standard, a modest repayment at the BLS moderate standard, and an increasing repayment percentage above the BLS moderate standard." All repayment would be tax deductible.

The program is not intended to be redistributive. All students, whether in high-paying jobs or low-paying jobs, would be required to fully repay their loans, though those in low-paying jobs could take longer. It is at best a modest proposal. The annual tithing mechanism might slightly reduce poorer students' anxieties about borrowing. Federal guarantees might make private borrowers more willing to extend loans. But since the program excludes undergraduate students, it is not likely to appreciably reduce the inequality of educational opportunity. And since the program does not offer any incentive for law students to take low-paying or public-service jobs, it will not reduce the financial pressure for students to accept the highest-paying private law firm jobs.

Far more promising and egalitarian federal funding approaches are being ignored. It is characteristic of federal support of medical education that it is not like a charitable contribution but is rather in the form of a purchase of medical research or the hiring of medical students to provide clinical services to the poor. Medical schools have, in effect, sold the public services they can perform for public subsidy.

Law schools should do so as well. Even with the growth of the Legal Services Corporation, the legal needs of the poor and lower-middle classes will not be fully met. Law schools are a logical base for supplementary legal assistance. By allowing law students to work off a portion of the cost of their legal education in a legal-services office, both the law schools' impending financial crunch and the cost of delivering legal services to the poor might be reduced. A Health Manpower bill proposed in 1976 suggests a particularly efficient way in which this might be done. The proposed legislation would have required medical schools to admit 25 percent of their students pledged to serve four years providing primary medical care in medically deprived areas after graduation. In return, the students would receive a free medical education and the medical schools would receive capitation grants.

The advantages of a comparable legal services program are plain. The Legal Services Corporation would receive attorneys pledged to serve long enough to be fully effective. Law students and law schools would be relieved of some of their financial burden.

Further arrangements with the Legal Services Corporation might be effected in the area of law research. Late in 1976, the corporation began funding test projects to study alternative models for the delivery of legal services. Such studies suggest far more comprehensive research concerning the substance of American law, ethical standards, and the attorney's role, which the corporation ultimately might explore. Law school–affiliated research institutes could provide effective centers for such research. Alternatively, Thomas Ehrlich, president of the Legal Services Corporation, has proposed that a new institution, perhaps called the National Institute of Justice, "should undertake a coordinated attack on the range of recurring legal hassles that plague average citizens." Like its analogues, the National Institutes of Health and the National Institute of Mental Health, a justice institute might, in part, be staffed by professors on leave from teaching institutions.

Initial steps toward the formation of schools of public law could be undertaken at existing law schools. But the six-year deanship of Harvard Law School's current Dean, Albert Sacks, suggests that such innovations are likely to fail unless they are sharply segregated from traditional training programs. By remaining flexible, nondoctrinaire, and pluralist in his approach, Sacks has converted Harvard Law School into a laboratory for experimentation in such areas as clinical legal education, critical scholarship, alternative career placement, and faculty affirmative action. But the value of these experiments has been limited by the fact that they occurred within a School whose basic structure and psychological climate has not changed.

For an effective public-law program to be administered by a law school like Harvard would require the formation of the equivalent of a separate school to coexist within the larger school. Only by providing a public-law program with separate admissions procedures, curriculum, faculty, incentives, research funding, and placement apparatus could the morale problems that consistently have beset students in conventional law programs interested in training for public-service careers be significantly reduced. Further, it would be essential that graduates of public-law programs earn degrees equal in value to those of conventional law programs. The most important consequence of establishing new public-law programs would be to symbolize that public service is a law career of equal dignity to any other — but with distinctive intellectual and methodological requisites.

Students in a public-law program might be selected in part on the basis of past commitment to public-interest or community activities. They could study with a class of students sharing their convictions, led by teachers equally concerned with a critical view of existing law, focusing on a curriculum specifically designed to provide students with an intellectual framework and practical experience appropriate for government and public-service careers. It might be noted that under the Fourteenth Amendment such a separate-program approach may be one of the few lawful ways that leading law schools will be able to promote directly greater representation of racial minorities and the poor.

Faculty selection and role would remain the root of the problem. Underlying the vision of Langdell was the theory of the scholar-generalist. As the legend went, a Harvard Law professor could teach anything. And considering how much time Harvard Law professors spend grading papers, drafting law review articles, and engaging in various forms of extraschool activities, it is apparently still believed that they can do everything. It is this Faustian belief, as much as anything else, that has held back the internal reforms that individual American law schools can achieve.

Unlike medical schools, which decades ago began hiring faculty specialists in classroom instruction, clinical training, and original research, law schools generally have limited their faculty selections to law review editors who seem to possess potential classroom teaching ability. Only occasionally have members of the law review clubs proved to have equivalent talents in clinical training or writing and research.

Separate public-law programs might best be served by adopting a fundamentally different approach. As in medical schools, public-law programs might hire a core of professors primarily to teach classroom topics and perform research. These professors would be augmented by a much larger part-time faculty supervising clinical training. Such a division of labor would better rationalize faculty selection and training. Currently, young professors are chosen before their writing and teaching abilities are proven. In the future, research professors in public-law programs might be expected to earn advanced degrees in law or related social sciences and be hired primarily on the basis of an outstanding writing. Future part-time clinical instructors could be selected on the basis of their success in public-law programs or law practice. Since they would be part-time instructors, it would be easier for a school to sever relations with instructors who do not work out. By the same token, effective clinical instructors could be encouraged to earn advanced degrees and ascend to research and classroom teaching roles.

The employment of a large part-time faculty would have the further advantage of providing a public-law program the opportunity to create small classroom sections in all introductory courses. Even Dean Sacks acknowledges that "major needs in the first year [of Harvard Law School] are improvement of feedback and reduction of tension." Both needs could be substantially met in a public-law program by providing beginning law students regular opportunity to meet in small groups with junior faculty. Not only would these sections provide students the reassurance of direct human contact with instructors, but they would also expose them to far more detailed criticism of their oral and written work during the months they need constructive criticism most. Similar sections during the senior years of law study could provide a bridge between class and field work.

Crucially, a public-law program could change the patterns of rewards in law study. In the research for this book, no single fact emerged quite so jarringly as the pain many extraordinarily talented Harvard Law students experienced because of the first-year *Law Review* competition. Experience at Stanford and Northeastern Law Schools illustrates that this competition is simply not necessary to motivate beginning law students to study arduously. Far preferable would be a system of incentives such as early opportunities to serve in poverty-law clinics that vivified to future attorneys the fundamental ethical responsibilities of their profession. Even above Archibald Cox's "unreachable goal of excellence in disciplined intellectual performance," a public-law program should elevate the goal of improving the distribution of legal services in the profession it helps form. A law school that in its first-year training eliminated the law review grading competition and required students to spend some time in community legal services would not only be more humane but also might be more effective.

Harvard Law School graduate Oliver Wendell Holmes, Jr., in his 1886 address, "The Uses of Law Schools," explicitly stated what most law students and law scholars intuitively know: "You cannot make a master by teaching. He makes himself by aid of his natural gifts. Education, other than self-education, lies mainly in the shaping of men's interests and aims." For most students in law schools today, it is direct contact with clients and actual legal problems, not the *in terrorem* motivation of a law review competition, that feeds their enthusiasm for learning law. The earlier law students experience the law in action, the sooner will they recognize the importance of the law in books.

Over three centuries ago, Sir Edward Coke, upon completing one of the most ambitious works ever written about English law, contemplated the humility that any reformer must bring to his task:

> And for that we have broken the ice, and out of our owne industry and observation framed this high and honourable building . . . I shall heartily desire the wise hearted and expert builders . . . to amend both the method or uniformity and the structure it selfe, wherein they shall finde either want of windowes or sufficient lights, or other deficiency in the architecture whatsoever. And we will conclude with the aphorisme of the great lawyer and sage of

the law (which we have heard him often say) *Blessed be the amending hand.*

No serious student of law schools could fail to see that for close to a century there has been but one dominant intellectual structure of legal education, the high citadel of Langdell and his progeny. It is hoped that this small book has identified sufficient "want of windowes or . . . lights" to further the contemplation of an alternative structure.

ACKNOWLEDGMENTS

NOTES ON SOURCES

INDEX

ACKNOWLEDGMENTS

This study was supported by Ralph Nader. It began in June 1975, when Mark Green, Director of Nader's Corporate Accountability Research Group, hired Greg Smith, a second-year Harvard Law student, to prepare a preliminary report concerning Harvard Law School and American legal education. Greg Smith's report was completed in September 1975. Shortly thereafter, Nader and Green asked me to assume direction of the project. During the final week of September 1975, I made a trip to Cambridge and selected five Harvard Law students to begin research. They were: Lynne Bernabei, Elizabeth Bernstein, Gail Bowman, Bruce Howard, and Roger Howard. Alan Jakimo, a first-year student, was asked to work with the five students in designing and analyzing a survey of student opinion at Harvard Law School. Don Russell joined the research group in January 1976.

By July 1976, the seven students had assembled over 500 pages of typed interview notes based on some 200 interviews with Harvard Law School students and faculty. The efforts of Lynne Bernabei, especially, were crucial to the study. Not only did she prepare an extensive draft of what ultimately was rewritten to become the faculty chapter of this book, but she also prepared a draft on teaching methods and worked throughout the second year as a reader and critic of the rest of the book. During the first year, Bruce Howard served as student director of the project and did research on the history of Harvard Law School. Elizabeth Bernstein produced over 100 pages of analysis concerning grading, placement, and the culture of the Law School. Gail Bowman studied Northeastern Law School and grading, among other topics. Don Russell researched the governance of Harvard Law School. Roger Howard and Alan Jakimo administered the student opinion survey.

I began full-time work writing the book in July 1976. During the next thirteen months I conducted an additional 100 or so interviews at Harvard Law School, Antioch Law School, the London School of Economics, England's Warwick Law School, and the national headquarters of the Legal Services Corporation, the Council on Legal Education for Professional Responsibility (CLEPR), the Council on Legal Educational Opportunity (CLEO), and the Association of American Law Schools. During the second year of the project, I was aided by first-year Harvard Law student Paul Rosenberg, who served as my principal research associate, and Howard Learner, who conducted imaginative research concerning the Law School's placement facilities. Janet Shaffro, a student at Northeastern Law School, helped me complete the final check of the sources cited in the book. A total of close to 400 live or telephone interviews were a primary basis for the facts and opinions presented in this book.

Throughout the two years of our research, the administrators, faculty, and students of Harvard Law School, virtually without exception, were unstintingly generous in affording us the opportunity to interview them and study relevant background documents. Especially gracious was the cooperation provided by the Law School's administrators: Dean Albert Sacks, Assistant Dean Russell Simpson, Assistant Dean Patricia Lydon, Assistant Dean Alfred Daniels, Director of Placement Eleanor Appel, Alternative Careers Administrator Doug Phelps, Vocational Counselor Mark Byers, Registrar Mary Upton, Librarian and Professor Morris Cohen, Treasure Room Curator Edith Henderson, Senior Reference Librarian Leonard Klein, Reference Librarian Zena Friedman, Ellen Bernstein of the *Harvard Law School Bulletin,* and Dean Sacks's Executive Secretary, Donna Chiozzi.

A little better than half of the Law School's emeritus professors, professors, assistant professors, visiting professors, lecturers on law, and teaching fellows were interviewed. Particularly appreciated was the opportunity to conduct lengthy interviews with the following faculty members: former Dean and Emeritus Professor Erwin Griswold, Dean Albert Sacks, Emeritus Professor David Cavers, Emeritus Professor Paul Freund, Professor Robert Keeton, Professor David Shapiro, Professor Milton Katz, Professor — now Emeritus Professor — A. James Casner, Professor Louis Loss, Professor Clark Byse, Professor Roger Fisher, Professor David Herwitz, Professor Alan Stone, M.D., Professor Phillip Areeda, Professor Andrew Kaufman, Professor Derrick Bell, Professor Charles Fried, Professor Gary Bellow, Professor Frank Michelman, Professor Morton Horwitz, Professor Charles Nesson, Professor Lance Liebman, Professor Duncan Kennedy, Professor Detlev Vagts, Professor Roberto Unger, Professor Vern Countryman, Professor Alan Dershowitz, Professor Harry Edwards (who has since returned to the University of Michigan Law School), Assistant Professor Richard Parker, Assistant Professor Sally Neely, Assistant Professor Lewis Sargentich, Visiting Professor Robert Pitofsky, Stanford Law School Assistant Professor Richard Danzig, Michael Zander of the London School of Economics, Assistant Dean Jeanne Kettleson, Lecturer on Law David Rosenberg, Lecturer on Law Diane Lund, Lecturer on Law John Cratsley, Lecturer on Law Michele Hermann, and Teaching Fellow Susan Kupfer. The generous aid of the close to 200 other Harvard Law faculty members, administrators, students, and alumni who were interviewed during this research is also appreciated.

After the drafts of this book were completed, part or all of the manuscript benefited from the criticism of Erwin Griswold, Albert Sacks, Mark Green, Public Citizen Litigation Director Alan Morrison, Stanford Law School Assistant Professor Richard Danzig, Tulane University Provost Robert Stevens, Professor Duncan Kennedy, Professor Gary Bellow, Assistant Dean Jeanne Kettleson, Assistant Dean Russell Simpson, Assistant Dean Patricia Lydon, Professor Derrick Bell, Professor David Shapiro, Alternative Careers Administrator Doug Phelps, CLEPR President William Pincus, University of Southern California Law School Dean

Dorothy Nelson, and University of Southern California Law School Professor Louis Brown. Although the manuscript was significantly improved by their criticisms, none of these readers nor any of the students who worked with me on this project is ultimately responsible for either the facts or opinions presented in this work.

Finally, I wish to express my special gratitude to Ellen Joseph, my editor at Houghton Mifflin. Two years is a long time to work on a book, and the fresh perspective that she brought to the assembling of the final manuscript was particularly helpful. Any writer would benefit from having an editor as patient, exacting, and thoughtful as Ellen.

J.S.

NOTES ON SOURCES

MUCH OF THIS BOOK was developed from live interviews. In virtually every instance where an interview resulted in a quotation used in the final text, the person quoted was contacted, read, or shown the quoted material, and confirmed that it was accurate and in fair context. The balance of the data and opinions presented in this book was developed from written sources. As the following notes imply, a comprehensive study was made of Harvard Law School's records, including dean's reports, faculty reports, catalogs, the School's newspaper, the *Harvard Law Record*, and the School's magazine, the *Harvard Law School Bulletin*. Additionally, a careful study was made of relevant secondary sources concerning legal education. In a relatively small number of instances, the source of a fact or quotation is identified in the text itself — for example, on the first page of the Preface, a quotation from A. Z. Reed is identified as being from his work, *Training for the Public Profession of the Law*. The following notes are meant to identify the basis of all facts and opinions not derived from a live interview or previously identified in the text. Since these are not formal, numbered footnotes, conventional abbreviations such as "Ibid" or "supra" have not been used.

Chapter 1   Dissolution Then Drift: The Last Ten Years at Harvard Law School
(Pages 3–19)

Page

3   Greater than 160 law schools in the United States. James P. White, "Legal Education: A Time of Change," *American Bar Association Journal* 62 (1976): 355–58. Describes American Bar Association approval procedures and data as of March 1976.

3   20 or 25 "national" law schools. It has been conventional, at least since the Reed Report, to distinguish law schools that prepare their students for a "national" practice from those that prepare students for a more local practice. See A. Z. Reed, *Training for the Public Profession of the Law* (New York: The Carnegie Foundation for the Advancement of Teaching, Bulletin No. 15, 1921), pp. 414–20; and David F. Cavers, "Legal Education in a Forward-Looking Perspective," in *Law in a Changing America*, ed. Geoffrey C. Hazard, Jr. (Englewood Cliffs, New Jersey: Prentice-Hall, Inc., 1968), pp. 142–43.

4   Number of Harvard Law partners in named law firms. *1977 Martindale-Hubbell Law Directory* (Summit, New Jersey: Martindale-Hubbell, 1977), I: 3261B–3265B; III: 452B–454B; and IV: 225B–229B.

4   Griswold remark concerning practice in "the grand manner." Erwin N. Griswold address, "Hopes — Past and Future," to the Visiting Committee of Harvard Law School, Cambridge, Massachusetts, on April 18, 1970, pp. 16, 20. On file at the Harvard Law Library.

4   *Law Review* on desk by tenth of the month. *Harvard Law Record*, September 21, 1973, p. 5. Griswold added: "They never failed me during all the time I was Dean."

4–5   Descriptions of the sesquicentennial celebration. *Harvard Law Record*, October 5, 1967, p. 1; *Harvard Law School Bulletin*, November 1967, p. 18.

5   *Harvard Law Record* on "Blitzkrieg attack." *Harvard Law Record*, October 13, 1967, p. 1.

5   Byse recommends "intensive" questioning. *Harvard Law Record*, October 14, 1966, p. 5.

5   Byse makes his criticisms more personal. *Harvard Law Record*, February 1, 1968, pp. 14–15.

5   Griswold appoints Byse to chair committee. *Harvard Law Record*, November 10, 1966, p. 1.

5–6   Griswold leaves Harvard Law School. *Harvard Law School Bulletin*, November 1967, p. 5; *Harvard Law Record*, September 21, 1973, p. 5.

6   Griswold remarks, September 22, 1967. Reprinted in *The Path of the Law from 1967*, ed. A. Sutherland (Cambridge, Massachusetts: The Belknap Press of Harvard University Press, 1968), pp. 150–51.

6–7   Harvard University Hall occupation precipitates Law School all-night meeting. Accounts appear in Dean Derek Bok's letter to the alumni dated May 12, 1969, and the *Harvard Law Record*, April 24, 1969, p. 1.

7   325 students left because of draft. *Harvard Law Record*, November 21, 1968, p. 1.

7   Hundreds marched against war. See, for example, *Harvard Law Record*, October 23, 1969, p. 3.

7   Resolution after Kent State. *Harvard Law Record*, May 21, 1970, p. 1.

7   Before 1950, not one woman at Harvard Law School. Arthur E. Sutherland, *The Law at Harvard* (Cambridge, Massachusetts: The Belknap Press of Harvard University Press, 1967), pp. 319–20.

7   1967, class 4 percent female. *Harvard Law Record*, October 13, 1967, p. 7.

7   1975–1976, figure grew to 21 percent. *Harvard Law Record*, December 5, 1975, p. 3.

7   Similar increase in minority enrollment. *Harvard Law Record*, September 26, 1968, p. 6; *Harvard Law Record*, December 5, 1975, p. 3.

8   1960 and 1974 admissions competition. *Harvard Law Record*, November 13, 1970, p. 10; *Harvard Law Record*, March 17, 1975, p. 1. Correlative percentiles for 1960 and 1974 supplied by the Educational Testing Service.

8   Stone on interstudent relations. Alan A. Stone, "Legal Education on the Couch," *Harvard Law Review* 85 (1971): 415–16.

8   1964–1965 and 1975–1976 tuition increase. *Harvard Law Record*, February 15, 1970, p. 3, compared with *Harvard Law School Catalog 1975–1976*, p. 57.

8   $7000 per year budget estimate. *Harvard Law School Financial Aid Guide* (1976–1977), p. 25.

8   College Board estimates. Quoted in the *Washington Post*, June 1, 1976.

9   First female faculty and administrators. See articles in *Harvard Law Record*, January 28, 1972, p. 1; February 4, 1972, p. 3; March 17, 1972, p. 1; and January 26, 1973, p. 1.

9   Walter Leonard chosen. *Harvard Law School Bulletin*, December 1969, p. 19.

9   Parietal hours all but abandoned. *Harvard Law Record*, November 16, 1967, p. 3.

9   Epidemic of venereal disease. *Harvard Law Record*, May 4, 1973, p. 3.

9   Male students stop wearing coats and ties. Stone, "Legal Education on the Couch," p. 396, n. 25.

9   Saturday classes ended. *Harvard Law Record*, May 1, 1969, p. 11.

9–10   *Harvard Civil Rights-Civil Liberties Law Review* established. *Harvard Law Record*, March 7, 1968, p. 4.

10   1970 legal aid societies. *Harvard Law Record*, October 8, 1970, p. 1.

10   Voluntary-defender organizations. *Harvard Law Record*, November 6, 1969, p. 12.

10   Black Law Students Association. *Harvard Law Record*, September 26, 1968, p. 6.

10   Women's Law Association. *Harvard Law Record*, November 14, 1969, p. 5.

10   Environmental Law Society. *Harvard Law School Bulletin*, Spring 1975, p. 9.

10   Student-run law firm to advise governments. *Harvard Law Record*, December 3, 1971, p. 5.

10   Committee for Research on the Draft. *Harvard Law Record*, February 9, 1973, p. 13.

10   Underground newspaper. *Harvard Law Record*, November 19, 1970, p. 13.

10   Women win right to shower. *Harvard Law Record*, November 9, 1973, p. 4.

10   Bok proposals. Bok's first dean's report, reprinted in the *Harvard Law School Bulletin*, December 1969, p. 5.

10–11   Fried, on possibility higher learning too long. *Harvard Law Record*, March 11, 1971, p. 6.

11   Cavers, Keeton, Bator, and Breyer voice interest. David F. Cavers, memorandum, "A Design for an Experimental Accelerated Section" (June 1, 1971). On file with Professor Cavers; *Harvard Law Record*, October 15, 1973, pp. 3, 13.

11   Carrington Committee model curriculum. The Carrington Report was reprinted in Herbert L. Packer and Thomas Ehrlich, *New Directions in Legal Education*, Report prepared for The Carnegie Commission on Higher Education, Berkeley, California (New York: McGraw-Hill Book Company, 1972)

12 $175,000 grant. *Harvard Law Record*, February 6, 1969, p. 6.

12   Student determination to retain clinical training. See, for example, *Harvard Law Record*, February 1, 1972, p. 1.

12   Short-lived fund cutback. *Harvard Law Record*, October 1, 1971, p. 4; January 28, 1972, p. 1.

12   Griswold's icy admonition. *Harvard Law Record*, April 24, 1970, p. 1.

13   Protest-letter concerning grades. Described in *Harvard Law Record*, September 22, 1967, p. 6.

13   *Record* comments concerning grades. *Harvard Law Record*, September 22, 1967, p. 28.

13   Other students make a more telling point. *Harvard Law Record*, December 8, 1966, p. 1.

13   Grade "inflation." *Harvard Law Record*, September 12, 1968, p. 1.

13   Bok on "fuzzing it up." *Harvard Law Record*, September 12, 1968, p. 2.

13-14 Student report on "The Trouble with Grades." Reprinted in Faculty Committee memorandum, "Views on Grades and Related Matters at Harvard Law School" (March 19, 1969), on file at the Harvard Law School Library.

14   Bok agrees with thrust of criticisms. *Harvard Law Record*, March 6, 1969, p. 1.

14   Faculty Committee recommendations. *Harvard Law Record*, September 18, 1969, p. 1.

14   Cox dissent. Reprinted in Faculty Committee memorandum, "Views on Grades and Related Matters."

14-15 1969-1970 students just as upset. *Harvard Law Record*, October 2, 1969, p. 3; January 29, 1970, p. 3.

15   1972 protest after student suicide. *Harvard Law Record*, May 5, 1972, p. 1.

15   Next year, 69 percent, same preference. *Harvard Law Record*, January 26, 1973, p. 7.

15   *Record* editorial attacked. *Harvard Law Record*, February 9, 1973, p. 10; February 16, 1973, p. 7.

15   Law School Council also weighed in. *Harvard Law Record*, March 2, 1973, p. 2.

15   Cohen committee recommendations. *Harvard Law Record*, May 4, 1973, p. 1.

15   Faculty eliminates pass-fail grading. *Harvard Law Record*, September 21, 1973, p. 1.

15   Decision gnaws at students. See, for example, *Harvard Law Record*, December 7, 1973, p. 3.

15-16 Milbank, Tweed picketed. *Harvard Law Record*, January 30, 1969, p. 2.

16   Questionnaire to firms. *Harvard Law·Record*, September 18, 1969, p. 1; *Harvard Law School Bulletin*, December 1969, p. 19.

16   Pro bono opportunities. *Harvard Law Record*, November 22, 1974, p. 4; February 28, 1969, pp. 11-12. On the issue of *pro bono* practice generally, see Joel F. Handler, Ellen Jane Hollingsworth, Howard E. Erlanger, and Jack Ladinsky, "The Public Interest Activities of Private Practice Lawyers," *American Bar Association Journal* 61 (1975): 1388-94; and Sharon Tisher, Lynne Bernabei, and Mark Green, *Bringing the Bar to Justice: A Comparative Study of Six Bar Associations* (Washington, D.C.: Public Citizen, 1977), pp. 118-41.

16   Other firms fell in line. *Harvard Law Record,* September 12, 1968, pp. 1, 11; October 24, 1968, p. 3.

16   1973 employment figures. *Harvard Law Record,* December 7, 1973, p. 11.

16–17   Solomon criticism. Letter to *Harvard Law Record,* December 7, 1973, p. 11.

17   Kennedy "Polemic." Published in *Yale Review of Law and Social Action* 1 (Spring 1970): 71–90.

18   Byse on reforms. Clark Byse, address on "The Future of Legal Education at Harvard" on March 4, 1971.

18   Kirp on reforms. D. Kirp, "David Kirp Sees Few Major Changes," *Harvard Law School Bulletin,* April 1973, p. 36.

18–19   1975 Visiting Committee meeting. Described in report of the committee, which was distributed with Dean Sacks's list of actions taken in response. On file in the Office of the Dean, Harvard Law School.

Chapter 2   Laying the Foundations: The Law School Model of Christopher Columbus Langdell (Pages 20–46)

21   English origins of American legal education. A. Z. Reed, *Training for the Public Profession of the Law* (New York: The Carnegie Foundation for the Advancement of Teaching, Bulletin No. 15, 1921), pp. 11–24, 29–35; William Holdsworth, *A History of English Law* (London: Methuen & Co. Ltd., 1938), Vol. 12, pp. 77–100: Sir William Blackstone, *Commentaries on the Law of England* (Philadelphia: Rees Welsh & Company, 1897), Vol. 1, pp. 1–26.

21–22   Judge Reeve and the Litchfield school. Reed, *Training for the Public Profession,* pp. 128–133; Roscoe Pound, "The Law School," in *Development of Harvard University 1860–1929,* ed. Samuel Eliot Morison (Cambridge, Massachusetts: Harvard University Press, 1930), pp. 473–74; Horace L. Wilgus, "Legal Education in the United States," *Michigan Law Review* 6 (1908): 649; James Willard Hurst, *The Growth of American Law* (Boston: Little, Brown & Company, 1950), pp. 258–59.

22   Jefferson reorganizes William and Mary to include a chair in law. Reed, *Training for the Public Profession,* pp. 116–17.

22   St. George Tucker and the Blackstone tradition. Reed, *Training for the Public Profession,* p. 117.

22   James Kent's commentaries. Reed, *Training for the Public Profession,* p. 121.

23   Royall's bequest and the founding of Harvard Law School. Arthur E. Sutherland, *The Law at Harvard* (Cambridge, Massachusetts: The Belknap Press of Harvard University Press, 1967), pp. 32–43.

23   Between 1817 and 1829, Harvard Law School foundered. Suther-

land, *Law at Harvard*, pp. 43–91; Reed, *Training for the Public Profession*, pp. 137–40.

23–24 Justice Story at Harvard Law School. Sutherland, *Law at Harvard*, pp. 92–139; Reed, *Training for the Public Profession*, pp. 453–55.

24–25 Early antagonism to common law. Perry Miller, *The Life of the Mind in America, from the Revolution to the Civil War* (New York: Harcourt, Brace & World, Inc., 1965), pp. 105–7; Maxwell H. Bloomfield, *American Lawyers in a Changing Society 1776–1876* (Cambridge, Massachusetts: Harvard University Press, 1976), p. 139.

25 Perry Miller on Blackstone. Miller, *Life of the Mind*, pp. 224–25.

25–26 Over time, Kent and Story Americanized Blackstone. Roscoe Pound, *The Formative Era of American Law* (Gloucester, Massachusetts: Peter Smith, 1938); Miller, *The Life of the Mind in America*, pp. 131–32, 156–64; Morton J. Horwitz, "The Conservative Tradition in the Writing of American Legal History," *American Journal of Legal History* 17 (1973): 281–82.

26 Jacksonian reaction. Miller, *The Life of the Mind in America*, pp. 231–35. On general incorporation statutes, see Justice Brandeis in dissent, *Ligget* v. *Lee*, 288 U.S. 517, 541 (1933).

26 Bar admission standards eased. Reed, *Training for the Public Profession*, pp. 86–88.

26–27 Lincoln on own bar examination. Lawrence M. Friedman, *A History of American Law* (New York: Simon and Schuster, 1973), p. 525; Hurst, *Growth of American Law*, p. 282; Jack Nortrup, "The Education of a Western Lawyer," *American Journal of Legal History* 12 (1968): 294–305.

27 Harvard Law School, a holding operation before Civil War. Robert Stevens, "Two Cheers for 1870: The American Law School" in ed. Donald Fleming and Bernard Bailyn, *Law in American History* (Boston: Little, Brown & Company, 1971), pp. 418–19; Charles Warren, *History of the Harvard Law School* (New York: Lewis Publishing Company, 1908), Vol. 2, p. 348; Sutherland, *Law at Harvard*, pp. 148, 155–56; *The Centennial History of the Harvard Law School 1817–1917* (Harvard Law School Association, 1918), pp. 22–23; Reed, *Training for the Public Profession*, p. 140.

27 The janitor, John Sweetnam. Warren, *History of Harvard Law School*, vol. 2, pp. 317–18.

27–28 The textbook method. Friedman, *History of American Law*, p. 529.

28 Holmes's bitter recollection. Quoted in Catherine Drinker Bowen, *Yankee from Olympus* (Boston: Little, Brown & Company, 1944), p. 216.

28 Parsons and Washburn report school "eminently satisfactory." Warren, *History of the Harvard Law School*, Vol. 2, pp. 357–58.

28–29 Holmes and Sedgwick, unsigned article. "Harvard University. Law

School," *American Law Review* 5 (1870): p. 177. Their second unsigned article concerning the library was entitled, "The Law School of Harvard College," *American Law Review* 5 (1871): p. 563.

29 1869 Visiting Committee report prompts Parsons to resign. Warren, *History of the Harvard Law School*, Vol. 2, pp. 358–59.

29 1889 photograph of Langdell. Appears in Louis D. Brandeis, "Harvard Law School," *The Green Bag*, January 1889, pp. 10, 23.

29–30 Ames biography of Langdell. James Barr Ames, "Christopher Columbus Langdell," in *Great American Lawyers*, ed. William Draper Lewis (1909), Vol. 8, pp. 465–89.

30 1848, Langdell remarks to classmate, "I prefer to study." Samuel F. Batchelder, "Christopher C. Langdell," *The Green Bag* 18 (1906): 438.

30–31 Fifty years later, fellow student remembered Langdell. Quoted in Ames, "Christopher Columbus Langdell," pp. 470–71.

31 As a student, Langdell referred to as a genius. Batchelder, "Christopher C. Langdell," p. 439.

31 Langdell initially an unsuccessful lawyer. Batchelder, "Christopher C. Langdell," p. 439.

31–32 Langdell describes Harvard Law School finances and library. Christopher Columbus Langdell, "The Harvard Law School, 1869–1894," *Harvard Graduates Magazine* 2 (1894): 491–94.

32 Langdell's arrival at Harvard Law School. Warren, *History of the Harvard Law School*, Vol. 2, pp. 354–59, 362; Sutherland, *The Law at Harvard*, pp. 166–67. Eliot quoted in Ames, "Christopher Columbus Langdell," pp. 474–75.

32–33 Langdell restores examinations. Warren, *History of the Harvard Law School*, Vol. 2, p. 364; Franklin G. Fessenden, "The Rebirth of the Harvard Law School," *Harvard Law Review* 33 (1920): 497–98.

33 Simultaneous with investment as dean, Langdell imposes degree requirement. Warren, *History of the Harvard Law School*, Vol. 2, pp. 365, 379, 344, and 398; *The Centennial History of Harvard Law School*, Harvard Law School Association, 1918, p. 32. See also Langdell, "Harvard Law School," pp. 493–94.

33–35 Langdell's most controversial innovation. Warren, *History of the Harvard Law School*, Vol. 2, pp. 372–73; Fessenden, "Rebirth of the Harvard Law School," pp. 498–501; *The Centennial History of Harvard Law School*, p. 36; Batchelder, "Christopher C. Langdell," p. 440.

35 Attendance fell more than anticipated. Charles W. Eliot, "Langdell and the Law School," *Harvard Law Review* 33 (1920): 522; Fessenden, "Rebirth of the Harvard Law School," pp. 509–10; Warren, *History of the Harvard Law School*, Vol. 2, p. 520.

35 Rumors Langdell would be fired. Fessenden, "Rebirth of the Harvard Law School," p. 510.

35–36 Brandeis glorifies Langdell's method. Brandeis, "Harvard Law School," pp. 10, 19–20.

36 Langdell on law as a science. C. C. Langdell, *A Selection of Cases on the Law of Contracts*, 2d. ed. (Boston: Little, Brown & Company, 1879), Vol. 1, "Preface to First Edition," p. viii. See also "Teaching Law as a Science," *American Law Review* 21 (1887): pp. 123–25.

37 One law review wondered why equity studied as it existed prior to 1827. Review quoted in Friedman, *History of American Law*, p. 533.

37 Nathaniel Holmes resigns. Sutherland, *Law at Harvard*, p. 183.

37 Langdell campaigns for a new type of law professor. Langdell, "Teaching Law as a Science," p. 124; Warren, *History of the Harvard Law School*, Vol. 2, pp. 388–94; Sutherland, *Law at Harvard*, pp. 184–90; *The Centennial History of Harvard Law School*, Harvard Law School Association, 1918, p. 31.

38 With Washburn retired, old order passed away. Warren, *History of the Harvard Law School*, Vol. 2, p. 403.

38 Langdell presses for college-degree requirement. Fessenden, "Rebirth of the Harvard Law School," pp. 496–97; Warren, *History of the Harvard Law School*, Vol. 2, pp. 387, 394–95; Sutherland, *Law at Harvard*, pp. 168–70.

38–39 President Eliot delighted. Eliot quoted in Warren, *History of the Harvard Law School*, Vol. 2, pp. 396–97.

39 Board of Overseers outraged. Warren, *History of the Harvard Law School*, Vol. 2, p. 398.

39 Brandeis persuades Weld to contribute $90,000. Alpheus Mason, *Brandeis: A Free Man's Life* (New York: The Viking Press, 1946), pp. 64–65.

39 Financial support regularized through Harvard Law School Association. *The Centennial History of Harvard Law School*, p. 41.

39–40 Elective system begun. Reed, *Training for the Public Profession*, pp. 306–11; Warren, *History of the Harvard Law School*, Vol. 2, p. 438.

40 Harvard Law Review organized. *The Centennial History of Harvard Law School*, pp. 139–43.

40–41 Frankfurter on Law Review. Dr. Harlan B. Phillips, *Frankfurter Reminisces* (New York: Reynal & Company, 1960), pp. 17–18, 26–27.

41 Enrollment soared. Warren, *History of the Harvard Law School*, Vol.2, p. 520.

41 New admissions requirement provokes national outcry. Pound, "The Law School," p. 498; "The Law School," *Harvard Law Review* 7 (1893): pp. 231–33; Wilgus, "Legal Education," p. 654; "The Harvard Departure," *American Law Review* 28 (1894): pp. 68–69; *The Centennial History of the Harvard Law School*, pp. 50–51, 138–39; "Law School Dean's Report," *Harvard University Annual Report* (1908–1909), p. 168.

42 Growth of Law School under Langdell. The *Centennial History of Harvard Law School*, p. 46.

42 Langdell answered Brandeis question. Brandeis, "Harvard Law School," p. 10. See also James Bryce, *The American Commonwealth*, (New York: The Macmillan Company, 1894), Vol. 2, p. 623.

42–43 Early users of the case method. Warren, *History of the Harvard Law School*, Vol. 2, pp. 506–12.

43 Taft adopts Harvard Law School courses. Taft quoted in Warren, *History of the Harvard Law School*, Vol. 2, p. 509.

43 Beale goes to Chicago. Edward Levi, "The Political, the Professional and the Prudent in Legal Education," *Journal of Legal Education* 11 (1959): 464–67.

43–44 Most law schools adopted Harvard curriculum without a struggle. Stevens, "Two Cheers for 1870," in ed. Fleming and Bailyn, *Law in American History*, pp. 432–35; and A. Z. Reed, *Present-Day Law Schools in the United States and Canada* (New York: The Carnegie Foundation for the Advancement of Teaching, Bulletin Number 21, 1928), pp. 230–35.

44 Three-year course standard by 1920s. Reed, *Present-Day Law Schools*, p. 111.

44 Even practice of hiring full-time teachers made headway. Wilgus, "Legal Education," p. 663; Harold D. Hazeltine, "Law Schools and Legal Practitioners in the United States of America," *Law Quarterly Review* 34 (1918): 85, n. 4.

44 Only college-degree requirement not swiftly adopted: Stevens, "Two Cheers for 1870," p. 432. See also Jerold S. Auerbach, *Unequal Justice* (New York: Oxford University Press, 1976), p. 95.

44 Post–Civil War change in legal profession. Hurst, *Growth of American Law*, pp. 297–304; Friedman, *History of American Law*, pp. 549–61.

44 Harvard Law School considered most effective preparation for new corporate partnerships. See Brandeis, "Harvard Law School," especially pp. 22–23; Richard Ames, "Suggestions from Law School Graduates as to Where and How to Begin Practice," *Harvard Law Review* 27 (1914): 260–67.

44 Harvard Law School attracted students from every state. Pound, "The Law School," p. 499. At the same time, other law schools increasingly began hiring Harvard law graduates to teach. The "Law School Dean's Report" in the *Harvard University Annual Report* of 1925–1926 notes on p. 188 that 143 of the 605 professors in the previous Association of American Law School Directory were trained in whole or in part at Harvard Law School.

45 Increase in number of printed reports. Reed, *Training for the Public Profession*, pp. 373–74; Friedman, *History of American Law*, p. 539.

45 Langdell's theory brought order out of chaos. Hurst, *Growth of American Law*, p. 264.

45–46 Proliferation of casebooks. *The Centennial History of Harvard Law School*, pp. 80–83; Warren, *History of the Harvard Law School*, Vol. 2, p. 512.

46 Beale's theory. Described and criticized in Jerome Frank, *Law and the Modern Mind* (New York: Brentano's, 1930), pp. 48–56.

46 Williston's work as draftsman. Bruce Wyman, "Samuel Williston, Professor of Law," *The Green Bag* 23 (1911): 613–18; Sutherland, *Law at Harvard*, pp. 214, 217.

46 The influence of the American Law Institute. Friedman, *History of American Law*, p. 582; Calvin Woodard, "The Limits of Legal Realism: An Historical Perspective," in Herbert L. Packer and Thomas Ehrlich, *New Directions in Legal Education*, Report prepared for The Carnegie Commission on Higher Education, Berkeley, California (New York: McGraw-Hill Book Company, 1972), p. 345; and Thurman Arnold, *Fair Fights and Foul* (New York: Harcourt, Brace, & World, Inc., 1951), p. 58, who pungently observed, "Professors were recruited from all over the United States — principally from Harvard, which was then the high church of abstract legal theology."

46 Pound on a taught tradition. Pound, *Formative Era of American Law*, p. 164.

Chapter 3   The Early Assaults on the Citadel, and Roscoe Pound (Pages 47–67)

47–48 Holmes impressed by Langdell's method. Oliver Wendell Holmes, "The Uses of Law Schools," in *Collected Legal Papers* (London: Constable & Company, Ltd., 1920), p. 45.

48 But Holmes never considered teaching methods important. Holmes, "The Path of the Law," in *Collected Legal Papers*, p. 200.

48 Holmes deprecated Langdell's contracts casebook. Unsigned book note written by Oliver Wendell Holmes, *American Law Review* 14 (1880): 233–35.

48 Law's source is not "brooding omnipresence in the sky." See Jerome Frank, *Law and the Modern Mind* (New York; Brentano's, 1930), p. 55.

48 No "transcendental body of law . . ." Justice Brandeis, quoting Holmes in *Erie Railroad Company* v. *Tompkins*, 304 U.S. 64, 79 (1938), which overruled Story's decision in *Swift* v. *Tyson*.

48–49 To master law, must habitually consider the forces outside of it which make it what it is. Unsigned book note written by Oliver Wendell Holmes, pp. 233–35.

49 Holmes attempts to redirect the path of the law. Holmes, "Path of the Law," pp. 187, 195.

49-50 Pound on sociological jurisprudence. Roscoe Pound, "The Need of a Sociological Jurisprudence," *The Green Bag* 19 (1907): 612.

50 Legal Realists. See, generally, Karl N. Llewellyn, "Some Realism about Realism — Responding to Dean Pound," *Harvard Law Review* 44 (1931): 1222–64; Frank, *Law and the Modern Mind;* William Twining, *Karl Llewellyn and the Realist Movement* (London: Weidenfeld and Nicolson, 1973); and G. Edward White, "From Sociological Jurisprudence to Realism: Jurisprudence and Social Change in Early Twentieth-Century America," *Virginia Law Review* 58 (1972): 999.

50-51 Columbia Law School functional approach. Herman Oliphant, ed., *Summary of Studies in Legal Education* (New York: Columbia Law School, 1928); Brainerd Currie, "The Materials of Law Study," published in an abridged version in Herbert L. Packer and Thomas Ehrlich, *New Directions in Legal Education,* Report prepared for The Carnegie Commission on Higher Education, Berkeley, California (New York: McGraw-Hill Book Company, 1972), pp. 296–312.

51 Twining on Llewellyn casebook. Twining, *Karl Llewellyn,* p. 132.

51 Columbia Law faculty sought to render unique service. Oliphant, ed., *Summary of Studies,* pp. 20–21.

51-52 Wechsler recalls being law student. Herbert Wechsler, "The Law Schools and the Law," *Harvard Law School Bulletin,* July 1967, p. 4.

52 By 1932 Columbia Law School had added functional courses. See "Report on Certain Recent Tendencies in Law School Teaching," by a committee of the faculty of Harvard Law School (1932), especially pp. 17–22, 26–30, and 70–72. Report on file in Harvard Law Library.

52-53 Yale Law School's Institute of Human Relations. Twining, *Karl Llewellyn,* pp. 67–68.

53 Stevens on intellectual excitement for the few. Robert Stevens, "Two Cheers for 1870: The American Law School" in ed. Donald Fleming and Bernard Bailyn, *Law in American History* (Boston: Little, Brown and Company, 1971), p. 481.

53 Harvard Law School report. "Report on Certain Recent Tendencies in Law School Teaching," by A Committee of the Faculty of Harvard Law School (1932), pp. 52–64. On file in Harvard Law Library.

53-54 Frank assault on Langdell's methods. Jerome Frank, "Why Not a Clinical Lawyer-School," *University of Pennsylvania Law Review* 81 (1933): 907–23; and "A Plea for Lawyer-Schools," *Yale Law Journal* 56 (1947): 1303–44. Frank was not alone in making this criticism. See also A. Z. Reed, *Training for the Public Profession of the Law* (New York: The Carnegie Foundation for the Advancement of Teaching, Bulletin No. 15, 1921), p. 281; *Present Day Law Schools in the United States and Canada* (New York: The Carnegie Foundation for the Advancement of Teaching, Bulletin Number 21, 1928), pp. 216–19; and Karl N. Llewellyn, "On What Is Wrong with So-Called Legal Education," *Columbia Law Review* 35 (1935): 651–78.

55   1938 Survey of National Resources Committee. Cited in, James Willard Hurst, *The Growth of American Law* (Boston: Little, Brown & Company, 1950, pp. 255, 316).

56   Lewis criticizes the bar. Lewis quoted in Jerold S. Auerbach, "Enmity and Amity: Law Teachers and Practitioners, 1900–1922," in ed. Donald Fleming and Bernard Bailyn, *Law in American History*, pp. 557–58.

56   Brandeis on law school professorship. Brandeis quoted in Auerbach, "Enmity and Amity," p. 558.

56   Why Frankfurter joined Harvard Law School faculty. Dr. Harlan B. Phillips, *Frankfurter Reminisces* (New York: Reynal & Company, 1960), p. 167; Auerbach, "Enmity and Amity," p. 554.

56   Opening of Legal Aid Bureau. The *Centennial History of Harvard Law School 1817–1917* (Harvard Law School Association, 1918), pp. 151–52.

57   Increase in student body. Compare Charles Warren, *History of the Harvard Law School*, Vol. 2, p. 520, with Arthur E. Sutherland, *The Law at Harvard* (Cambridge, Massachusetts: The Belknap Press of the Harvard University Press, 1967), p. 232.

57   Pound background. Sutherland, *Law at Harvard*, pp. 236–37; and David Wigdor, *Roscoe Pound* (Westport, Connecticut: Greenwood Press, 1974).

57–58   Leach observes Pound tolerated no opposition. Wigdor, *Roscoe Pound*, p. 249.

58   Pound supported Brandeis nomination. Alpheus Mason, *Brandeis: A Free Man's Life* (New York: The Viking Press, 1946), p. 164.

58   Pound seeks Brandeis advice after Frankfurter criticized. Phillips, *Frankfurter Reminisces*, pp. 168–70.

58–59   Pound, Chafee, and the "heresy trial." Wigdor, *Roscoe Pound*, pp. 236–38; Arthur E. Sutherland, *The Law at Harvard* (Cambridge, Massachusetts: The Belknap Press of Harvard University Press, 1967), pp. 250–59; Phillips, *Frankfurter Reminisces*, pp. 175–77.

59   Pound considers resigning. Wigdor, *Roscoe Pound*, pp. 235–36.

59   Pound terms Wigmore attack "a disgrace." Wigdor, *Roscoe Pound*, pp. 249–50.

59   Others objected that Pound did not combat anti-Semitism. Wigdor, *Roscoe Pound*, p. 251.

59–60   Pound's trip to Austria and its aftermath. Wigdor, *Roscoe Pound*, pp. 250–51.

60   "As the 1930s wore on, the law school creaked a bit." Sutherland, *Law at Harvard*, pp. 288–89.

60–61   By conventional criteria, Pound a successful dean. Sutherland, *Law at Harvard*, pp. 262–70, 277–78; and Wigdor, *Roscoe Pound*, p. 248.

61   Pound sought to study law in action. Law School Dean's Report, *Harvard University Annual Report* (1925–1926), p. 190.

62   1925–1927 fund drive. Sutherland, *Law at Harvard*, p. 269.

62–63   Why Pound opposed radical changes in curriculum. Dean's Report, *HU Annual Report* (1920–1921), pp. 203, 208; Wigdor, *Roscoe Pound*, pp. 253–54; Dean's Report, *HU Annual Report* (1927–1928), pp. 202–4; Dean's Report, *HU Annual Report* (1915–1916), p. 142; Dean's Report, *HU Annual Report* (1930–1931), p. 204.

63   Throughout Pound's deanship no important revisions of the curriculum. See "Report on Certain Recent Tendencies in Law School Teaching," by A Committee of the Faculty of Harvard Law School (1932), pp. 70–72.

63–64   Pound article on Legal Realists. See Llewellyn, "Some Realism about Realism," 1222–64.

64   Professors leave to serve in New Deal. Sutherland, *Law at Harvard*, p. 287.

64   28 of 43 *Law Review* editors served in federal government. Jerold S. Auerbach and Eugene Bardach, "Born to an Era of Insecurity: Career Patterns of *Law Review* Editors, 1918–1941," *American Journal of Legal History* 17 (1973): 12; Jerold S. Auerbach, *Unequal Justice* (New York: Oxford University Press, 1976), p. 181.

64–66   1934–1935 curriculum report. The Committee on the Curriculum, *Committee on the Harvard Law School, 1935*. On file at the Harvard Law Library. See also Sutherland, *Law at Harvard*, pp. 283–86. The curriculum report included memoranda written by the Student Advisory Group, Felix Frankfurter, the *Law Review*, and David Riesman.

66   Pound resigns. Sutherland, *Law at Harvard*, pp. 296–97.

67   Landis and his innovations. Dean's Reports, *HU Annual Reports* (1938–1939), p. 229; (1939–1940), pp. 227–28, 234; (1941–1942), p. 226; (1945–1946), p. 345. See also Esther Lucile Brown, *Lawyers, Law Schools and the Public Service* (New York: Russell Sage Foundation, 1948), p. 130.

Chapter 4   Synthesis: Griswold's Deanship (Pages 68–92)

68–71   On Landis generally. Arthur E. Sutherland, *The Law at Harvard* (Cambridge, Massachusetts: The Belknap Press of the Harvard University Press, 1967); Erwin N. Griswold, "James McCauley Landis — 1899–1964," *Harvard Law Review* 78 (1964): 313–28; and Victor S. Navasky, *Kennedy Justice* (New York: Atheneum, 1971), pp. 378–91.

68 Landis imbibed the faith of Frankfurter and Brandeis. The quotation is from James B. Thayer, "The Origin and Scope of the American Doctrine of Constitutional Law," *Harvard Law Review* 7 (1893): 129. Biographer Liva Baker has termed this Felix Frankfurter's favorite description of the Court's institutional role, "a map to Frankfurter's judicial mind." Liva Baker, *Felix Frankfurter* (New York: Coward-McCann, Inc., 1969), pp. 223-24.

69 Roosevelt considered appointing Landis to Supreme Court. Baker, *Frankfurter*, p. 201.

71-72 Griswold deanship. Much of the material on Griswold deanship was derived from interviews with Harvard Law School faculty members. But two published accounts of his deanship should be noted: Henry Friendly, "Erwin N. Griswold — Some Fond Recollections," and the other tributes appearing in *Harvard Law Review* 86 (1973): 1365-79; and Sutherland, *The Law at Harvard*.

72-73 Griswold's defense of school desegregation decision. E. Griswold, address, "The Function of the Supreme Court," before the City Club, Cleveland, Ohio, December 7, 1957. All of Griswold's speeches and written statements cited in this manuscript are on file at the Harvard Law Library. On desegregation, see similar statements of Griswold in address, "Fools Rush In," before the State Bar of California, Coronado, California, October 9, 1958; statement filed by Griswold with the Internal Security Subcommittee on the Judiciary of the United States Senate, March 3, 1958; and brief reprinted in *Minnesota Law Review* 34 (1950): 289-329.

73 Griswold criticism of the bar. Erwin N. Griswold, address, "The Legal Profession," before the Cleveland Bar Association, on December 9, 1953.

73 Griswold on function of the dean. *Harvard Law Record*, November 6, 1946, p. 3.

73 Griswold on preparing for bar exams. See, for example, *Harvard Law Record*, November 30, 1949, p. 1.

73-74 Griswold on how to take law school tests. *Harvard Law Record*, May 3, 1950, p. 2.

74 Griswold on lavatory soap. *Harvard Law Record*, July 9, 1947, p. 2.

74 Griswold on basic values of legal education. Law School Dean's Report, *Harvard University Annual Report* (1948-1949), p. 422; *Harvard Law Record*, November 6, 1946, p. 3.

74-75 Disinterest in broad social questions. See, for example, Dean's Report, *HU Annual Report* (1951-1952), p. 491.

75 Surge in enrollment after war. See Dean's Reports, *HU Annual Reports* (1945-1946), p. 345; (1949-1950), p. 451, and (1946-1947), p. 398. See also *Harvard Law Record*, March 23, 1949, p. 1.

75-76 Griswold's program for the Law School. Dean's Report, *HU Annual Report* (1947-1948), pp. 377-99.

76 Griswold recalls state of Harvard Law School Fund. Erwin N. Griswold, address, "Hopes — Past and Future," to the Visiting Committee of Harvard Law School, Cambridge, Massachusetts (April 18, 1970), p. 6.

76–77 Griswold regularized fund collecting. See *Harvard Law Record,* March 15, 1962, pp. 11–12; and *Harvard Law Record,* November 1, 1962, p. 13. On answering correspondence, see "Erwin Griswold as Seen by His Staff," *Harvard Law Review* 86 (1973): p. 1378.

79 G. E. White on consensual decision making. G. Edward White, "The Evolution of Reasoned Elaboration: Jurisprudential Criticism and Social Change," *Virginia Law Review* 59 (1973): 279–302.

80–81 Fuller committee report. Besides the report itself, see Dean's Report, *HU Annual Report* (1945–1946), pp. 342–43; "Preliminary Statement of the Committee on Legal Education at the Harvard Law School" (March 1, 1947); *Harvard Law Record,* February 16, 1949, and February 23, 1949; Dean's Report, *HU Annual Report* (1948–1949), pp. 420–22; and "Report of the Committee on the Third Year Program" (November 17, 1949). On file at the Harvard Law Library.

82 Problem method in Hart-Sacks materials. See David F. Cavers, "In Advocacy of the Problem Method," *Columbia Law Review* 43 (1943): 449–61 for views of one early advocate of method.

82 Concept of "reasoned elaboration." See White, "Evolution of Reasoned Elaboration," pp. 279–302.

83–84 Debate on Casner report and development of Legal Institutions course. Individual faculty members' views are included as a supplement to the 1960 Curriculum Report. See also Dean's Report, *HU Annual Report* (1960–1961), p. 322.

85–89 The Lubell incident. Almost all of the material included was developed from approximately thirty separate interviews. Griswold, Kaufman, the Lubells, and other principals in the incident were given the opportunity to comment on the drafts of this section — as was customary in each instance in this book when material that was critical, or could be construed as critical, of an individual was included. See also articles on the Lubells in *Harvard Law Record,* April 1953 issues; William Manchester, *The Glory and the Dream* (Boston: Little, Brown & Company, 1974), pp. 491–92, 562, and 627; and views of Griswold and Leach included in collection of memoranda concerning the Lubells (March 1953), on file in the Harvard Law Library.

89–90 Surge of applicants after World War II. Dean's Report, *HU Annual Report* (1955–1956), pp. 392–93; Sutherland, *Law at Harvard,* p. 316.

90 Griswold on maintaining high standards. Dean's Report, *HU Annual Report* (1957–1958), pp. 321–22.

90 Students on "rat race." *Harvard Law Record* articles, March 12, 1947, p. 2; March 11, 1954, p. 2; and March 31, 1955, p. 2. See also Louis A. Toepfer, "Marks and the Man," *Harvard Law School Bulletin*, April 1958, p. 4.

90–91 Bleicher on corporate-law practice. S. Bleicher, quoted in "In Praise and Blame, Comments on Harvard Law School by Graduating Students" (1966). Memorandum on file in Harvard Law Library.

91–92 Post-World War II job placement. See *Harvard Law Record*, October 9, 1969, p. 3; May 3, 1950, p. 1; April 12, 1956, p. 3; October 18, 1962, pp. 1 and 9; February 25, 1960, p. 15; November 19, 1964, p. 5; and October 28, 1965, p. 15 (re: Nixon). See Dean's Reports, *HU Annual Reports* (1949–1950), p. 472, and (1961–1962), p. 409.

Chapter 5   Admissions: A Meritocracy for the Few (Pages 95–121)

95–101 Kenneth Krohn's story. Derived from interviews and the complaint Krohn filed in Federal District Court.

101 State bar requirements. See *Rules for Admission to the Bar* (St. Paul, Minnesota: West Publishing Company, 1975).

101 137 law schools require college degrees. *Law Schools and Bar Admission Requirements — A Review of Legal Education in the United States —* Fall 1975, published by the American Bar Association, Section on Legal Education and Admissions to the Bar (Chicago).

101 20 or so "national" law schools. Throughout the manuscript, references to "national law schools" are based on data derived from 1975–1976 catalogs of the law schools of: Boston College, University of California at Berkeley, University of California at Los Angeles, University of Chicago, Columbia, Cornell, Duke, Georgetown, George Washington, Harvard, Hastings, University of Michigan, University of Minnesota, New York University, University of Pennsylvania, Rutgers (Newark), University of Southern California (1974–1975 catalog), Stanford, University of Texas, University of Virginia, University of Wisconsin (Madison), and Yale.

101 Only 24 percent of teenagers earn college degrees. W. Vance Grant and C. George Lind, *Digest of Educational Statistics*, 1975 Edition, United States Department of Health, Education, and Welfare, Education Division, (Washington: U.S. Government Printing Office, 1976).

101–102 1976–1977 College Board estimates. *Washington Post*, June 1, 1976. See also *Newsweek*, April 26, 1976, p. 63; Caroline Bird, *The Case Against College* (New York: D. McKay Co., 1975) pp. 35–36; The Carnegie Commission on Higher Education, *Higher Education: Who Pays? Who Benefits? Who Should Pay?* (McGraw-Hill Book Company, 1973), p. 179.

102 Purpose of Education Act. See *1972 Congressional Quarterly Almanac*, pp. 385–87; and David Mundell and Jay K. Wright, "The Federal Basic Educational Opportunity Grant Program: Some Issues in Program Design," *Harvard Journal on Legislation* 10 (1973): 431–66.

102 1969–1973 enrollment data. U.S. Bureau of the Census, "Characteristics of American Youth: 1974" (1975), and Current Population Reports, Series No. 51, p. 23; Jerome Karabel, "Community Colleges and Social Stratification," *Harvard Education Review* 42 (1972): 521–62.

103 1972 and 1976 income data respecting Harvard Law School students. According to the Bureau of the Census, Current Population Report on Consumer Income (Series P-60, No. 105), June 1977, p. 43, 5.8 percent of American families earned $25,000 or more in 1972 and 18.2 percent earned $15,000 to $24,999. To determine the percentage of families earning $21,000 or more, the Bureau suggested that I extrapolate a proportionate figure through a "linear interpolation." Employing the alternative standard statistical technique, which is called a "Paretto interpolation," the percentage of families earning $21,000 or more would have seemed smaller. I employed an identical approach to the 1976 data. According to Harvard Law School's Registrar, 544 students registered in 1976. The Office of Financial Aids informed me that of the 284 students who received financial aid, 81 had parents with income of $30,000 or more. If the assumption is made that 90 percent of the parents of the 260 students who did not receive financial aid also had income of $30,000 or more, it would appear that 315 students (or 58 percent of the class) had parents with income of $30,000 or more. According to the Bureau of the Census, Current Population Report of Consumer Income (Series P-60, No. 107), September 1977, p. 2, 1.9 percent of all American families earned $50,000 or more and 15.9 percent earned $25,000 to $49,999 in 1976. To determine the percentage of families earning $30,000 or more, I again employed a "linear interpolation." The Office of Financial Aids also informed me that 80 students of the 284 who applied for financial aid had parents with income of less than $14,999. Assuming that none of the parents of the students who did not apply for financial aid had incomes below $14,999, it would appear that 80 students of a class of 544 (or 16 percent) had parents who earned income of less than $14,999. According to the September 1977 Current Population Report, p. 2, 50.3 percent of all American families earned less than $14,999 in 1976.

103 Data from other law schools similar. Robert Stevens, "Law Schools and Law Students," *Virginia Law Review* 59 (1973): 689. See also Seymour Warkov, *Lawyers in the Making: The 1961 Entrants to*

American Law Schools, Report No. 96 (Chicago: National Opinion Research Center, University of Chicago, 1963), p. 59; Leonard L. Baird, *The Graduates: A Report on the Plans and Characteristics of College Seniors* (Princeton: Educational Testing Service, 1973), p. 24; and Law School Admission Council (hereinafter LSAC), *Annual Council Report* (1973), p. 654.

104 1975, 85,000–90,000 sought admission; 39,038 were admitted. James White, "Legal Education: A Time of Change," *American Bar Association Journal* 62 (1976): 356.

104 LSAT validity studies in general. Patricia W. Lunneborg and Donna D. Radford, "The LSAT: A Survey of Actual Practice," *Journal of Legal Education* 18 (1966): 313–24; LSAC, *Annual Report* (1974), p. 362; LSAC, *Annual Report* (1972), pp. 423–31; Kelso, "What We Know and Don't Know About the LSAT Test: A Review of LSAT Test Development and Research by One Who Is Not an Expert," LSAC, *Annual Report* (1972), pp. 517, 518; amicus curiae brief of the Association of American Law Schools in *DeFunis* v. *Odegaard,* 416 U.S. 312 (1973) reprinted in *DeFunis* v. *Odegaard and the University of Washington, The Record,* ed. Ann Fagan Ginger (Dobbs Ferry, New York: Oceana Publications, 1974), Vol. 2, p. 621.

105 Law school admission decisions solely on "numbers." See, for example, LSAC, *Annual Report* (1972), p. 90; and John A. Winterbottom, "Comments on A Study of the Criteria for Legal Education and Admission to the Bar: An Article by Dr. Thomas M. Goolsby, Jr." *Journal of Legal Education* 21 (1968): 78. Section 503 of the American Bar Association Standards for the Approval of Law Schools requires the use of the LSAT or its equivalent. There is no equivalent. Not surprisingly, the ABA's *1975–1976 Prelaw Handbook* reported (pp. 26–29) that all 160 of their approved law schools require applicants to take the LSAT test; 144 require college grades to be processed by the Law School Data Assembly Service.

105 History of law school admission processes. See Arthur E. Sutherland, *The Law at Harvard* (Cambridge, Massachusetts: The Belknap Press of Harvard University Press, 1967), p. 322; Robert R. Ramsey, Jr., "Law School Admissions: Science, Art, or Hunch?" *Journal of Legal Education* 12 (1960): 503–20; Charles E. Consalus, "The Law School Admissions Test and the Minority Student," *University of Toledo Law Review,* 1970 volume, pp. 501, 508; and amicus curiae brief of the Association of American Law Schools in *DeFunis* v. *Odegaard,* reprinted in *DeFunis* v. *Odegaard,* ed. A. Ginger, p. 619.

106 LSAT only predicts ability to do well on law school examinations. The Educational Testing Service has begun to attempt to measure the correlation between LSAT scores and professional skills in its ongoing "Becoming a Competent Lawyer" study.

106   Jencks on college examinations. Christopher Jencks, *Inequality* (New York: Basic Books, Inc., 1972), p. 57.

106   "Gut" courses receive as much credit as academic courses. LSAC, *Annual Report* (1975), pp. 407-9.

106   Stephenson on "cake" courses. D. Grier Stephenson, Jr., "Why Law Schools Shouldn't Play the Numbers," *American Bar Association Journal* 59 (1973): 492.

106   1965 Report on grades and adult achievement. Donald P. Hoyt, "The Relationship between College Grades and Adult Achievement," ACT Research Report No. 7 (Iowa City, Iowa: American College Testing Program, Research and Development Division, 1965), pp. 49-50.

107   True aptitude and earned score vary by thirty points in two out of three cases. See, for example, LSAC, *Annual Report* (1972), p. 106.

107   Test less reliable at leading law schools. LSAC, *Annual Report* (1972), p. 90.

107   Griswold on Law School Admission Test. Amicus curiae brief of the Association of American Law Schools in *DeFunis* v. *Odegaard*, reprinted in *DeFunis v. Odegaard*, ed. A. Ginger, p. 620.

107   1973 study of LSAT scores for blacks and whites. Educational Testing Service, "Law School Admission Test, Comparisons of Black Candidates and Chicano Candidates with White Candidates" (Princeton, 1973), p. 2. See also S. Warkov, *Lawyers in the Making*, especially p. 21.

107   Educational Testing Service denies cultural bias. Robert L. Linn, "Test Bias and the Prediction of Grades in Law School," *Journal of Legal Education* 27 (1975): 293-323.

107-108   Jencks on cognitive score inequality. Jencks, *Inequality*, p. 109.

108   Douglas on LSAT. *DeFunis* v. *Odegaard* 416 U.S. 312, 340 (1973). (Justice Douglas, in dissent.)

108   LSAT scores increase second and third times test taken. LSAC, *Annual Report* (1975), p. 433.

108   Sexton's LSAT centers. *Harvard Law Record*, January 30, 1976, p. 4.

109-110   Association of American Law Schools on diverse society. Amicus curiae brief in *DeFunis* v. *Odegaard*, reprinted in *DeFunis v. Odegaard*, ed. A. Ginger, p. 624. See similar views of Harvard University in their amicus brief, reprinted in the same volume.

111   Winograd on hiding behind the numbers. Peter A. Winograd, "Law School Admissions: A Different View," *American Bar Association Journal* 59 (1973): 864.

112   Less than 1 percent of students in 145 law schools black in 1964-1965. Robert M. O'Neil, "Preferential Admissions: Equaliz-

ing Access to Legal Education," *University of Toledo Law Review*, 1970 volume, pp. 281–321.

112 Harvard among first law schools to open doors to blacks. Walter W. Leonard, *"DeFunis* v. *Odegaard:* An Invitation to Look Backward," *Black Law Journal*, 3, No. 3 (1973): 226, *n.* 19.

112 Before 1963, a typical Harvard Law class had one black. See, for example, *Harvard Law Record*, September 26, 1968, p. 1.

112 Harvard Law School's 1965 program. Louis A. Toepfer, "Harvard's Special Summer Program," *Journal of Legal Education* 18 (1966): 443–51.

112 UCLA program. See description of UCLA's and several other programs in American Bar Association Law Student Division Report, *Equal Rights Project Report* (Chicago: American Bar Association, 1972). See also American Bar Association, *Report of the Task Force on Professional Utilization* (1973), pp. 3, 5; Cruz Reynoso, Jose Alvarez, Albert Moreno, Mario Olmos, Anthony Quintero, and William Soria, "La Raza, the Law, and the Law Schools," *University of Toledo Law Review*, 1970 volume, pp. 809–46; and Rennard Strickland, "Redeeming Centuries of Dishonor: Legal Education and the American Indian," *University of Toledo Law Review*, 1970 volume, pp. 847, 861–66.

112–113 CLEO. See Nancy Fulop, "The 1969 CLEO Summer Institute Reports: A Summary," *University of Toledo Law Review*, 1970 volume, pp. 633, 635; Kenneth J. Burns, Jr., "CLEO: Friend of Disadvantaged Minority Law Students," *American Bar Association Journal* 61 (1975): 1483–86; *Prelaw Handbook, The Official Guide to Law Schools*, prepared and published by the Association of American Law Schools and the Law School Admission Test Council, Washington, D.C., 1975–1976, pp. 26–29; and Sanford Jay Rosen, "Equalizing Access to Legal Education: Special Programs for Law Students Who Are Not Admissible by Traditional Criteria," *University of Toledo Law Review*, 1970 volume, pp. 321–76.

113 Money is barrier to minority admissions. See LSAC, *Annual Report* (1974), pp. 393–94; and *Flanagan* v. *President and Directors of Georgetown College*, 417 F. Supp. 377 (D.D.C., 1976).

114–118 *DeFunis* case. See record, briefs, and decision in *DeFunis v. Odegaard*, ed. A. Ginger. See also Martin Fassier, "Another DeFunis, Reviving the Quota Question," *Juris Doctor*, May 1976, pp. 15–23.

119 Data on Harvard Law School students admitted. *Harvard Law Record*, December 5, 1975, p. 1 and November 22, 1974, p. 1; *Harvard Law School Bulletin*, May 1968, p. 9. These figures parallel national figures. See Robert Stevens, "Law Schools," especially p. 691; and LSAC, *Annual Report* (1975), pp. 23–24.

120 Kennedy on emotions at Yale Law School. Duncan Kennedy,

"How the Law School Fails: A Polemic" *Yale Review of Law and Social Action*, 1 (Spring 1970): 79.

120   Law students' reasons for coming to law school seem confused. Stevens, "Law Schools," pp. 551, 616, and 623–24; and *Harvard Law School Bulletin*, May 1968, p. 14.

120–121   Underlying psychological conflict. Warkov, *Lawyers in the Making*, especially p. 13; Baird, *The Graduates*, especially p. 41; Stevens, "Law Schools," pp. 551, 632, 634, and 579; Alan A. Stone, "Legal Education on the Couch," *Harvard Law Review* 85 (1971): 398–401. Our own survey was administered to fifty students chosen at random from each of the three classes attending Harvard Law School in the fall of 1976. Of the 150 students who received our 13-page questionnaire, 27 of the 50 first-year students, 31 of the 50 second-year students, and 15 of the 50 third-year students, responded with fully completed questionnaires. The primary purpose of the survey was to give students an opportunity to suggest research themes and express the intensity of their feelings about widely discussed aspects of legal education and proposals for reform. Throughout this book answers to particular questions are cited only when consistent with other similar surveys — such as that of Stevens — or when they are suggestive of intensely held sentiments.

Chapter 6   Faculty Selection and Faculty Role: The Root of the Problem (Pages 122–136)

122   Riesman on significance of faculty selection. Riesman, "Some Observations on Legal Education" in ed. Arthur Sutherland, *The Path of the Law from 1967* (Cambridge, Massachusetts: The Belknap Press of Harvard University Press, 1968), p. 174.

123   Griswold on "vicious circle." Erwin N. Griswold, "Intellect and Spirit," in *The Path of the Law*, pp. 151–52.

124   Frank criticizes lack of experienced practitioners. Jerome Frank, "A Plea for Lawyer-Schools," *Yale Law Journal* 56 (1947): 1314.

124   Hutchins scorned how-to-do-it law school. Robert Hutchins, "The University Law School," in *The Law School of Tomorrow*, ed. David Haber and Julius Cohen (New Brunswick, New Jersey: Rutgers University Press, 1968), pp. 5–24.

125–126   Bergin on "men divided." Thomas F. Bergin, "The Law Teacher: A Man Divided Against Himself," *Virginia Law Review* 54 (1968): 638.

127   1970 House subcommittee testimony. See Steven H. Leleiko, "Legal Education —Some Crucial Frontiers," *Journal of Legal Education* 23 (1971): 502–27.

127–128   Women's Law Association complaint and Sacks's response that charge was groundless. Alice W. Ballard and Rosalind A. Lazarus, "Women v. Harvard: Admissions and Placement," in the *Harvard Law School Yearbook* (1973): 18–21; *Harvard Law Record*, January 26, 1973, p. 1.

128   Owens and Lund urged greater affirmative action in 1973. *Harvard Law Record,* March 9, 1973, p. 3. See also *Harvard Law Record,* November 12, 1971, p. 2, regarding argument that Harvard University was bound by 1964 Civil Rights Act and subsequent Executive Orders because it received federal funds.

129   Bell threatened to resign in November 1974. *Harvard Law Record,* November 22, 1974, p. 1.

129   Bok contends Bell complaint was not legitimate. *Harvard Law Record,* December 13, 1974, p. 1.

130   Griswold called trial practice "a lark." *Harvard Law Record,* February 13, 1958, p. 2.

132   Cavers organized meetings on research needs of fields of American law. David F. Cavers, memorandum, "A Report to the Faculty Concerning Research Activities in the Harvard Law School and Some of the Problems They Present" (October 1, 1955), on file with Professor Cavers at Harvard Law School.

133   Student lack of contact with professors. *Harvard Law Record,* April 18, 1975, p. 8. On unpopularity of large classes, see *Harvard Law School Bulletin,* May 1968, p. 16, and Robert Stevens, "Law Schools and Law Students," *Virginia Law Review* 59 (1973): 591.

134   Educational Testing Service survey. Leonard L. Baird, *The Graduates: A Report on the Plans and Characteristics of College Seniors.* (Princeton: Educational Testing Service, 1973), p. 118.

134   October 1968 editorial. *Harvard Law Record,* October 24, 1968, p. 8.

134   Bok on an important by-product. "Report on the Second Year Curriculum," by the Continuing Committee on Legal Education (1967), p. 26.

34-135   Origins of teaching-fellow program. Sutherland, *Law at Harvard,* p. 323; Richard Field, "The Teaching Fellows," *Harvard Law School Bulletin,* November, 1966, p. 13.

135   Law School report on Fried experiment. "Report and Recommendations of the Legal Methods Study Committee," Harvard Law School (April 22, 1977), p. 33.

136   "Nine [classroom] hours a week." R. S. Stubbs, II, "Only Nine Hours a Week!" *Journal of Legal Education* 21 (1969): 566–68.

Chapter 7   Curricula: Beyond the Hairy Hand (Pages 137–148)

138   Legal education abroad. See W. R. Lederman, "Canadian Legal Education in the Second Half of the Twentieth Century," *University of Toronto Law Journal* 21 (1971): 141–61. *The Legal Systems of England,* a pamphlet prepared for the British Information Services by the Central Office of Information, London, England (1976), pp. 30–31; John Henderson McNeill, "Legal Education in England," *American Bar Association Journal* 57 (1971): 673–75; Philip A. Thomas and Geoff M. Mungham, "English Legal Education: A

Commentary on the Ormrod Report," *Valparaiso Law Review* 7 (1972): 87–131; Rainer M. Kohler, "The Study and Practice of Law in West Germany," *American Bar Association Journal* 54 (1968): 992–94; and Dr. Wilfried Schluter and William O. Morris, "A Comparison of Legal Education in the United States and West Germany," *West Virginia Law Review* 72 (1970): 317–25.

138–139 Griswold criticism. *Harvard Law Record*, October 6, 1955, p. 1.

139 Kingman Brewster believes for many education takes too long. Quoted in Caroline Bird, *The Case Against College* (New York: D. McKay Co., 1975), p. 159.

139 Packer and Ehrlich report. Herbert L. Packer and Thomas Ehrlich, *New Directions in Legal Education*, Report prepared for The Carnegie Commission on Higher Education, Berkeley, California (New York: McGraw-Hill Book Company, 1972), pp. 77–78.

139 Carrington proposal. Reprinted in Packer and Ehrlich, *New Directions*.

139 1951, only 16 percent of law schools required degree; 1948, only 37 percent of lawyers had degrees. John C. York and Rosemary D. Hale, "Too Many Lawyers? The Legal Services Industry: Its Structure and Outlook," *Journal of Legal Education* 26 (1973): 1–31.

139–140 Current college degree requirements. *Law Schools and Bar Admission Requirements, A Review of Legal Education in the United States — Fall 1975*, published by the American Bar Association, Section on Legal Education and Admissions to the Bar (Chicago, Illinois), pp. 48–53.

140 Hutchins proposal. Robert Hutchins, *The Higher Learning in America* (New Haven: Yale University Press, 1936), especially pp. 16–18.

140 Same curricula as Langdell required. See E. G. Gee and D. Jackson, *Following the Leader? The Unexamined Consensus in Law School Curricula*, a pamphlet published by the Council on Legal Education for Professional Responsibility (New York, 1975).

141 Carrington Report recommendations. Reprinted in Packer and Ehrlich, *New Directions*, pp. 110–13.

141–142 1975–1976 catalog survey of twenty law schools. The law schools were: Antioch, Boston University, University of California at Berkeley, University of Chicago, Columbia, Cornell, Duke, Georgetown, George Washington, Hastings, University of Michigan, New York University, Northeastern, University of Pennsylvania, Rutgers (Newark), University of Southern California (1974–1975 catalog), Stanford, Texas, University of Wisconsin (Madison), and Yale.

143 1973–1975 Harvard Law School enrollment figures. Supplied by the Law School's registrar.

144 Fiduciary relations and trusts permeated by "ethical presuppositions." Dr. Harlan B. Phillips, *Felix Frankfurter Reminisces* (New York: Reynal & Company, 1960), p. 19.

144–145 Kaufman, Keeton, and Rosenberg memorandum. Andrew Kaufman, Robert Keeton, and David Rosenberg, memorandum to the Committee on Legal Education, Re: Required Instruction in Professional Responsibility (October 30, 1974), p. 2. On file with Professor Kaufman.

145–146 20 leading law schools similar. Same law schools as listed above in notes to this chapter. See also James Huffmann, "Is the Law Graduate Prepared to Do Research?" *Journal of Legal Education* 26 (1974): 520–27; and Irvin C. Rutter, "A Jurisprudence of Lawyers Operations," *Journal of Legal Education* 13 (1961): 301–99.

146 Burger conclusion. Warren E. Burger, "The Special Skills of Advocacy: Are Specialized Training and Certification of Advocates Essential to Our System of Justice?" *Fordham Law Review* 42 (1973): 234.

146 Bazelon characterization. Quoted in Ralph Nader and Mark Green, eds, *Verdicts on Lawyers* (New York: Thomas Y. Crowell Company, 1976), pp. 120–21.

146 Second Circuit proposal. See "New Admission Rules Proposed for Federal District Courts," *American Bar Association Journal* (1975) 61: 945.

147–148 Advocates of two-year law school plans. See Burger, "The Special Skills of Advocacy," *Fordham Law Review* 42 (1973): 232; *New York Times*, August 12, 1976, p. 18; R. Stevens, "Two Cheers for 1870: The American Law School," in *Law in American History*, ed. Donald Fleming and Bernard Bailyn (Boston: Little, Brown and Company, 1971), p. 544; William Pincus, "A Small Proposal for a Big Change in Legal Education," *University of Toledo Law Review*, 1970 volume, p. 913; Bayless Manning, "Law Schools and Lawyer Schools — Two-Tier Legal Education," *Journal of Legal Education* 26 (1974): 379–84; Packer and Ehrlich, *New Directions*, p. 98; and David F. Cavers, "A Proposal: Legal Education in Two Calendar Years," *American Bar Association Journal* 49 (1963): 475–81.

Chapter 8   Teaching Methods: Birds Sing Better Than Books Know How (Pages 149–175)

154–155 Llewellyn on case instruction. Karl N. Llewellyn, "The Place of Skills in Legal Education," *Columbia Law Review* 45 (1945): 351.

155–156 Miller incident. The account of this incident was based on interviews with the participants, including Miller. But see also *Harvard Law Record*, November 21, 1975, p. 1.

156–157 Kennedy's "Polemic." Duncan Kennedy, "How the Law School Fails: A Polemic," *Yale Journal of Law and Social Change* 1 (1970): 76.

157 Two generations of legal scholars have joined Frank. See, for example, Lon Fuller, "What the Law Schools Can Contribute to the Making of Lawyers," *Journal of Legal Education* 1 (1948): 195; and Quintin Johnstone, "Student Discontent and Educational Reform in the Law Schools," *Journal of Legal Education* 23 (1970): 266.

158–159 Llewellyn criticism of case class. Karl Llewellyn, "The Current Crisis in Legal Education," *Journal of Legal Education* 1 (1948): 215.

159 Bickel on Socratic method. Bickel quoted in Martin Mayer, *The Lawyers* (New York: Harper & Row, 1967), p. 85.

159 Packer and Ehrlich on large classes. Herbert L. Packer and Thomas Ehrlich, *New Directions in Legal Education,* Report prepared for The Carnegie Commission on Higher Education, Berkeley, California (New York: McGraw-Hill Book Company, 1972), p. 32. On similar point, see Walter Gellhorn, "The Second and Third Years of Law Study," *Journal of Legal Education* 17 (1964): 1–15.

159–160 Stevens survey. Robert Stevens, "Law Schools," *Virginia Law Review* 59 (1973), 699–701. See also Erwin N. Griswold, "Law Schools and Human Relations," *Chicago Bar Record* 37 (1955): 199–208; and Louis M. Brown, "Teaching the Low Visible Decision Processes of the Lawyer," *Journal of Legal Education* 25 (1973): 386–402.

160 Frank excoriates "library" law schools. See Jerome Frank, "A Plea for Lawyer-Schools," *Yale Law Journal* 56 1947: 1303–44.

160 Cantrall's controversial article. Arch M. Cantrall, "Law Schools and the Layman: Is Legal Education Doing Its Job?" *American Bar Association Journal* 38 (1952): 907–10, 972.

160–164 Pincus and CLEPR. Description derived from interview and the president's reports in the Council of Legal Education for Professional Responsibility's (CLEPR) first three biennial reports; William Pincus, "Clinical Legal Education in the United States, 1968–1975," *Australian Law Journal* 49 (1975): 420–27; William Pincus, "Clinical Training in the Law School: A Challenge and a Primer for the Bar and Bar Admission Authorities," *St. John's Law Review* 50 (1976): 479–93; William Pincus, "Legal Education in a Service Setting," in CLEPR, *Clinical Legal Education for the Law Student: Legal Education in a Service Setting* (1973); CLEPR study, *The Education and Licensing of Lawyers* (1976): CLEPR, *Survey and Directory of Clinical Legal Education* (1975–1976); C. D. Putz, "Including Clinical Education in the Law School Budget," in *Clinical Education for the Law Student: CLEPR Conference Proceedings,* Buck Hill Falls, Pa., June 1973, pp. 101–5; H. Packer and T. Ehrlich, *New Directions,* pp. 46, 134; and *CLEPR Newsletter,* 9, No. 1 (January 1977): 1.

164–173 Bellow and clinical program at Harvard Law School. Much of this description was derived from interviews and observing classes and field operations. The following written sources were also quoted: Gary Bellow quoted in A. Pye, "On Teaching the Teachers: Some Preliminary Reflections on Clinical Education as Methodology," in *Clinical Education for the Law Student: CLEPR Conference Proceedings,* 1973, p. 23; G. Bellow, "On Teaching the Teachers: Some Preliminary Reflections on Clinical Education as Methodology," in CLEPR, *Clinical Legal Education*, pp. 374, 384–385; Jeanne Kettleson, memorandum, "Field Supervision in the Lawyering Process Course," prepared for an Association of American Law Schools study of field supervision, July 1975, pp. 19–20. On file with Jeanne Kettleson; George S. Grossman, "Clinical Legal Education: History and Diagnosis," *Journal of Legal Education* 26 (1974): 176; and *CLEPR Fourth Biennial Report* (1975–1976), pp. 25–26.

173–175 Descriptions of Antioch and Northeastern Law Schools. Derived from interviews with faculty and students of the two law schools.

175 Stanford and Hastings farm-out programs. Described in 1975–1976 bulletins of the law schools. See also Thomas Ehrlich and Thomas E. Headrick, "The Changing Structure of Education at Stanford Law School," *Journal of Legal Education* 22 (1970): 452–68.

Chapter 9 Grades, Law Review, and Placement: The Rewards System (Pages 176–200)

177 Students believe "everything is riding on these seven days." Quotation from John Jay Osborn, Jr., *The Paper Chase* (Boston: Houghton Mifflin Company, 1971), p. 177. Scott Turow's recent narrative of the Law School's first year, *One "L"* (New York: G. P. Putnam's Sons, 1977), similarly characterized the consequences of first-year competition as "the enemy."

177–178 Cox on grading. Archibald Cox letter to Mr. Jonathan Brent, January 3, 1969, reprinted in faculty memorandum, "Views on Grading and Related Matters at Harvard Law School" (March 19, 1969). On file at Harvard Law Library.

178 Some evidence students study more conscientiously with competitive grade system. Richard Lempert, "Law School Grading: An Experiment with Pass-Fail," *Journal of Legal Education* 24 (1972): 284.

178 Some professors have suggested exams can be graded with mathematical precision. See, for example, Dr. Harlan B. Phillips, *Felix Frankfurter Reminisces* (New York: Reynal & Company, 1960), p. 27.

179 Bok's midyear exam. Bok quoted in *Harvard Law Record*, February 8, 1968, p. 5.

179 1969 faculty report. *Report of the Special Committee on Examinations, Grading and Related Matters*, Harvard Law School, June 4, 1969, p. 16.

179–180 "The Trouble with Grades." Memorandum prepared by the Harvard Law class of 1971 and included in faculty memorandum, "Views on Grading," pp. 1–19.

180 Stone on student's self-esteem. Alan A. Stone, "Legal Education on the Couch," *Harvard Law Review* 85 (1971): p. 426.

181 1973 survey of graduate students. Leonard L. Baird, *The Graduates:*

A Report on the Plans and Characteristics of College Seniors (Princeton: Educational Testing Service, 1973), p. 122.

181   Visiting Committee heard students prefer pass-fail. A. Sacks, memorandum to faculty and students, January 19, 1976, including the report of May 5, 1975, to the Subcommittee on Student Concerns to the Harvard Law School Visiting Committee. Poll results in Appendix to report marked "Law School Council Questionnaire."

182   Other law school approaches to grading. Derived from 1975–1976 catalogs of respective law schools.

182–185   *Harvard Law Review.* Much of the material derived from interviews. An early history of the *Review* appears in *The Centennial History of the Harvard Law School, 1817–1917* (Harvard Law School Association, 1918), pp. 139–43. Havighurst's view is quoted from "Law Reviews and Legal Education," *Northwestern Law Review* 51 (1956): 24; Llewellyn's view may be found in "The Crisis in Legal Education," *Journal of Legal Education* 1 (1948): 216; Rodell's in "Goodbye to Law Reviews," *Virginia Law Review* 23 (1936): 38–45.

185–186   Harvard Law School alumni employment. American Bar Foundation, *1971 Lawyer Statistical Report* (Chicago: American Bar Foundation, 1972), p. 103.

186   5.5 percent located public-interest jobs. National Association for Law Placement press release, dated November 1, 1976.

186   1976 Harvard Law School class employment. Data supplied by Harvard Law School Placement Office. See their pamphlet, *What to Do, Where to Go* (Fall 1976), p. 43.

187   Mark Green's view. Mark Green, "The Young Lawyers, 1972: Goodbye to Pro Bono," *New York Magazine*, February 21, 1972, p. 29.

188   Instead Sacks appointed Phelps. Albert M. Sacks, *Harvard Law School Bulletin*, Winter, 1976, p. 11.

189–192   Description of Phelps. Derived from interviews with Phelps.

193–194   Views of Byers. Derived from interview with Byers.

196–200   Gail Bowman's case. Derived from interviews; Robert Gorman, *Report to the Harvard Law School Committee on Placement: The Complaint of Gail Bowman Against the Firm of Kirkland and Ellis* (1976); and *Harvard Crimson*, March 23, 1976, p. 8.

Chapter 10   Toward a New Model for American Legal Education (Pages 201–216)

202   Changes in employment patterns. American Bar Foundation, *The 1971 Lawyers Statistical Report*, pp. 10–12.

203–204   Ehrlich and Frank view. Thomas Ehrlich and Jane Lakes Frank, memorandum, "Planning for Justice" (May 9, 1977). On file with Thomas Ehrlich.

204 Louis Brown's point. Louis M. Brown, "Teaching the Low Visible Decision Processes of the Lawyer," *Journal of Legal Education* 25 (1973): 386–402.

204 Data on legal profession. See articles by T. Goldstein in *New York Times*, May 16–18, 1977; and remarks of T. Ehrlich, before the Annual Meeting of the Association of American Law Schools, December 28, 1976.

205 Pertschuk on lobbying. Michael Pertschuk, in Ralph Nader and Mark Green, eds., *Verdicts on Lawyers* (New York: Thomas Y. Crowell Company, 1976).

206 Kelso's conclusion. J. Kelso, "Solving Our Credentialing Problems by Drawing on the Medical Analogy: A Coordinating Council and Alternative Routes to Licensure and Certification," in CLEPR, *The Education and Licensing of Lawyers* (1976), p. 152.

207 Yale Law School's divisional program. Robert H. Freilich, "The Divisional Program at Yale: An Experiment for Legal Education in Depth," *Journal of Legal Education* 21 (1969): 443–60.

210 Rockefeller Foundation support of medical education. See CLEPR, *Third Biennial Report*, 1973–1974, pp. 14–15.

210 Harvard Medical School budget. See Dean's Report, Harvard Medical School, 1975–1976.

210 1974–1975 Harvard Law School Expenditures. Derived from Albert Sacks, memorandum to the faculty, "Tuition for the school year 1976–1977," March 9, 1976.

210–211 Memorandum prepared for Simpson. Stephen Dresh, memorandum, "Outline for a Proposed Federal Program of Loan Assistance to Graduate and Professional School Students" (March 23, 1976). A less well publicized memorandum, presenting a more egalitarian approach, was prepared by Harvard Law Professor Stephen Breyer for the School's Financial Aid Committee on March 2, 1977. It was entitled, "A 'Forward Looking' Financing System."

212 Legal Services Corporation research. See *Legal Service Corporation News*, August-September 1976, p. 3; Ehrlich and Frank, "Planning for Justice"; Ehrlich, remarks before the Association of American Law Schools"; Legal Services Corporation, memorandum, "To Those Interested in Legal Services for the Poor" (May 10, 1977), describing demonstration projects for the Legal Service Corporation's Delivery Systems Study; and Alan Houseman, director of Research Institute on Legal Assistance, Legal Services Corporation, memorandum, "Initial Proposals and Ideas for Research with the Research Institute" (April, 1977).

INDEX

Acheson, Dean, 78, 122

Administrative Law (course), 141

Admission(s), HLS: admission committees determining, 103-4; and *De-Funis* case, 114-19; democratic principle in policies of, 109-10; and distribution of graduating attorneys, 110-11; increase in, during Griswold's deanship, 89-90; increasing competitiveness of, 7-8; Kenneth B. Krohn's suing of HLS over denial of, 99-101; money as barrier to, 101-3; process, described, 95-99; standards raised by Langdell, 38-40, 41-42; validity of LSAT scores to determine, 104-9, 111; of women and minorities, 7, 112-14

Admission Council Committee on Student Aid, HLS, 210

Admissions Committee, 9, 97, 98, 100; and admission of minorities, 113-14

Admissions Office, 95, 99, 104

AFL-CIO, 116

Alumni Association, 20, 39

Alumni Fund Office, 198

American Bar Association (ABA), 47, 85, 144, 174, 202; and CLEO, 112; and clinical legal education movement, 162; and completion of undergraduate education for law students, 139-40; Council on Legal Education and Admissions to the Bar of, 11; and *DeFunis* case, 116;

Standards for the Approval of Law Schools of, 206-7

American College Testing Program, 106

American Economic Operations, 70

American Indian Movement, 191

American Jewish Congress, 116

American Law Institute, 46, 61

American Law Review, 28, 38, 41

Ames, James Barr, 8, 29, 30, 37; succeeds Langdell as HLS dean, 42, 55

Antioch Law School, 18, 142, 173-74, 207

Anti-Riot Act, Federal, 191

Appel, Eleanor, 91, 186, 188

Aristotle, *Nichomachean Ethics*, 157

Arnold and Porter (Washington), 16

Aspinall, Wayne, 190

Association of American Law Schools, 11, 85, 109-10, 139; Carrington Report of, 141, 147; and CLEO, 112; and *DeFunis* case, 116

Austin Hall, 4, 39, 65-66

Bailments (course), 33

Baird, Leonard, 120

Baker, Russell, quoted, 95

Bar admission standards, easing of, 26-27

Bator, Paul, 11

Bazelon, David, 146

Beale, Joseph, Jr., 43, 46, 57, 61, 66-67

Bell, Derrick, 9, 128-29

Bellow, Gary, 9, 130-31, 208, 209; and